PENGUIN BOOKS

THE PENGUIN HISTORY OF THE CHURCH

Volume One

Henry Chadwick has been Regius Professor at both Oxford and
Cambridge, and has been head of Christ Church, Oxford, and
Peterhouse, Cambridge. He is a Fellow (former Vice-President) of
the British Academy and a corresponding member of the American
Academy of Arts and Sciences, the American Philosophical Society,
the French Académie des Inscriptions et Belles Lettres and the
Göttingen and Rhineland Academies. He was made a knight in
1989. Several of his books on early Christian history are now in
paperback.

D0048215

HENRY CHADWICK

The Early Church

REVISED EDITION

PENGUIN BOOKS

PENGUIN BOOKS

Published by the Penguin Group
Penguin Books Ltd, 27 Wrights Lane, London W8 5TZ, England
Penguin Books USA Inc., 375 Hudson Street, New York, New York 10014, USA
Penguin Books Australia Ltd, Ringwood, Victoria, Australia
Penguin Books Canada Ltd, 10 Alcorn Avenue, Toronto, Ontario, Canada M4V 3B2
Penguin Books (NZ) Ltd, 182–190 Wairau Road, Auckland 10, New Zealand

Penguin Books Ltd, Registered Offices: Harmondsworth, Middlesex, England

First published in Pelican Books 1967
Reprinted in Penguin Books 1990
Revised edition 1993
7 9 10 8 6

Printed in England by Clays Ltd, St Ives plc
Set in Monotype Baskerville

The Penguin History of the Church
(formerly *The Pelican History of the Church*)

GENERAL EDITOR: OWEN CHADWICK

1 *The Early Church*. By Henry Chadwick, Honorary Fellow and former Master of Peterhouse, Cambridge and Regius Professor Emeritus of Divinity, Cambridge University.

2 *Western Society and the Church in the Middle Ages*. By Sir Richard Southern, formerly President of St John's College, Oxford.

3 *The Reformation*. By Owen Chadwick, formerly Chancellor of the University of East Anglia and Regius Professor of Modern History, Cambridge.

4 *The Church and the Age of Reason, 1648–1789*. By Gerald R. Cragg, formerly Professor of Church History at Andover Newton Theological School, Boston, Mass.

5 *The Church in the Age of Revolution*. By Alec R. Vidler, formerly Fellow and Dean of King's College, Cambridge.

6 *A History of Christian Missions*. By Stephen Neill, formerly Professor of Philosophy and Religious Studies at the University of Nairobi and Assistant Bishop in the Diocese of Oxford.

7 *The Christian Church in the Cold War*. By Owen Chadwick, formerly Chancellor of the University of East Anglia and Regius Professor of Modern History, Cambridge.

Contents

Contents

I

From Jerusalem to Rome

THE first Christians were Jews. They differed from their fellow-countrymen by their faith that in Jesus of Nazareth the Messiah of the nation's expectation had now come. They took it for granted that his coming, being a fulfilment, must be continuous with the past revelation of God to his people and could not mean a break either with the old covenant made with Abraham, symbolized by circumcision, or with the Law given to Moses on Mount Sinai. If something new had happened, it was the action of one and the same God, Creator of the world, Lord of history, the God of Abraham, Isaac, Jacob, and the twelve patriarchs. His new word to his people must be consistent with that spoken in the past by the prophets.

Because of this deep sense of continuity, various ideas and attitudes characteristic of traditional Judaism became and have largely remained integral to the structure of Christian thought. The Jews believed in God's election: God had chosen Israel to be an exclusive society, uncorrupted by heathen influences, yet with the two qualifications that this particularity of providence was not grounded upon any merit in the people chosen but in the sovereign, inscrutable will of God, and that Israel was called to exercise a priestly function in relation to mankind as a whole. Intensely tenacious of their Law, which they held to have been given by God to Moses on Mount Sinai, the Jews adopted a negative attitude towards pagan religion, which they regarded as the cult of evil spirits. In Graeco-Roman society they were a race apart, the object of some degree of vulgar distrust and at times hostile prejudice. They refused to participate in the

imperial cult, though they offered daily sacrifice on behalf
of the emperor in the temple at Jerusalem and were ready to
dedicate synagogues 'to God in honour of the emperor'.
They were socially distinctive, marked out by circumcision
and notorious for their abstinence from pork and other unclean food. In the second century B.C. the Maccabean martyrs
had preferred to die rather than eat pork. Jews could not
eat with Gentiles and could not compromise with any recognition of pagan deities in official ceremonial.

Foreign domination and the poor economy of Palestine
had led to a general emigration of Jews all over the Mediterranean world, the 'Dispersion', so that Jewish colonies could
be found almost anywhere from Cadiz to the Crimea. At
Rome in the first century A.D. they had eleven or twelve
synagogues. At Alexandria they formed a particularly large
proportion of the population; there were a million Jews in
Alexandria and Egypt altogether, and they were always a
factor in municipal politics, even though their social exclusiveness prevented them from becoming a pressure-group for
the acquisition of power. Everywhere they refused to be
merged with the Gentile inhabitants, but adhered to their
own beliefs and practices, meeting each Saturday for psalms,
readings from their Scriptures followed by an exegetical
sermon, and prayers. Users of the Latin Breviary or the
English Prayer Book are in important respects legatees of
this way of worship. Though dispersed far afield, they retained their sense of unity with the land of their fathers by
frequent pilgrimage to the holy city of Zion and by sending
annual contributions for the upkeep of the temple. Sometimes this export of currency from provinces where Jews were
numerous caused difficulty for the Roman fiscal authorities;
but in this as in other matters it was always easier to let the
Jews have their own way when a principle of their religion
was at stake. There was no area of public life from which the
Jews were excluded except by their own choice. But of course
not all Jews were as strict as their own religious authorities
would have liked; and there were not a few who felt the
pressure to conform to the manners of surrounding society.

Nevertheless, the pull was not all in one direction. Although circumcision was repellent to Greeks and Romans, there were many Gentiles attracted by monotheism, by the purity of Jewish morality, and by the antiquity (if not by the style) of their sacred books. Without being ascetic, except in some deviationist groups,[1] Judaism stood for chastity and stable family life; and among themselves the Jews practised works of charity, visiting the sick, caring for the dead, showing hospitality to strangers, giving alms for the poor. Round many synagogues of the Dispersion there gathered a penumbra of devout Gentiles commonly called 'God-fearers' (the term applied to *any* good synagogue member). A Gentile might undergo circumcision and, more commonly, the baptism required of would-be proselytes, but this was rare and the hellenized Jews of the Dispersion, to the regret of the stricter Palestinian authorities, were normally content to welcome Gentile adherents without insisting on circumcision as generally necessary to salvation. Among these Gentile groups the Christian missionaries found their first converts outside the number of the circumcised. They were indeed ripe fruit, for they had the advantage not only of high moral education, but also of instruction in the Hebrew Scriptures.

Judaism was the religion of a book in a way that no other ancient religion was. The reconstruction of Israelite society after the catastrophe of the Babylonian deportation had been firmly based on the Law of Moses. There were no more prophets to proclaim the immediate word of God. God's revelation to his people was in writing, and needed to be interpreted by learned scribes and 'lawyers', so that the original documents were supplemented by exegetical tradition in the rabbinical schools. (The status of this tradition became a matter of sharp controversy between church and synagogue in the first century.) As the Jews outside Palestine needed the Bible in Greek, a number of translations came into existence. One of these, the Septuagint, or version of the Seventy translators, became the authorized version of the

1. According to Philo and Josephus, the Essenes of the Dead Sea region held celibacy in high regard. The documents of the community at Qumran say nothing of this subject.

early Gentile churches. This version had been produced at Alexandria in the third century B.C., according to the tradition (which there is no very good reason to doubt) under the sponsorship of king Ptolemy Philadelphus of Egypt. For the Alexandrian Jews the translation became surrounded by an aura. They had an annual liturgical festival to commemorate its production; and some told wonderful tales of its origin, notably that Ptolemy had appointed seventy-two translators and that they produced their version in seventy-two days. Philo believed that the version had been granted divine assistance. The legend of the seventy-two was widely credited and, even where it was not, the Septuagint often ranked as an inspired version enjoying an authority that no other translation possessed. Only after the Christian appeals to its text became embarrassing to the Jews were alternative, more literal translations favoured by the Greek synagogue (below, p. 101); and some Rabbis, almost as hostile to liberal or hellenized Judaism as to Christianity, regretted that the Bible had ever been translated into Greek and denounced the making of the Septuagint as a sin like the worship of the golden calf.

THE EARLIEST CHURCH

From the first the Church was deeply conscious of its solidarity with Israel, and of the continuity of God's action in the past with his present activity in Jesus of Nazareth and in his followers. In St Matthew's Gospel Christ is the new Moses, with a stormy nativity prefigured by that of Moses in Egypt, and in his teaching laying down ethical principles that were in line with the highest traditions of the best Judaism. The Lord had come not to destroy but to fulfil; and the mission of the Christians was to bring their fellow-Jews to acknowledge as God's anointed or 'Messiah' him whom in ignorance the authorities had brought to a shameful judicial murder under Pilate the Roman governor. By raising him from the dead, God had vindicated him as 'Lord and Christ', the Messiah of expectation. To the objection that the prophets had expected the Messiah to come in glory and power, not in the weakness of crucifixion, the reply was that Jesus' sufferings, like those of the Suffering Servant in Isaiah's prophecy, were redemptive. His death inaugurated a 'new covenant' between God and his people, in accordance with the hope of Jeremiah (xxxi, 31–34).

At first Christianity must certainly have appeared only as one more sect or group within a Judaism that was already accustomed to considerable diversity in religious expression. Judaism was not monolithic. There were differences between the Pharisees and the Sadducees that could become sharp. The Pharisees were the party most anxious to preserve the distinctively religious and theocratic character of Jewish life in defiance of hellenistic influences and Roman domination; they were strict in their observance not only of the Mosaic law but also of the scribal tradition of interpreting the law. The Sadducees, who tended to be drawn from the leading aristocratic families, held only to the Mosaic law and did not feel bound by scribal tradition; moreover, they rejected belief in the resurrection of the dead as a doctrine only found in writings like the book of Daniel, composed long after Moses' time, which in their view lacked authority. The dis-agreement of the Pharisees and Sadducees concerning the after-life enabled St Paul on one occasion to extricate himself from an awkward situation (Acts xxiii, 6–10). Despite the apparently violent conflict with the Pharisees reflected in passages like Matt. xxiii, a number of Pharisees, of whom St Paul was to be the most famous, became Christians.

In addition to the Pharisees and Sadducees there was also a group, perhaps a number of related groups, to whom the title 'Essene' was given. A description of their life is given in Pliny the elder, Philo, and Josephus, of whom the last had some direct contact with them. They were a rigidly separatist society, whose principal settlement lay near the western shores of the Dead Sea, though adherents could be found elsewhere in Judaea. It is probable, but not certain, that the Essenes were, or rather included, the community for whom the Dead Sea Scrolls were written and who had their house at Qumran near the western shores of the Dead Sea. This community rejected the sacrifices and priesthood of the

officially recognized worship in the temple at Jerusalem, and
looked back to their founder-hero, 'the Teacher of Righteousness', who had been harried by a 'wicked priest' who
ruled over Israel. In certain respects the Essenes resembled
the early church. They were a close-knit body which practised property-sharing and distributed money to each according to his need. Their life was frugal, and any member who
had two coats gave one away to his needy brother and wore
his remaining coat until it was threadbare. They appear to
have been divided among themselves about the question of
passive resistance. Most of them rejected the carrying of
arms, but some of them were Zealots dedicated to the
nationalist cause of resistance to the occupying Roman
power. The site at Qumran became the scene of bloody
fighting in the Jewish war of 66–70. The Essenes rejected
slavery in principle as incompatible with the equality of
all men before their Creator; and though they did not condemn marriage as wrong, they expected full members of the
community to be celibate. Entrance to the community was
hedged about with tests and solemn vows preceded by a
novitiate, and any delinquency led to expulsion. They practised very frequent ritual washings, and had a sacred common
meal to which the uninitiated were not admitted. They rejected the use of oaths.

On the other hand, there are important differences between the Essenes and the early Church. The Essenes were
particularly precise about keeping the sabbath day, and
exercised extreme care to avoid any ceremonial pollution.
According to our Greek sources, they rose before dawn to
offer prayer to the rising sun, and had esoteric teachings
about the properties of roots and stones and about the secret
names of the angels. They devoted much attention to the
exegesis of the inner meaning of scripture, and made predictions of the future. The Qumran texts and the Greek sources
are not in complete harmony in their accounts; but perhaps
the Greek documents present a portrait of the Essenes that
reshapes their likeness to resemble Pythagorean ascetics of
the hellenistic world. The material from the Dead Sea Scrolls
provides relatively little evidence for the immediate back-

ground of the early Church except in the broad sense that it reveals the existence of a group fervently studying Old Testament prophecy, especially Messianic prophecy, and expecting a great divine intervention in world history. There is a kinship in atmosphere; as for example in the so-called 'War Scroll' describing a final battle between the sons of light and the sons of darkness which is reminiscent of the Armageddon of the Apocalypse and perhaps also of Ephesians vi. But it is fair to say that in points of detail the number of analogies and parallels between the Qumran documents and the New Testament is not very numerous or impressive; and 'The Teacher of Righteousness' does not play a role in the thought of the Qumran community which is closely comparable to that of Jesus in the faith of the early Church. In short, the New Testament writings and the Qumran Scrolls mutually illuminate one another, but neither group of documents can be said to 'explain' the other. That individual Essenes became Christians is probable enough, but it is most unlikely that there was any institutional continuity. Surprisingly the first Christians appear to have adopted a much more positive attitude than the Qumran community towards the temple worship at Jerusalem (cf. Acts vi, 7). At the same time there is much to suggest that the Christians would have been very impatient with a community so obsessed by the need for ceremonial purity that their day was punctuated at frequent intervals by ritual lustrations.

The initial impact of Christianity on the Jewish people seems to have been fairly considerable. The church probably drew its membership from most of the diverse elements within the heterogeneous society of first century Judaism, apart from the Sadducees. It appealed both to the Pharisees' sense that the revealed will of God was a matter demanding to be taken with the most intense seriousness and also to the ordinary Jew's feeling that too much of the Pharisaic scrupulousness about the law had ended in niggling ceremonial niceties that missed the central point of religion. Before long there were substantial groups of Christian Jews not only in Jerusalem but also in the surrounding countryside of Judaea. That there were also important groups in the north in Galilee is probable enough, but of their relation to the Judaean churches and of their later history we can only guess. They were rural communities in a backward area, and disappear from history. We know, however, that the faith rapidly reached not only Damascus but Antioch, the capital of Syria and third city of the Roman Empire, where the pagans soon gave them the nickname 'Christians', which quickly spread as the popular term. (The Jewish term for them remained 'Nazarenes'; below, p. 21.) Even some of the strictest adherents of the Mosaic Law and of its traditional interpretation, the Pharisees, were associated with the movement. Nevertheless, neither the authorities nor the people as a whole came to follow 'the Way'. On the one hand Christianity offered no encouragement to the nationalistic Zealots, awaiting the hour for revolt against Rome; on the other hand, it was far too revolutionary for the Jewish 'Establishment', which pursued a compromising policy of political collaboration and religious conservatism. Above all, there was the delicate problem of the Christian attitude towards the Gentiles. This was an issue of principle causing deep division of opinion within the Church itself, the beginnings of which may be traced in the story of the 'Hellenists' and Stephen told by Luke in Acts vi–vii.

The spread of Christianity northwards into Syria and Cilicia caused such acute anxiety to the synagogues that a counter-movement was provoked, armed with authority from Jerusalem and led by a Cilician Jew who had been a pupil of the famous Rabbi Gamaliel at Jerusalem – Saul or Paul of Tarsus, a Pharisee convinced of the finality and perfection of the Mosaic Law and accordingly a zealous persecutor of the infant church. Travelling to Damascus he was suddenly confronted by the risen Christ, and thenceforth was an equally convinced Christian – and once again a man of zeal: he had a burning sense of mission to take the Gospel to the Gentiles. Paul was probably not the first to conceive of a Christian mission to the non-Jewish world. But from the start he was undoubtedly the dominant figure in the work, and believed himself to be called in a particular and unique degree as the apostle of the Gentiles, exercising authority

over the Gentile churches by visits and especially by letters
(he found that he was more effective on paper than when
speaking), and representing their interests in his negotiations
with the mother-church at Jerusalem.

While the Pauline letters and the Acts of the Apostles tell
us something of the development of the Gentile communities,
we know relatively little of the mother-church in Judaea.
Most of the twelve disciples disappear from history. Only
Peter, John, and James the Lord's brother are more than
names. By the third century romantic legends began, describing the missionary travels of the twelve, Thomas in
Persia and India, Andrew to the Scythians of South Russia,
and so on. But these stories are like the medieval legends
which associate James the Apostle with Compostela or
Joseph of Arimathea with Glastonbury. They are derived
from the apocryphal romances about the apostles which
became widespread popular reading in the latter half of the
second century.[1] Second century traditions with more claim
to respect relate that John the son of Zebedee lived in his
old age at Ephesus, and that Philip the evangelist with his
four prophetess-daughters (Acts xxi, 9) died in Phrygia. This
exodus of the Jerusalem church to Asia Minor may have
been caused by the Jewish War of 66–70. The fourth Gospel
comes from a group of St John's disciples for whom it en-
shrined the beloved disciple's teaching. About 200 we find
the churches of Asia Minor looking back to St John as their
founder and treasuring his tomb at Ephesus.[2]

The Ephesians seem to have supposed that the Virgin Mary
had lived in St John's house there (see John xix, 27), and in
the fifth century were the first to dedicate a church in her
honour. But according to another view, first formulated in
375 by Epiphanius, who speaks of it as a highly esoteric

1. These are translated in M. R. James, *The Apocryphal New Testament*
(Oxford, 2nd edn., 1955). See also E. Hennecke's *New Testament Apo-
crypha* (ed. W. Schneemelcher, transl. R. M. Wilson, 2 vols., London,
2nd edn., 1991).

2. Latin writers follow Tertullian and Jerome in relating that St John
was cast into boiling oil at Rome and escaped unhurt; in the seventh
century this scene was located at the Latin Gate and commemorated
on 6 May. The legend is not known to Greek writers.

mystery of which he is not at all confident, Mary did not go to Ephesus and indeed did not taste death at all.

James the Just, 'the Lord's brother', was president of the Jerusalem Church until his martyrdom in 62 (an event which gave many non-Christian Jews a very bad conscience), when he was succeeded by a cousin of the Lord. The exact relation between James and Peter, the leading apostle to whom the Lord had specially entrusted the church's mission, is obscure. In the Pauline letters and the Acts the Holy Family and the Apostles appear as distinguished authorities side by side; if there was at any time tension between them (as Mark iii, 31–5 may imply) it was quickly ironed out. According to one strand of tradition (Matt. xvi, 18) the Lord nominated Peter as the rock on which the Church was to be built; perhaps there were some Christians who believed Peter rather than James to be the supreme authority in the Church after the Ascension. The eirenic account of the earliest Church in Acts, probably written a generation or more later, does not allow us to do more than ask unanswerable questions.

Peter's relation to Paul is also ambiguous. The battle royal between them at Antioch was evidently exceptional or it would not have been recorded in the way it is (Gal. ii, 11ff.); and at least in their death they were not divided – both died at Rome as martyrs in the persecution under Nero.[1] No doubt Peter's presence in Rome in the sixties must indicate a concern for Gentile Christianity, but we have no information whatever about his activity or of the length of his stay there. That he was in Rome for twenty-five years is third-century legend.

THE GENTILE CHURCH

In the ancient world everyone knew at least three things about the Jews: they would not be associated either directly

---

1. The martyrdom of St Peter is alluded to in St John's Gospel (xiii, 36; xxi, 18). That it took place at Rome is highly probable from the epistle of Clement to the Corinthians, Ignatius' letter to the Romans and the unanimous tradition of second century writers, besides the memorial monument at the cemetery on the Vatican hill, built about A.D. 160–70 and recently excavated (below, p. 162).

or indirectly with any pagan cult (which seemed antisocial), they refused to eat not only meat that had been offered in sacrifice to the gods but also all pork (which seemed ridiculous), and they circumcised their male infants (which seemed repulsive).

If the Church was to undertake a mission to the Gentiles, a ruling on these questions was necessary: Were the same prohibitions to apply to Gentile converts to Christianity? A conservative group thought that Gentile converts must not merely keep clear of food defiled by idolatrous associations but also accept circumcision as the covenant sign of admission to the people of God. Other Christian Jews who believed that the Gospel must be preached to all the world absolutely rejected this conservative view. Circumcision together with the entire ceremonial law of the Pentateuch was limited to the Jewish people, whereas in Christ God had acted for the reconciliation of humanity, to break down the barriers not only between sinful man and his Creator but between one man and another.

The cleavage between conservatives and universalists led to an acute and at times passionate controversy, resulting in a general conference in Jerusalem (Acts xv). The outcome was in some respects a compromise but one which in all decisive points was bound to favour the universalists. The Gentile converts were recognized as truly within the covenant by the mother-church at Jerusalem even if they were uncircumcised; but they must be careful not to eat food with idolatrous associations (it was customary for Greek dinner-parties to be held in temples, the god himself being considered as the host) and not to allow sexual relations outside marriage, this being a matter on which Jewish ethic was much stricter than pagan. St Paul's Corinthian correspondence casts a vivid light on the social background of these conditions.

The controversy turned on the continued validity of the Mosaic Law. Paul saw that at bottom the question was whether a man attains to heaven on the ground of his merit achieved by obedience to God's commandments. To this idea of Law Paul opposes the idea of divine mercy and

forgiveness, which are freely offered to us in Christ: by baptism the believer is united with Christ and is 'justified'; we
are put into a right relationship with God on the ground of
which we do 'good works' and advance in holiness. From the
law of Moses the Christian is therefore free. Its status is not
fixed but provisional: it was a 'childminder to bring us to
Christ'.

It was Paul's achievement to vindicate the freedom and
equal status of Gentile Christians and to win from the Jerusalem leaders the recognition of his converts as full members of the Church. He understood this also to imply recognition of his own standing as the apostle of the Gentiles. The
claim involved him in painful controversy, in which his
most potent argument was the concrete fact of the existence
of numerous Gentile converts. Perhaps the chief reason for
Paul's success was his extraordinary versatility and capacity
for adapting himself to the situation of his audience: he had
the power to translate the Palestinian Gospel into language
intelligible to the Greek world, and thereby became the first
Christian apologist. The first generation of Palestinian
Christians expected the Lord to return with glory very
shortly. Paul perceived that the doctrine of the imminent
end of the world was a liability rather than an asset in evangelizing the Greek world where the dominant speculative
interest was in the beginning of things. He transferred the
emphasis from Christ as the end to Christ as the Wisdom of
God in creation, pre-existent from eternity and the immanent
power by which the manifold diversity of the cosmos is saved
from disintegration. In particular (he taught) the Lord is
immanent within his Church, as the soul in the body, which
is therefore ever growing until the final consummation when
it is to be coterminous with the human race itself. In these
terms the epistle to the Ephesians formulates the idea of the
universal Church, one, holy, catholic and apostolic. For
according to this full Pauline doctrine all Christians are
united to one another through union with the Lord in faith
and baptism; by him the Church is made a holy society,
called out of the world to exercise a priestly function, media-
ting the Gospel to humanity, universally extended in space

and looking back in time to its apostolic founders. The mother-church of this universal society is Jerusalem. But already in Paul's mind there is formed the westward look towards the capital of the Gentile world as the potential focus of Gentile Christendom, and as a centre for a mission to Spain (which perhaps he may have succeeded in reaching).

Paul thought of the Church as a society where the barrier between Jew and Gentile is broken down but which retains a quasi-dual character. But Jewish Christianity failed to convert the Jewish people. Jerusalem was terribly damaged in A.D. 70 and especially in 135, when by Hadrian's edict all Jews were henceforth excluded by law from Judaea, and Jerusalem became a Greek city, renamed Aelia Capitolina, with pagan temples and theatres. This meant an emancipation of Gentile Christendom from its Jewish Christian roots; its sheer weight of numbers and geographic extent over the Mediterranean world ensured its self-confidence and sense of catholicity, while it could look for continuity with the apostles not only to the churches of the East but also to Rome, the scene of the martyrdom of Peter and Paul. Paul's concept of the quasi-independent status of Gentile Christendom standing over against Jerusalem, existing side by side with Jewish Christendom within the one Church, was in time developed into the idea of the independence (and potential rivalry) of the West over against the East.

Although persecuted by the Jews (1 Thess. ii, 14) the Christians in Palestine long remained a group within Judaism. But the break became inevitable. A sentence in Suetonius' *Life of Claudius*[1] could mean that as early as 50 rioting between Jews and Christians had broken out at Rome. In Judaea the Jewish Christians kept the bridges open as long as they could, but they were severely harried and about 85, to make sure of their exclusion, a formal anathema was incorporated in the synagogue liturgy: 'May the Nazarenes and the heretics be suddenly destroyed and removed from the Book of Life.' The existence of the Gentile mission was an embarrassment in the mission of the Jewish Christians

1. 'Since the Jews continually made disturbances at the instigation of Chrestus, Claudius expelled them from Rome.' (Cf. Acts xviii, 2.)

to their own countrymen (Rom. xi, 28 illustrates this point); and their position was not helped by the attitude of some of their Gentile brethren who had no desire to stress their debt to Judaism and were inclined to the unconciliatory view that the destruction of Jerusalem by the hated Romans in A.D. 70 was nothing but the merited judgement of providence for the murder of Jesus, which was itself only the last of a long line of stiff-necked refusals of God's word in the prophets. The Jewish nation's rejection of the Messiah was discovered to be the subject of Old Testament prophecy just as much as the world-wide mission of the Church as the people of the Messiah. Accordingly, there came into being a tradition of interpretation of the Old Testament which concentrated upon prophetic denunciations of mere externalism in religion and upon the observance of feasts and ceremonies. The Old Testament was seen as the history of a people with an ineradicable capacity for apostasy, despite the continual warnings of the prophets. The Mosaic Law was not God's permanent will, but a temporary and provisional measure given by God to a hard-hearted people to prevent lapses into worse things, perhaps even an actual punishment for the worship of the golden calf. In short, the Old Testament itself was seen to imply a negative judgement on Judaism.

The Jewish Christians, excluded by their fellow-countrymen, continued to observe sabbaths, circumcision, and other Jewish feasts. As this distressed many Gentile Christians, they became lonely, unsupported groups. In the fourth century and later there were small Jewish churches in Syria. Jerome translated into Latin their *Gospel according to the Hebrews*, preserving traditions slightly diverging from the canonical Greek gospels, and magnifying the position of James the Lord's brother. But the orthodox Jews could not forgive them for being Christians, and the Gentile majority in the Church could not comprehend their continued observance of the traditional customs and rites of Judaism. Slowly the communities lost importance. In Justin Martyr's *Dialogue with Trypho* (below, p. 75) written about 160 it appears that they were still a force. Justin believed that a Jewish Christian was quite free to keep the Mosaic law without in any way com-

promising his Christian faith, and even that a Gentile Christian might keep Jewish customs if a Jewish Christian had
influenced him to do so; only it must be held that such observances were matters of indifference and of individual conscience. But Justin had to admit that other Gentile Christians
did not take so liberal a view and believed that those who
observed the Mosaic law could not be saved. From Irenaeus
onwards Jewish Christianity is treated as a deviationist sect
rather than as a form of Christianity with the best claims to
continuity with the practice of the primitive church at Jerusalem. The Jewish Christians called themselves Ebionites, a
name derived from the Hebrew word meaning 'the poor'; it
was probably a conscious reminiscence of a very early term
which is attested by St Paul's letters as an almost technical
name for the Christians in Jerusalem and Judaea. Since
some of them had never accepted the tradition of the virgin
birth of Christ, Irenaeus classified the Ebionites with other
heresies that denied this; soon Tertullian was supposing that
they originated with a person named Ebion, and later anti-
heretical writers even felt able to quote from Ebion's alleged
writings.

ENCOUNTER WITH THE ROMAN EMPIRE

A Roman procurator had condemned the Lord to crucifixion
like a common criminal. But he had done it to placate the
Jews, not because he actually believed Jesus to be guilty of
crime against the Roman State. There was still hope of a
rapprochement. The Lord himself had said it was possible
to render loyal service to Caesar while still being loyal to
God. The primitive Church refused to identify itself with the
nationalist Jewish 'zealots'. The Jerusalem community had
left the city when the resistance started the war in 66, and
they were again harried as potential traitors during the
Hadrianic war under Bar-Cochba in 133–5. Committed to
the approval of the Gentile mission, they were not disposed
to quarrel with the Gentile authorities for whose conversion
they prayed. Paul, who possessed dual citizenship both of Tarsus and of Rome, regarded the magistrates as the ministers

of divine justice in restraining crime; and on the express authority of the Lord himself, Christians faithfully paid their taxes. The Gentile mission had every interest in the maintenance of public order, and none whatever in adopting an attitude of disaffection towards the State. In the Acts of the Apostles it is already implied that the Empire, under the providence of God, could be the instrument for the furtherance of the Gospel. By the middle of the second century Christians were discerning the hand of God in the fact that Augustus had established the Roman Peace at the very time when Christ's gospel of universal peace and goodwill was given to mankind. What was wrong with the State was its old paganism. Change its religion and all would be well.

The Empire, however, was not disposed to abandon the old gods by whose favour the legions had conquered the world. Philosophic criticism might have destroyed the faith of many; Epicureans like Lucretius could denounce religion as based on the fear of non-existent bogies after death. But no one proposed to act on his scepticism and to initiate a social revolution. To refuse to participate in the pagan emperor-cult was a political as well as a religious act, and could easily be construed as dangerous disaffection.

Side by side with the official cults of the deified emperor and of the old local deities, the priesthoods of which were held by ordinary citizens, there flourished the eastern mystery religions, which normally possessed a professional priesthood. The most important of these were the cults of Isis (the Egyptian mother-goddess), Mithras (the Persian god of light), and the grim Anatolian cult of Attis and Cybele. These cults had some popular appeal. The profound emotions evoked by initiation into the exotic mysteries of Isis, the mother nursing her holy child like the Madonna, may be seen in the last book of *The Golden Ass* by Apuleius. Mithraism, an ascetic religion for men only, appealed especially (but not exclusively) to officers in the army; it had sacred meals not unlike the Christian eucharist and offered souls a way through the seven planetary spirits which bar the ascent to the Milky Way after death. But it was not a religion of the people. The cult of Cybele was well known for its flagellant, mendicant priests and for the public ceremonies of 15–27 March when, after fasting and the Day of Blood (22 March) on which Attis was mourned, sorrow was turned into joy with the Hilaria celebrating his resurrection on 25 March (a striking parallel to the Christian Holy Week and Easter).[1]

No pagan cult was exclusive of any other and the only restriction on initiation into many cults was the expense. By supposing that the various deities were either the same god under different names or local administrators for a supreme deity it was possible to give all cults a loose unity.

The Roman government was in practice tolerant of any cult provided that it did not encourage sedition or weaken morality. Indeed, one reason for Roman military success was believed to be the fact that, while other peoples worshipped only their own local deities, the Romans worshipped all deities without exclusiveness and had therefore been rewarded for their piety. The God of the Jews, who had no images and no sacrifices except at Jerusalem, was harder for the Romans to assimilate. Although the Jews were monotheists and in theory understood that belief to invalidate all forms of religion other than their own, until the revolt of 66–70 they were treated with marked toleration and under Augustus were granted privileges which, after an awkward crisis with Caligula who wanted to set up his statue in the temple at Jerusalem,[2] were renewed by Claudius. There seemed no necessary reason why the Christians should not also achieve toleration. They came into conflict with the State in the first instance by accident, not on any fundamental point of principle. In 64 a great fire destroyed much of Rome. Nero had made himself sufficiently unpopular to be suspected of arson, and turned to the Christians to find a scapegoat. The historian Tacitus, writing about fifty years later, did not believe that the Christians were justly accused of the arson, though he saw no harm in the execution of a contemptible, anti-social group 'hated for their vices' – for by his

1. In the fourth century pagan critics accused the Church of plagiarism on this count. Both festivals had an all-night vigil with lights.

2. For the reverberations of this crisis in the New Testament see Mark xiii, 14; II Thess. ii, 3–4.

time, if not by Nero's, the Christians were vulgarly thought
to practise incest and cannibalism at their nocturnal meetings. (These charges probably arose from language about
universal love and the eucharist.) The Neronian persecution was confined to Rome and was not due to any sense of
deep ideological conflict between Church and State; it was
simply that the emperor had to blame somebody for the fire.
Nevertheless, it was a precedent that magistrates had condemned Christians to death because they were Christians
and on no other charge.

Probably pressure against the Church continued inter-
mittently, and no doubt many wavered. Jews and Gentiles
who after peaceful adherence to the synagogue had passed
over to the Church must have felt tempted to retrace their
steps. To some such situation the anonymous Epistle to the
Hebrews is addressed; the author, who is evidently a member
of the Pauline circle, exhorts the hesitating Roman community to remain confident of the inferiority of Judaism and of
the finality of Christianity on the ground that Christ is the
unique Son of God; to be mindful of the example of its past
leaders and loyal to those now occupying their position; to
continue its care for imprisoned brethren; and to take heart
from the lull in actual executions.

Under Domitian (81–96) the situation seems again to
have become grave. Except for Caligula and Nero the emperors had traditionally discouraged over-enthusiastic subjects from offering them divine honours. Domitian took the
opposite view, styling himself 'Master and God', and inclined to suspect of treachery those who looked askance at
his cult. The customary oath 'by the genius of the emperor'
became officially obligatory. There is good evidence that
this created a crisis for the Jews. It is probable (though not
quite certain) that the Church was no less embarrassed.
According to the third-century historian Dio, several emi-
nent Romans with Jewish sympathies were accused of
'atheism', and on this charge action was taken against Titus
Flavius Clemens, consul in 95, and his wife Domitilla. Fourth
century Christian tradition counted Domitilla a Christian,
and perhaps the phrase 'atheism and Jewish sympathies' is

Dio's polite circumlocution for Christianity.[1] The Revelation of St John, with its denunciations of idolatrous, persecuting Rome as the scarlet woman drunk with the blood of saints, may reflect the tension in the churches of Asia Minor at this time.

The emperor Trajan (98–117) did not like his cult being made a compulsory loyalty-test, and the crisis passed. Nevertheless, about 112 the governor of Bithynia in Asia Minor, Pliny the younger, asked Trajan for guidance about the procedure for dealing with Christians. His letter is very revealing. In his province, it appears, Christianity had spread widely not only in towns but also in the countryside; the pagan temples had become empty and the meat of sacrificial animals practically unsaleable. Local interests had been affected and representations were made to Pliny, who executed some Christians who were not Roman citizens while keeping others who possessed citizenship to be sent to Rome for trial. Pliny was aware that by precedent Christians were executed and had acted without hesitation; but he was puzzled about the exact nature of their crime. He asked Trajan whether the mere profession of Christianity was in itself culpable, or if they were charged with the vices associated with the name; whether some mitigation of the punishment was appropriate in the case of the young or infirm; whether if a man was proved to be a Christian he could purge his crime by recanting. Pliny had no conscience about the executions since the accused had been contumacious in refusing to recant which was much worse than being a Christian. But the sequel had been a tiresome increase in accusations, not merely from an informer, but also from an anonymous pamphlet. On examination, those now accused had either denied that they were Christians at all or, admitting that they had been so in the past (in some cases twenty years previously), denied that they were any longer, and proved

1. Another personage of high rank, Acilius Glabrio, consul in 91, was also executed on this charge – but also on that of fighting as a gladiator. The cruelty and murder of gladiatorial combats were anathema to the Church; but it is conceivable that he was interested in Christianity enough to open himself to Domitian's attack.

their point by offering incense and wine before images of the emperor and the gods and by cursing Christ. These inquiries of lapsed Christians, however, elicited the disconcerting information that no enormities were practised. The accused declared that their normal practice had been to attend a meeting before daybreak on a particular day (no doubt Sunday is meant) at which they sang a hymn to Christ as a god, and took an oath (i.e. the baptismal promise?) to abstain from crime rather than to commit it; thereafter they dispersed, but met again later to eat, not a murdered infant, but ordinary food. This common meal they had suspended of their own accord when Pliny published an imperial edict forbidding secret societies. Disturbed by the discovery that Christianity could appear so innocuous Pliny had examined under torture two deaconesses; he found only 'squalid superstition', nothing vicious. But at least, he felt, his severity had been justified by the result: the population had returned to the temples.

Trajan's reply to Pliny shows a reluctance to take the matter too seriously. Pliny, he thought, had proceeded sensibly, but should pay no heed to anonymous accusations and was not to organize any general inquisition himself. If a proper charge was brought by a responsible individual (who under Roman law had the tables turned on him if his accusations were found to be slanderous, which made people chary of bringing a capital charge), then the person accused of Christianity could be tried and, if found guilty, punished. Only, Trajan added, he might be pardoned if he showed that he was not a Christian by offering prayers to the gods, whatever he might have done in the past. Pliny's principal question Trajan left unanswered. But at least it was clear that the emperor did not regard the Christians as dangerous. The essentials of his reply were reaffirmed by Hadrian about 123 in a letter to Minucius Fundanus, proconsul at Ephesus.

The authorities had now discovered that the Christians were virtuous folk, but inexplicably hostile to the old religious tradition and so obstinate in their dissent as to forfeit sympathy and preclude toleration. Christianity remained a capital offence, and several in the second century suffered martyrdom: Ignatius bishop of Antioch, Telesphorus bishop of Rome, Polycarp bishop of Smyrna, Justin 'the Christian philosopher' at Rome some time between 162 and 168. In 177 an ugly persecution broke out with savage violence against the Christians at Lyons and Vienne in the Rhône valley; the emperor Marcus Aurelius had directed that they should be tortured to death, and no refinement of cruelty was spared. The mob was always ready to believe that catastrophes like floods or bad harvests or barbarian invasions were a sign of the gods' displeasure at their neglect under the influence of Christian 'atheism'. Tertullian sarcastically commented: 'If the Tiber rises too high or the Nile too low, the cry is "The Christians to the lion". All of them to a single lion?' The vulgar charges of incest and cannibalism died slowly. Even as late as the middle of the third century, by which time the main teachings of Christianity were a matter of universal knowledge and discussion, it was possible to meet virtuous pagans who still believed in the stories of secret vice. But persecution was far from being continuous or systematic. Both Trajan and Hadrian had discouraged governors from taking any personal initiative. Much was left to private informers, and action remained in the discretion of individual governors, which some exercised in the manner of Gallio who 'cared for none of these things' (Acts xviii, 15). A few provincial governors actually protected the church, and grateful Christians believed that despite their paganism they might be rewarded hereafter. By the end of the second century Christianity was penetrating the upper classes of society, and more than one highly placed personage might wake up to find his wife embarrassing him by disappearing to nocturnal vigils and prayers. Marcia, the concubine of the emperor Commodus (180–92), was a Christian, and was able to gain for the church in Rome a considerable measure of relief (below, p. 88). Because the early persecutions were limited they did not seriously slow down the expansion of Christianity, but on the contrary tended to give the church the maximum of publicity. Tertullian observed that 'the blood of the martyrs is the seed of the church'. Many of the records of the early martyrs have a heroic quality about them. At the same time they reveal the temptations of peculiar subtlety to which the martyrs were exposed. Not all were able to rise to the Christ-like simplicity of Stephen who followed his Lord's example in praying for the forgiveness of his murderers. Judicial murder is never an easy thing to bear, and the martyrs were at times inclined to seek satisfaction in the thought that they would be avenged in the world to come, or even that it would be an element in the felicity of heaven to contemplate the appropriateness of punishments justly meted out to those responsible for acts of gross injustice in this present life. Moreover, the conviction that martyrdom granted immediate admission to paradise and conferred a victor's crown, combined with a sombre evaluation of the Roman empire as a political institution, led to a tendency towards acts of provocation on the part of over-enthusiastic believers, especially among the Montanists (below p. 52) who were especially prone to identify reticence with cowardice and moral compromise. Hotheads who provoked the authorities were soon censured by the church as mere suicides deserving no recognition. As, from the middle of the third century onwards, the private commemorations of the martyrs began to pass into the official and public liturgy of the church, control had to be exercised and the claims of an individual martyr were subjected to examination and scrutiny. Even so there were difficulties, mainly because there were different interpretations of what constituted provocation. Ignatius of Antioch, martyred at Rome before A.D. 117, was a man of intense devotion; his warnings that the influential Roman Christians should not try to obtain his release so as to deprive him of suffering in union with his Lord, could easily pass into an attitude that would appear provocative to a magistrate. His friend Polycarp, bishop of Smyrna, who was martyred at the age of 86 not long after the middle of the century (the evidence regarding the date is conflicting)[1]

1. Eusebius of Caesarea places it in 167–8. A late note appended to the account of the martyrdom dates it 'in the proconsulship of Statius Quadratus', i.e. probably 155–6. This earlier date, though attested by inferior evidence, better coheres with Polycarp's extant correspondence with Ignatius of Antioch and with Irenaeus's statement that Polycarp had known St John at Ephesus.

was held up as a model on the specific ground that he did
nothing to provoke the authorities but quietly waited for
them to come and arrest him. The Stoic emperor, Marcus
Aurelius, who regarded suicide as ethically unobjectionable,
felt that it must be done in good style 'not, like the Christians,
in a spirit of theatricality'.

But there were also temptations in the opposite direction.
Some who were influenced by the radically spiritualizing
tendencies of Gnostic dualism (below, p. 36) argued that
pagan gods were not devils, but simply non-existent; so it was
a matter of complete indifference whether one ate meat that
had been offered in sacrifice to idols (cf. 1 Corinthians,
viii) or if one offered incense in honour of the emperor. It
was a mere formality, and merely external acts did not affect
the inner devotion of the mind. One's conscience could not
be held to be polluted by a mere act of respect and loyalty.
In the second century most of those who thus argued belonged to gnostic sects. But in Spain by A.D. 300 there were
Christians happily holding the distinguished office of *flamen*
in the cult of the emperor. They greatly distressed more
puritan brethren. At times even the most serious-minded
among the orthodox believers were tempted to doubt whether
perhaps they were not cranks dying for trivialities, and to ask
themselves at what point they could no longer compromise.
Between the two extremes of provocation and compromise
there were many, such as the twelve simple Christians of
Scilli in North Africa condemned at Carthage on 17 July
180, the record of whose trial leaves a deep impression of
moral protest and integrity. The same may be said of the
Acta Proconsularia of Cyprian, or the minutes of Justin's
trial at Rome.

The sporadic nature of persecution, which often depended
on local attitudes, and the fact that before the third century
the government did not take Christianity seriously, gave the
Church breathing space to expand and to deal with critical
internal problems.

2

Faith and Order

THE unity of the scattered Christian communities depended on two things – on a common faith and on a common way of ordering their life and worship. They called each other 'brother' or 'sister'. Whatever differences there might be of race, class or education, they felt bound together by their focus of loyalty to the person and teaching of Jesus. The pattern of worship derived all its meaning from its reference to him. The rite of baptism by which they were admitted to the Church was both a commemoration of the moment at the river Jordan when Jesus was filled with the Spirit for his life work, and a once for all renunciation of evil, which St Paul in a powerful metaphor described as 'being buried with Christ'. Each Sunday they met for their 'thanksgiving' in which the baptized ate bread and drank wine in a sacred meal which they spoke of as 'eating the body' and 'drinking the blood' of Christ. To share in this sacred meal was so deeply felt to be the essential expression of membership of the society that fragments of the broken bread were taken round to any who were absent through illness or imprisonment. A serious moral fault entailed exclusion from sharing in the meal, either permanently or for a time; but those so excluded continued to attend the first part of the service, consisting of psalms, readings and prayers, together with those who were not yet baptized but were 'receiving instruction' (*catechumenoi*). The penitent under discipline prayed that by the intercession of the faithful they might be granted mercy for their fault.

The determination of which moral faults did or did not involve exclusion, and for how long, was a pastoral problem that deeply exercised the minds of the Church's leaders well into the third century. Not less difficult was the thorny question whether and at what point intellectual deviation should lead to censure. The translation of the Gospel into the religious language of the hellenistic world was a task of great intricacy calling for the highest sensitivity and awareness of responsibility if its structure was not to be altered. The missionaries to the Gentile world were not speaking in a vacuum to people without existing prejudices and expectations. The moment they passed outside the ambit of the synagogues of the Jewish dispersion and their loosely attached Gentile adherents, the missionaries were in a twilight world of pagan syncretism, magic, and astrology. Even the apparently exclusive religion of Judaism had been welcomed into the loose amalgam of polytheism by identifying the God of the Jews with Dionysus or (since they reverenced Saturday) with Saturn. The pagan world was quite accustomed to myths of great heroes, like Heracles or Asclepius, who were elevated to divine rank as a reward for their merits. The Christians amazed the world by the extraordinary claim that the divine redeemer of their story had lately been born of a woman in Judaea, had been crucified under Pontius Pilate, had risen again, and at the last (which they believed to be in the near future) would judge the world. It would all have been less startling to the ancient mind if only the story could be cut free of its historical anchorage and interpreted as a cosmic or psychological myth attached to an esoteric mystery-cult.

GNOSTICISM

Among his Gentile converts Paul soon met doctrinal tendencies of which he did not approve and which called for delicate but firm correction. At Corinth a spiritual aristocracy were inclined to pride themselves on the possession of profounder wisdom and deeper mystical experiences than their brethren or even than the apostle himself. Believing themselves to be already perfect, they regarded their fellow-Christians as inferior beings who had not risen to the truly

supernatural heights. They were also dualists, believing that
the spirit is everything, the body nothing (if not actually evil).
This belief had immediate moral consequences. Some Corinthians concluded that physical acts were a matter of indifference; taking encouragement from Paul's doctrine of
freedom from the law, and regarding the sacraments as
magical guarantees of automatic bliss, they fell into moral
licence. A rival group adopted extreme ascetic opinions, so
that husbands and wives withheld conjugal rights from one
another and betrothed couples abstained from consumma-
ting their marriage. Consistent with this dualism they rejected as crude the Hebraic doctrine of the resurrection of
the body, preferring the Platonic doctrine of the immortality
of the soul; in any event, to those who were already perfect,
resurrection could add nothing. They saw no harm in eating
meat offered in sacrifice to idols, which they knew to be
non-existent.

At Colossae in Asia Minor Paul met with graver heresy, a
syncretistic amalgam of Christianity with theosophical
elements drawn partly from the mystery cults and partly
from heterodox Judaism. The Colossian Christians were
being persuaded to worship intermediate angelic powers,
identified with the heavenly bodies, and believed to possess a
power to determine human fate unbroken by the Gospel.
Special ceremonies and strict ascetic practices were enjoined, with feast-days drawn from the Jewish calendar.

Both these types of heresy, at Corinth and Colossae,
belong to the general category commonly labelled 'Gnosticism', a phenomenon which became an immense problem
and threat to the Church as the personal authority of the
first generation of Christian leaders receded into the past.
Gnosticism is a generic term used primarily to refer to theosophical adaptations of Christianity propagated by a dozen
or more rival sects which broke with the early church
between A.D. 80 and 150. The word is often used in a much
wider and vaguer sense to describe an imprecise, syncretistic
religiosity diffused widely in the Levantine world, and existing independently of and prior to Christianity. Behind this
double usage of the word there lies a complicated con-

troversy – whether and in what sense Gnosticism existed before Christianity. The question can be otherwise stated thus: Were the second century heresies the consequence of attempts to superimpose alien theosophical elements on a Christian substratum? or systems which resulted from fitting bits of Christianity into a prior religious entity, which might take several different forms and could assimilate Mithras or Attis or Judaism with as little trouble as it accepted Jesus? There is no dispute that many of the raw materials of Gnosticism, drawn from Platonism, hellenized Zoroastrianism, and Judaism, were present before Christianity; but it is unlikely that they had been blended into a systematic or organized body of 'doctrine' attached to any particular group or groups of people in space and time, or that a redemption myth closely resembling that of Christianity was widely current already.

The term Gnosticism is derived from the ordinary Greek word for knowledge (*gnosis*). The second century sects claimed to possess a special 'knowledge' which transcended the simple faith of the Church. But in fact their knowledge was not of a philosophical or intellectualist character, but rather a knowledge of human nature and destiny, especially Gnostic destiny, based on a grandiose revelation about the origin of the world which explained how evil had come into being and how one should act in order to gain deliverance from it. What they claimed to 'know' consisted of a myth about the creation of the world as the result of a pre-cosmic disaster which accounted for the present misery of our lot, and about the way in which the elect few may be redeemed. In the elect, they believed, there was a divine spark that had become imprisoned in matter and had lost its memory of its true, heavenly home. The content of the Gnostic gospel was an attempt to rouse the soul from its sleep-walking condition and to make it aware of the high destiny to which it is called. The present material world the Gnostics regarded as utterly alien to the supreme God and to goodness, and as therefore the creation of inferior powers, either incompetent or malevolent. The natural order of things reflected nothing at all of the divine glory and of the matchless heavenly beauty, and towards it the Gnostic initiate was taught to acknowledge no responsibility. His ethic was to be one of complete freedom from any constraint or any obligation towards society and government regarding which he entertained the most pessimistic opinions. The world was in the iron control of evil powers whose home was in the seven planets, and after death the elect soul would be faced by a perilous journey through the planetary spheres back to its heavenly home. Much time was therefore devoted to learning the correct magic passwords and the most potent amulets, which would enable the delivered soul to force the monstrous powers barring the ascent to open their doors and allow him to pass onward and upward to the realm of light. The rival sects, which hated one another as much as they hated orthodoxy, used to offer different sets of names and passwords to be learnt, each group claiming to possess the authentic forms, with which alone the soul's ascent could be successful. The details of the myths of the various sects were widely divergent. But the basic pattern can be seen to be constant. The Gnostic ethic, however, could take one of two forms, both based on the estimate of the natural order as wholly alien from God. The majority of the sects demanded an ascetic life with rules for the mortification of the flesh and a special prohibition on marriage (or at least on procreation), so that the divine soul might be liberated from the bonds of sense and bodily appetite and assisted to turn itself towards higher things. But some groups drew the opposite conclusion from the basic premise, and became notorious for their orgies of immorality. (In the New Testament the epistle of Jude warns against some Gnostic group which was exploiting the agape or love-feast and turning it into riotous licence.) The latter type liked to appeal to St Paul's doctrine that the Christian is free from the law and lives under grace as a son of the kingdom, and (so far were they from being uneducated crudities) subtly justified their eroticism by appeals to the *Symposium* of Plato as teaching that love is a mystical communion with God.

To the Gnostic myth the cosmogony of Plato's *Timaeus* and the first chapters of Genesis contributed in almost equal proportions. But the story of the Fall of Adam and Eve exercised a deep fascination over the Gnostic imagination. The Fall of Eve was taken to symbolize a pre-cosmic catastrophe in which a female power, the 'Mother', went astray from the divinely intended path. Or the story might suggest exciting speculations about the role of the serpent: the Ophites (i.e. serpent worshippers) argued that since through the serpent Adam and Eve had come to have knowledge of good and evil, he was a good power, the Leviathan encircling the cosmos with his tail in his mouth to symbolize eternity, who had out-manoeuvred the inferior creator and his son Jesus (whom the Ophites solemnly cursed in their liturgy). Apart from the book of Genesis the main ingredient which Gnosticism derived from Judaism was a transmuted apocalyptic. Jewish apocalyptic painted a dark picture of the present world as the bone of contention between rival angelic armies, good and evil, and as the expected stage of a dramatic divine intervention redeeming God's elect. The Gnostics eliminated any historical or literalist element from this notion and reinterpreted the apocalyptic world picture of Armageddon as a myth either about the origins of the world or about inward psychological experience.

The principal ingredient which Gnosticism derived from Christianity was the central idea of redemption. But not all the second-century sects included Jesus as the redeemer. Among the Samaritans a popular form of Gnosticism made Simon Magus the redeemer. In another system the Greek hero Heracles appears as the chief bringer of salvation, and Jesus plays a very subordinate role indeed. Even in those sects which stood closest to orthodox Christianity, such as the groups founded by the Egyptian Basilides and by the Platonist Valentinus of Rome, the Gnostic attitude to matter as alien to the supreme God required the rejection of any genuine incarnation. The divine Christ (they held) might have appeared to blinded worldlings as if he were tangible flesh and blood, but those with higher insight perceived that he was pure spirit and that the physical appearance was an optical illusion and mere semblance (*dokesis*, whence this doctrine is labelled Docetism). It was inconceivable that the divine Christ could have come 'in the flesh' in any ultimately true sense. What people would have seen if they had been there at the time would have differed according to their spiritual capacity.

It was the intense stress on the absolute necessity of a redeemer from the divine realm which led the Gnostics to place the natural order at so vast a distance in moral value from the supreme God. The influence of fatalistic ideas drawn from popular astrology and magic became fused with notions derived from Pauline language about predestination to produce a rigidly deterministic scheme. Redemption was from destiny, not from the consequences of responsible action, and was granted to a pre-determined elect in whom alone was the divine spark. Valentinus modified the division of humanity into light and darkness by allowing the existence of some grey twilight in between the two extremes. He took a lead from St Paul's phrase (1 Thess. v, 23) that we consist of spirit, soul, and body, and applied the threefold division both to humanity and to the entire cosmos. The Gnostic initiates were people of the spirit, the elect, whose salvation was certain and indefectible. Ordinary church members, with faith but not 'knowledge', were only of *psyche*, while the heathen were merely earthy clods without even the dimmest ray of light or the faintest hope of salvation. Valentinus allowed his followers to entertain hopes that some moderate degree of twilight happiness hereafter might be granted to those of *psyche*. But the three classes were determined from eternity. The natural person was constitutionally incapable of discerning the higher things of the spirit.

A further consequence of the Gnostic devaluation of the created order was the depreciation of the Old Testament. This was greatly accentuated by a thorough exploitation of the Pauline antithesis of law and gospel. The Gnostics liked to contrast the God of the Old Testament as the God of justice, whose principle was an eye for an eye and a tooth for a tooth, with the loving Father proclaimed by Jesus. This antithesis was especially worked out by Marcion, a figure who stands quite apart from the main stream of Gnosticism in that his system of thought did not include speculations about cosmogony or the names of the angels, but who in this one respect was the most radical and to the church the most formidable of heretics. Marcion came from Asia Minor to Rome, where the church excommunicated him in 144. He wrote a book entitled *Antitheses* (to which 1 Tim. vi, 20 could conceivably be an allusion) in which he listed contradictions between the Old and New Testaments to prove that the God of the Jews, the creator of this miserable world, was quite different from the God and Father of Jesus of whose existence the world had no inkling until the fifteenth year of Tiberius Caesar when Jesus suddenly appeared preaching the Gospel. It was inconceivable that the divine redeemer could ever have been born of a woman, and Marcion rejected the story of the birth and childhood of Christ as a falsification imposed on the authentic story.

Marcion's attack on the status of the Old Testament depended on two axioms: the rejection of allegorical interpretation and the assertion that the first generation of Jewish Christians had misunderstood and misinterpreted the mind of Jesus. If allegory was disallowed, there was much in the Old Testament which appeared distressing. The God of the Jews, Marcion argued, was vacillating: after forbidding the making of images, he told Moses to set up a brazen serpent. He was ignorant: he had to ask Adam where he was and descended to Sodom and Gomorrah to discover what was going on. Moreover, as the creator of Adam he was responsible for the entrance of evil into the world. In one text of the Old Testament God himself confesses 'I create evil'. It was congruous, thought Marcion, that he should so favour that bloodthirsty and licentious bandit, King David. Moreover, it was this creator who devised the humiliating method of sexual reproduction, the discomforts of pregnancy, and the pains of childbirth, the mere contemplation of which filled Marcion with nausea. The Marcionite community was accordingly strict in its rejection of marriage as helping the inferior creator in his repulsive business. Marcion's rejection of allegory destroyed any invocation of the argument from the fulfilment of prophecy, for the Old Testament prophets were not inspired by the kindly Father of Jesus. They expected a Jewish national Messiah, and their God was so limited in vision as to have a special favour for the Jewish people. In Marcion's evaluation of the Old Testament there lurks a constant overtone of anti-Semitism.

The assertion that the first Christians had misinterpreted their Master was necessary to Marcion because it was clear that the New Testament writings presupposed continuity between the Old and the New covenants. Marcion concluded that the documents had been considerably corrupted by the Judaisers of whose insidious methods St Paul complained in the epistle to the Galatians. He therefore set about the task of restoring the true text. St Paul was his hero, but the Pauline epistles he found interpolated and altered by Judaising interests anxious to make the apostle say that the Old Testament contained divine revelation. Even there cuts and restorations had to be made. In the case of the Gospels Marcion could take a shorter way. He took it for granted that only one could be authoritative, and decided that it must be St Luke's. But in its existing form St Luke's text showed every sign of acknowledging the validity of the Old Testament revelation and of assuming the continuity of the Gospel with the word spoken in time past to Moses and the prophets. This text also, therefore, had been corrupted by Judaisers. Moreover, the original text, Marcion believed, was the work of Paul himself, and he therefore undertook to establish the authentic text of Paul's Gospel as it was before his uncomprehending friends and disciples had altered it. Marcion thus became the first person to draw up an exclusive canonical list of Biblical books, which excluded all the Old Testament and large parts of the New, grounded on the basic assumption that the twelve apostles had not possessed the insight to comprehend the true meaning of Jesus.

Valentinus dealt with the Bible very differently. He did not reject allegory, which to his Platonist mind was profoundly congenial. Some Valentinians distinguished in the Old Testament between those parts inspired by God, certain sections inserted by Moses by way of concession to the hardness of men's hearts, and a third group of inferior passages that had been inserted by the Jewish elders and possessed no authority. But the Valentinians had no special interest in depreciating the Old Testament. Nor did they utter any breath of disparagement against the original apostles of Jesus. The Valentinian mythology, it was claimed, had been secretly taught by Jesus to the disciples, and from them had been passed down by an esoteric oral tradition side by side with the public teaching of the church.

THE MINISTRY AND THE BIBLE

The basic difficulty raised by these teachers was to know on what authoritative ground their doctrines could be refuted.

In a word the central issue was that of Authority. What was the true interpretation of the Old and New Testaments? Who now occupied the teaching chairs of the apostles and could give clear guidance to bewildered believers? Where could one find reliable evidence of what the apostles had really taught?

Ignatius of Antioch sought to answer the problem of centrifugal movements by insisting upon the local bishop as the focus of unity; without him the lifegiving sacraments could not be administered. He gave this, so to speak, a vertical justification by claiming that the bishop is God's representative on earth, an earthly counterpart corresponding to the heavenly Monarch, so that 'we ought to regard the bishop as the Lord himself'.

A more permanent justification of ministerial authority came from Rome. About the end of the first century there was a revolution in the Corinthian Church which deposed its old clergy and put new men in their place. In deep fraternal concern a formal and successful letter of protest was sent by the Roman Church, composed by Clement, probably the presiding presbyter or bishop of the Church. The letter, which was written with extreme care and solemnity and claimed to be inspired, besought the Corinthians to preserve ordered unity and to rectify the scandal caused by deposing members of the sacred order who stand in due succession from the apostles, even if not actually ordained by apostles, and who have 'blamelessly offered the gifts' in the holy rite of the eucharist.

At Corinth Clement found no doctrinal deviation, but in this idea of a succession from the apostles there was a weapon capable of being developed in the subsequent conflicts with Gnosticism. Against any heretical claim to possess secret traditions of what Jesus had told the apostles in the forty days after the resurrection, there was the clear argument that the apostles Peter and Paul could not have failed to impart such doctrines to those whom they had set over the churches, and that by the line of accredited teachers in those churches of apostolic foundation no such heretical notions had been transmitted. The succession argument carried the implication that the teaching given by the contemporary bishop of, say, Rome or Antioch was in all respects identical with that of the apostles. This was important, for two reasons. In the first place, the faithful were thereby in some sense assured that revelation was not only knowable by a retrospective historical knowledge derived from either the apostles' occasional writings or anecdotal gossip, but had in the bishop a contemporary authority, able and authorized to speak God's word in the present. In the second place, it enabled the defenders of orthodoxy, especially Irenaeus of Lyons, to oppose to the proliferating Gnostic sects, none of which agreed with one another and all of which were continually modifying their views, the concept of the monolithic church, universally extended in space and with unbroken continuity in time, unanimous in its possession of an immutable revelation (below, p. 82).

The second weapon of the orthodox defence was the gradual formation of the New Testament canon. In the first century the Christian Bible had simply been the Old Testament (read in the Septuagint version). Authority resided in this scripture and in the words of the Lord, which long circulated in oral tradition, as is apparent in the letter of Clement to the Corinthians. The authoritative standing of this oral tradition continued to be high even after the sayings and doings of the Lord had been written down in the 'gospel' according to Mark, Luke, Matthew, or John. Even as late as the time of Irenaeus (c. 185–90) this oral tradition of the words of the Lord was regarded as an authority that had not yet been wholly merged with the written gospels. But the controversy with Marcion and the Gnostics gave a sharp impetus to the control of authentic tradition which a written document possessed and which oral transmission did not. Justin Martyr, who probably knew all the four canonical gospels, seems to have used Matthew, Mark, and Luke in a gospel harmony, to which his pupil Tatian added St John to form his *Diatessaron* (below, p. 62). The synoptic gospels seem to have achieved general acceptance rather earlier than St John's gospel, the authority of which was disputed by some. The existence of four versions of the gospel was a troublesome puzzle in itself. Marcion (above, p. 39) accepted only one. The Valentinians accepted not only the well known four but many additional documents professing to contain traditions of the secret sayings of Jesus, like the *Gospel of Thomas* recently recovered from the sands of Egypt. Irenaeus ingeniously vindicated the fourfold gospel on numerological principles. Four, he urged, was a sacred number corresponding to the four winds, or the four faces of the cherubim in Ezekiel and the Johannine Apocalypse with faces resembling a lion, a calf, a man, and an eagle. But apart from accepted use in church lectionaries the prime criterion was apostolicity. Mark and Luke were set beside Matthew and John as being sanctioned by Peter and Paul respectively.

The Gospel of John caused some controversy because of its evidently discrepant account compared with the other three Gospels, but it was skilfully defended by Irenaeus as being the work of John son of Zebedee, to whom he also ascribed the Revelation.

The strict application of the criterion of apostolicity in Rome led to the exclusion from the western New Testament of the Epistle to the Hebrews, which Roman tradition knew to be non-Pauline, and it was only readmitted in the West more than 200 years later on the authority of the eastern churches. It also led to the eventual exclusion of writings like the Shepherd of Hermas and the epistle of Clement to the Corinthians which did not claim to be apostolic. A fragment giving the New Testament canon probably of Rome about 200 (the 'Muratorian canon')[1] explains that the Shepherd is good private reading, but as its author was neither apostle nor prophet but a recent writer it is disqualified for admission to the lectionary.

Naturally enough, orthodoxy and apostolicity were equated. This made it difficult to detect the non-apostolic authorship of orthodox documents like the second epistle of Peter (which, nevertheless, was debated for a long time). Other disputed and eventually successful documents were the Revelation of John, the epistles of James and Jude, and the second and third epistles of John. Likewise disputed but unsuccessful candidates on the orthodox side were the Acts of Paul and Thecla and the Apocalypse of Peter. Sometimes modern writers wonder at the disagreements. The truly astonishing thing is that so great a measure of agreement was reached so quickly.

The third and last weapon against heresy was the 'Rule of Faith', a title used by Irenaeus and Tertullian to mean a short summary of the main revelatory events of the redemptive process. Irenaeus declares that the whole Church believes 'in one God the Father Almighty, maker of heaven and earth and the seas and all that is therein, and in one Christ Jesus the Son of God, who was made flesh for our salvation, and in the Holy Spirit who through the prophets preached the dispensations and the comings and the virgin birth and the passion, and the rising from the dead and the assumption into heaven in his flesh of our beloved Lord Jesus Christ, and his coming from heaven in the glory of the Father . . . to raise up all flesh.' The crux of this summary for polemical purposes lies in its assertion of the unity of the divine plan from Old Testament to New, a theme which Irenaeus developed in his doctrine of 'recapitulation' or the correspondence between Adam and Christ. The heretics did not believe the supreme God to be maker of heaven and earth and, with their low valuation of the Old Testament, were not interested in the fulfilment of prophecy.

1. Some think it of fourth-century origin. First printed in 1740 by L. A. Muratori from an eighth-century manuscript at Milan.

This Rule (Irenaeus claimed) is what the bishops teach now and therefore comes down from the apostles. In content it is akin to the formulas used in the questions put to candidates for baptism and is simply the credal pattern based on the New Testament. Tertullian treated it as independent of Scripture because, in argument with heretics, it was a better defence than the Bible, over the interpretation of which one can argue long with the sole effect of bewildering simple folk who want a short and direct answer. Tertullian argued that the Bible is often difficult to interpret. Obscure passages must be interpreted by those which are plain. Moreover, the Bible is old. To appeal to the Rule of Faith is to appeal to what is now being taught by the churches of apostolic foundation. So Tertullian, following Irenaeus before him but going considerably further, seems here to have distinguished between Scripture and Tradition almost as if they were distinct sources of revelation. Nevertheless, Tertullian was also well aware that the Rule of Faith is derived from Scripture: for him to say that the Rule is the key for interpreting the Bible is no different from saying that obscure passages must be interpreted by the clear. The argument is of course circular: the tradition of Church teaching must be proved orthodox by the biblical revelation; yet doubtful books are admitted to the New Testament canon because they are orthodox by the standards of Church tradition, and only the tradition can ensure that the interpretation of Scripture is sound.

FORMS OF THE MINISTRY

The apostles derived their name and function from the fact of being sent by the Lord as missionaries. They were not the only ones to receive gifts of the Spirit. There were also 'prophets', like Agabus (Acts xi, 28; xxi, 7), and teachers, accredited as instructors in the faith. At Corinth the Church especially prized the gift of ecstatic irrational utterance ('speaking with tongues'). Paul could not afford to deny that the gift of ecstasy was a genuine manifestation of the Spirit, but was alarmed by its divisive possibilities (1 Cor.

xiii) and told the Corinthians that the enthusiastic utterance they especially prized was the last in the graded hierarchy of supernatural gifts: it is preceded by 'first apostles, second prophets, third teachers, next miracle-workers, then healers, helpers, and administrators' (1 Cor. xii, 28). The first three in this sevenfold hierarchy are the chief 'orders' of the first missionary generation.

Sixty or seventy years later Ignatius was speaking of Antioch and the Asian churches as possessing a monarchical bishop, together with presbyters and deacons. In his time there were neither apostles nor prophets. The exact history of this transition within two generations from apostles, prophets and teachers to bishop, presbyters and deacons is shrouded in obscurity, though our sources give occasional glimpses of the process. The epistle of Clement of Rome to the Corinthians implies the existence of two distinct orders of ministry, bishops *or* presbyters (the titles are applied to the same people) and deacons. This twofold order is also apparent in the New Testament: Paul addresses his Philippian epistle to the 'bishops and deacons'. Later New Testament writings (Acts xx, 17; Titus i, 5–7) likewise illustrate the application of 'presbyter' and 'bishop' to the same person. Evidently the churches established by the travelling missionaries soon came to have local, stationary clergy, subordinate to the general oversight of mobile apostolic authority. For a generation or more the apostles and prophets coexisted with this local ministry of bishops and deacons. This situation is in fact reflected in the *Didache* or 'Teaching of the Apostles',[1] a document reckoned as Scripture by many early Fathers but which disappeared until 1883 when Archbishop Bryennios printed it from a manuscript, now at Jerusalem, dated 1056. The text may have suffered some revision over the centuries before this date. From the beginning the *Didache* was a composite work, made up of bits and pieces. Its date and purpose have been much debated, and because of the mistaken opinion that it is dependent on the *Epistle of Barnabas* (probably an Alexandrian work of about 130–40) it has often been thought to be a late fiction. But the situation

1. The title might also be translated 'Instruction for missionaries'.

regarding Church order presupposed in the *Didache* makes it hard to find any plausible niche for it in early Christian history other than the period between about 70 and 110. It may be odd there, but it is much odder anywhere else.

The *Didache* begins with moral exhortation for converts, taken from an extant Jewish tract 'The Two Ways', followed by directions for baptism, fasts on Wednesdays and Fridays, the correct form of the Lord's Prayer (to be said thrice daily), and eucharistic prayers, notable (but not very astonishing) for the lack of reference to the redemptive death of Christ as interpreted by Paul. The last section (possibly a slightly later addition?) is especially sensitive about the danger of charlatans; it gives rules concerning hospitality towards apostles and prophets and other visitors with claims upon the community's generosity, and offers directions concerning the way to detect false prophets (see below, p. 57), concerning the proper stipend of a prophet who decides to settle permanently with a particular congregation, and concerning the parallel provision of a local ministry which is not itinerant:

Appoint for yourselves therefore bishops and deacons worthy of the Lord, men that are meek and not lovers of money, true and reliable; for they also perform for you the ministry of prophets and teachers. Do not despise them therefore; for they are your men of honour together with the prophets and teachers.

The writer evidently feared that the local ministers might not receive the same respect as the itinerant charismatics. As the congregations consolidated, the part played by travelling missionaries and prophets receded into the background. Inspired utterance in preaching was expected of the regular local ministry. To Ignatius of Antioch the wonder of divine grace was found in the sacramental life of the church gathered round its bishop, who spoke in the Spirit. It is noteworthy that in the *Didache*, as in the letter of Clement to Corinth and in the later New Testament writings (see 1 Tim. iii), the local ministry is two-tiered – bishops or presbyters and deacons. Between these two orders, according to all the evidence, there is a distinction in liturgical function: in the common eucharist the presbyter-bishop celebrates while the deacon assists. Deacons also helped the bishops in looking after any church property and in administering charitable relief. In the third century the congregations had swollen to such a size that deacons had to maintain proper order; in North Africa in Cyprian's time the deacon administered the chalice. At Rome in 150, according to Justin Martyr's evidence, the deacon used to take the consecrated elements to absent brethren who were imprisoned or sick. Later, in some but not in all churches, it was customary for the deacon to read the liturgical Gospel.

It was a natural missionary strategy for the Church to make the towns its first objective, and it became normal to serve the rural congregations, in the region under the civil administration of the city (which might be very large), by sending out deacons. During the second and third centuries there must have been many occasions when the deacons actually celebrated the eucharist. This practice was frowned upon and at the Councils of Arles (314) and Nicaea (325) explicitly forbidden. By then it was usual for rural congregations to be served by a resident presbyter.

St Luke's account of the Seven in Acts vi is probably intended to recount the origin of the diaconate, though this identification of the Seven with deacons is first made explicit by Irenaeus. It is noteworthy that the Roman church always had seven deacons; and the same number was common in the churches of Asia Minor in the third and fourth centuries.

The diaconate was not originally a probationary order for the presbyterate,[1] but normally lifelong, unless a deacon were made a bishop. In great cities like Rome the office was powerful. The earliest recorded 'archdeacon' appears in North Africa early in the fourth century. An ancient archdeacon was not as today a presbyter, but the senior deacon with large financial and administrative responsibility. Many

1. The first person known to have been promoted through all orders is Cornelius of Rome (251–3). By the fourth century the idea is well established that clergy may hope to be promoted through the successive grades as steps of a ladder.

deacons and especially archdeacons succeeded to the episcopate.

The charitable (but not the liturgical) side of the diaconate was shared with deaconesses who had special responsibilities for women.

The assistant status of the deacons is evident in the earliest known form of ordination in the *Apostolic Tradition* of Hippolytus (about 200–220):[1] while all the presbyters join with the bishop in laying hands on candidates for the presbyterate, the bishop alone lays hands on the deacon since 'he is not ordained for priesthood but for the service of the bishop'.

This two-tiered ministry is integrally linked to the eucharistic celebration. But among the presbyter-bishops one rose to a position of superiority, and acquired the title 'bishop' while his colleagues are called 'presbyters'. Four factors helped to bring this about. The first distinctive right naturally assigned to the senior member of the presbyteral college was the power to ordain. This became his prerogative. Secondly, correspondence between churches was normally carried on by the presiding presbyter-bishop. Thirdly, on the solemn occasion of an ordination, leaders from other communities would come as representatives of their own congregations and would take part in the laying on of hands and prayers which conferred the power of the Spirit and the authority of the community as the body of Christ. Frequent exchanges by correspondence and mutual visiting helped the concrete realization of the Church's unity and universality. Finally, the crisis of the Gnostic sects showed the manifest necessity of a single man as the focus of unity.

At Jerusalem the Church had had from the start a single figure at the head of the body of elders. The correspondence of Ignatius betrays no sign that at Antioch any other system had once prevailed, though the *Didache* (probably Syrian) would suggest otherwise. The elevation of the episcopate

1. This document survives in a fragmentary Latin version of about 400, and parts are incorporated in other church orders extant in Greek, Ethiopic, Coptic, Syriac, and Arabic. Unhappily the textual tradition cannot be traced back earlier than the second half of the fourth century; caution is therefore necessary in using its evidence (below, p. 262).

into an order standing above the presbyterate, while also
remaining on a level with it, was taking place in the period
when apostolic authority was going or gone. The process may
have been helped by the example of the churches of Jerusalem
and Antioch. The bishop among his presbyters remained
first among equals and for centuries continued to address
them as 'fellow-presbyters'; presbyters too had authority to
celebrate the eucharist and were entrusted with the disciplinary 'power of the keys' (Matt. xvi, 19; xviii, 18; John xx, 23)
by which the purity of the society was maintained and
sinning brethren excluded. At the same time the presbyter
inherited the lower role of the 'teacher', while the bishop
inherited those of the apostle and the prophet: it is primarily
the bishop who ordains presbyters, though the presbyters
join in the laying on of hands. Some variety of custom appears
on the question whether, when the bishop himself is being
consecrated, the presbyters of his church share in the laying
on of hands. At Alexandria we are told that they did so until
the third century and there is no mention of visiting bishops;
but at Rome by the time of Hippolytus only the bishops who
came from other churches laid hands on the one to be consecrated, the chief consecrator being chosen by the bishops
themselves. The service was held on a Sunday. The actual
choice of the candidate rested with the whole congregation,
clergy and people together, an idealistic system which
assumed unanimity but in practice led to faction. Election
by the people likewise played a large part in the ordination
of presbyters and deacons.[1] With the advent of a Christian
emperor in the fourth century, especially when the local
church was passionately divided, it began to become common
for the bishops of important cities to be imperially nominated;
it was soon discovered that no system of election or nomination is free of abuses and that even emperors were not always
disinterested.

1. The process of electing a new bishop could be sharply divisive.
Unanimity of choice was sufficiently unusual to be regarded as a special
grace. In a few cases the people's choice was settled by special considerations. In the middle of the third century Fabian of Rome owed his
election to the fact that a dove alighted on his head, and was taken to
symbolize the choice of the Spirit.

The transition from a missionary ministry to a local and pastoral ministry was going on at the time when the emergence of the bishop as transcendent among his fellow-presbyters was also beginning to become apparent. Partly because of the tendency to idealize the apostolic age, it is often supposed that, besides these two changes, there was also a parallel transition from vitality to formalism, from freedom to rigidity, or even from a lay democracy to a clerical authoritarianism. The truth is not so simple. In fact there have probably been few periods in church history when authority has had comparable difficulty in asserting itself and when freedom so nearly meant anarchy as in the sub-apostolic age. It is true that from the middle of the second century onwards there is a strong reaction towards standardization in both faith and order; diversities in dogmatic formulation, in matters of liturgical practice (such as the observance of Easter), and in the text of Scripture began to be smoothed out. The basic presupposition of the process on which all were in principle agreed, was the idea that since the Church is one, its beliefs and practices should be uniform. Variety in church order was a legacy of the missionary beginnings: in some churches one man would have been entrusted with sole authority, in others a single leader might not be available and it would then seem best to put a body of elders in charge. Much missionary enterprise was undertaken by individuals acting without special authority from any church or apostle, and the leading sub-apostolic churches had then the task of bringing these congregations into line as members of the federation. The three-tiered system of one bishop in one city, with presbyters and deacons, was attained in the second century without controversy. A further natural development was the provincial system by which in the third century special dignity came to be accorded to the bishop of the metropolis of the imperial province, and yet more transcendent honour to the bishops of the three greatest cities of the empire, Rome, Alexandria, Antioch, which are nominated in the sixth canon of the Council of Nicaea as possessing a jurisdiction beyond that of the civil province (below, p. 131). The whole development is a story of transition from unregulated church organization to a more close-knit arrangement.

The antithesis between immediate inspiration and mediated authority emerges sharply in the Montanist crisis in the seventies of the second century. A Phrygian named Montanus was seized by the Spirit and, together with two women, Prisca and Maximilla, delivered utterances of the Paraclete in a state of 'ecstasy', i.e. not being in possession of his faculties. It was the peculiar form of these utterances to which other Christians objected: this kind of ecstatic prophecy was not, like that of the biblical prophets, delivered in the third person, but was direct speech by the Spirit himself using the prophet's mouth as his instrument. The content of the 'New Prophecy' was hostile to the Gnostic elimination of eschatological expectation and insisted on the literal resurrection of the flesh and the nearness of the End. As prophesied in the Revelation of St John, the Lord would shortly come to reign on earth with his saints for a thousand years. Local patriotism led the three prophets to claim that the heavenly Jerusalem would descend in Phrygia. The Montanists did not expect all the Lord's people to be prophets, but rather required their fellow-Christians to 'acknowledge' the supernatural nature of the utterances of the Paraclete's chosen three: to reject them was blasphemy against the Holy Spirit. This demand split the churches in Asia Minor, some thinking the New Prophecy divine, others diabolical. The opposition to Montanism eventually won, but at a price. In Thyatira the entire church remained Montanist to a man for nearly a century; and inscriptions show how the sect lived on.[1] Though refused recognition by the Church at large (after some hesitations at Rome where both sides competed to win the bishop's support), its puritanism and revivalist ethics won for it a notable convert in the brilliant African orator Tertullian,

1. The inscriptions show that the Montanists were much more uncompromising than their Catholic brethren about making an open confession of their faith before the world. It is virtually only from central Phrygia, a Montanist stronghold, that we have explicitly Christian epitaphs of the third century, often with the challenging formula 'Christians to Christians'. Elsewhere neutral formulas are used on Christian tombs of this period.

who died fulminating against his former Catholic brethren
because they imagined that the Church was constituted by
bishops rather than spiritual men.

The orthodox reply, as formulated by Hippolytus of
Rome, was unerringly directed against Montanism's weakest
point, namely its divisiveness: the quest for miraculous gifts
is well (he thought), but the supreme miracle is conversion
and therefore every believer alike has the gifts of the Spirit;
the supernatural is discerned in the normal ministry of word
and sacrament, not in irrational ecstasies which lead to pride
and censoriousness.

The chief effect of Montanism on the Catholic Church was
greatly to reinforce the conviction that revelation had come
to an end with the apostolic age, and so to foster the creation
of a closed canon of the New Testament. Irenaeus is the last
writer who can still think of himself as belonging to the
eschatological age of miracle and revelation.

The prominence of women in Montanism revived the
relatively high participation of women in the life of the
early Church (e.g. Acts xxi, 9; 1 Cor. xi, 5, and their emphatic
presence in the Gospels). But already at Corinth excessive
feminine independence led Paul to ask for restriction (1
Cor. xiv, 34–5). In classical Greek society, 'silence is a
woman's glory' (Sophocles). The sub-apostolic churches
needed order, above all in ministry and procedures for
ordination at a time when the development of the
episcopate was among the conditions for Christianity's
coherence and survival. The leading role of women among
the sects may have encouraged the stress in 'the great
Church' on their exclusion from the presidential and public
functions of bishops and presbyters. In 375 Epiphanius observed polemically that Jesus did not call any women to be
apostles. In the third-century East (not West), women
deacons were receiving ordination from bishops by prayer
and imposition of hands and were fulfilling a pastoral role
in sick-visiting, anointing women at baptism, and giving
instruction. Paradoxically the West, under necessity, allowed women to baptize, the East not. The influence of
well-to-do women upon episcopal elections was notorious.

3

Expansion and Growth

EVEN to a writer as early as the author of Acts (probably c. 80), the expansion of the church seemed an extraordinary chain of improbabilities. Nothing could have been less likely to succeed by any ordinary standard of expectation. It appeared as a long story of strange coincidence in which human intentions played a subordinate role and where the eye of faith was entitled to discern the tranquil operation of a wiser providence.

The pagan writer Celsus (probably c. 180) saw it with the cold eye of a hostile external observer. He picked on the close-knit structure and coherence of the Christians as a social group, and saw in this the principal source of Christian strength. But in his view this social coherence was not the consequence of any internal principle but merely the result of being persecuted: 'Their agreement is quite amazing, the more so as it may be shown to rest on no trustworthy foundation. However they have a trustworthy foundation for their unity in social dissidence and the advantage which it brings and in the fear of outsiders – these are factors which strengthen their faith.' The opposition which the Christians provoked may certainly be accounted an important factor in producing their cohesion, though it is certainly too simple to explain their social drive as resulting from some inner compensation for being rejected by society. Celsus was also aware that the Christians worshipped in secret for fear of arrest. Publicity was dangerous, and sometimes the smell of a sip of insufficiently diluted wine at the eucharist might lead to betrayal. The earliest churches were simply private houses, gradually converted inside as the congregations grew. It was not till the fourth century that churches acquired a 'public' style of architecture and became recognizable as such. Nevertheless, it is an illusion to think that persecution drove the Church down to the catacombs and that the sacraments had to be celebrated in a kind of troglodyte life. Persecution, so far from driving the church underground, had the opposite effect. When one governor in Asia Minor in the second century began persecuting the Christians, the entire Christian population of the region paraded before his house as a manifesto of their faith and as a protest against the injustice. From the start the Christians were a society abnormally sensitive to outside opinion. The enemies that they had to conquer were prejudice and misinformation.

Motives which led to conversions were no doubt as various as they are today. Curiosity about a secretive sect suspected of immorality, the witnessing of a martyrdom, ordinary relations of friendship: all were causes for further inquiry. At a deeper level, the Christian Gospel spoke of divine grace in Christ, the remission of sins and the conquest of evil powers for the sick soul, tired of living and scared of dying, seeking for an assurance of immortality and for security and freedom in a world where the individual could rarely do other than submit to his fate. The terms were those of the baptismal vows: a renunciation of sin and everything associated with demonic powers, idols, astrology and magic; and a declaration of belief in God the Father, in the redemptive acts of Christ's life, death, and resurrection, and in the Holy Spirit active in the Church. Though it is improbable that all converts knew themselves to be sick souls (perhaps relatively few found their way by guilt and tears and there is no evidence that many were hag-ridden with anxiety in this age more than in others), baptism and admission to the sacred meal meant a break with the past and a gift of grace by which the individual could live up to ideals and moral imperatives recognized by his conscience. In a word, Christianity directly answered to the human quest for true happiness – by which more is meant than *feeling* happy. Ancient Stoicism, nobly represented in the writings of the aristocrat Seneca, in the slave Epictetus, and (with a markedly individual, introspective, brooding mood) in the emperor Marcus Aurelius, taught that happiness is achieved by the suppression of desire for everything that one cannot both get and keep: 'Before the external disorder of the world and bodily illness, retreat into yourself and find God there.' The Stoic soul stood proudly erect amidst a sea of troubles, untouched by emotion. The Christians found much that was congenial in Stoic ethics ('Seneca often speaks like a Christian,' remarked Tertullian), and were not disposed to deny their indebtedness to its wisdom. The divergence lay in the Christian stress on the grace of God as making the Christian life possible, on the love of God (rather than the individual's self-respect) as the object towards which human striving should be directed, and on the outgoing activity of 'charity' towards one's fellow men.

The practical application of charity was probably the most potent single cause of Christian success. The pagan comment 'See how these Christians love one another' (reported by Tertullian) was not irony. Christian charity expressed itself in care for the poor, for widows and orphans, in visits to brethren in prison or condemned to the living death of labour in the mines, and in social action in time of calamity like famine, earthquake, pestilence, or war.

A particular service which the community rendered to poor brethren (following synagogue precedent) was to provide for their burial. In the second half of the second century, at any rate in Rome and Carthage, the churches began to acquire burial grounds for their members. One of the oldest of these was south of Rome on the Appian Way at a place named Catacumbas (below, p. 88), from which these cemeteries in the form of underground corridors have received the name 'catacombs'.

Hospitality to travellers was an especially important act of charity: a Christian brother had only to give proof of his faith to be sure of lodging for a period of up to three nights with no more questions asked. The bishop had the prime responsibility of providing such hospitality, especially for travelling missionaries. The bishop accordingly controlled the church revenues.

At first clergy stipends were paid on a dividend system (monthly in the time of Cyprian of Carthage); it was only much later that the growth of endowments made fixed incomes possible at least in many churches. The proportions distributed among the different claimants on the church's resources varied in different places. At Rome in the fifth century a quarter of the revenue went to the bishop, while the remaining three quarters was equally divided between the remaining clergy, those on the official list of sick and poor, and the maintenance of the church buildings. The financial independence of each church meant that rural clergy were ill paid while those in great cities or attached to popular shrines became well off. It was always recognized that the prime responsibility of the church treasury was to provide for the needs of the poor, and bishops who preferred to spend money on rich adornments and splendid churches were generally disapproved; in any event, there was no question of such elaboration before the time of Constantine.

The distribution of alms was obviously open to abuse. In the first century the author of the *Didache* was already giving warnings about exploitation by false brethren. A vivid and cruel portrait was painted by the pagan satirist Lucian of Samosata (*c.* 170), describing how a charlatan named Peregrinus Proteus (of whom other second-century pagans wrote more kindly) became a Christian for very worldly reasons, was elevated to the office of bishop and was imprisoned by the governor of Syria; but he so traded on the devotion of his church to their noble confessor that he made a very substantial profit before gaining his release and going on to his next adventure. Lucian had a low opinion of the human race, and treated Christianity as merely additional evidence of human absurdity and folly. But he knew that the Christians were unbelievably generous with their money and preferred to be open-handed rather than inquire too closely into the recipients.

By the year 251 the resources of the church in Rome had grown so much that it was supporting from its common purse not only the bishop, 46 presbyters, 7 deacons, 7 subdeacons, 42 acolytes, and 52 exorcists, readers and doorkeepers, but also more than 1500 widows and needy persons, all of whom were 'fed by the grace and kindness of the Lord'. The same community was also well known for its generosity to less prosperous Christians in areas that suffered under the ravages of barbarian invasion during the crisis of the third century. The persecution of 250 under Decius brought a number of refugee bishops to Rome where they could hide in the vast city and rely on the wealth of the Roman church to support them. But the distribution of alms was not confined only to believers. The assistance provided by the church was impressive in a world where, except for a period during the second century and again during Julian the Apostate's brief attempt to incorporate the church's ideals within paganism (below, p. 157), the government did not expect to undertake a general programme of social welfare.

Christianity being illegal, the church could not own property as such. From early in the fourth century, perhaps even as early as Gallienus' edict of toleration in 260 (below, p. 120), money and land began to be bequeathed to the church by will. A law of Constantine of 321, legalizing such bequests, presupposes that already they were being made and that in some cases their validity had been disputed. In consequence of this law the fourth century saw a great increase in the endowment income of the churches. In Asia Minor and Syria by the end of the fourth century it was common to bequeath a determined proportion (often a third) of one's property to the church; in the West the proportion set aside for the church was reckoned as the share that would be given to an additional child, so that Western custom paid more regard to the family's needs. An unusual view was represented by Salvian, a presbyter of Marseilles (400–480), who, confronted by vast pauperism under the barbarian invasions, denounced inherited wealth and taught that to bequeath anything to one's family prejudiced one's eternal interests.

Christianity seems to have been especially successful among women. It was often through the wives that it penetrated the upper classes of society in the first instance. Christians believed in the equality of men and women before God, and found in the New Testament commands that husbands should treat their wives with such consideration and love as Christ manifested for his church. Christian teaching about the sanctity of marriage offered a powerful safeguard to married women.[1] The Christian sex ethic differed from the conventional standards of pagan society in that it regarded unchastity in a husband as no less serious a breach of loyalty and trust than unfaithfulness in a wife. The apostle's doctrine that in Christ there is neither male nor female (Gal. iii, 28) was not taken to mean a programme of political emancipation, which in antiquity would have been unthinkable. The social role of women remained that of the home-maker and wife. At the same time, Christianity cut across ordinary social patterns more deeply than any other religion, and encouraged the notion of the responsibility of individual moral choice in a way that was quite exceptional.

Christianity did not give political emancipation to either women or slaves, but it did much to elevate their domestic status by its doctrine that all are created in God's image and all alike redeemed in Christ; and they must therefore be treated with sovereign respect. What made the Church conservative about slavery as an institution was not political indifference but respect for the State and for Law as laid down in Romans xiii. That any one should possess property rights over another was recognized as an evil, and therefore held to be a consequence of the fallen state of humanity since Adam. According to St Paul slavery is like a mixed marriage in which the Christian partner should not take the initiative in seeking for its dissolution (1 Cor. vii, 17–24). When St

1. Difficult pastoral problems were raised when a marriage broke down. There were some differences of opinion whether unfaithfulness in a spouse required or only permitted divorce (the latter view prevailing). It was agreed, on the basis of Matt. v, 32 and xix, 9, that it was a ground for dissolution of marriage. There were greater differences of opinion about the remarriage of divorced persons; for an innocent party Augustine judged it a venial sin, and in the third century there were some bishops who thought that in certain pastoral circumstances it was possible for the church's blessing to be given. The legislation of the Christian emperors tended to make divorce more difficult out of consideration for the needs of the children, but was not based on a consistent doctrine of marriage, which could hardly be found before the writings of Augustine.

Paul wrote his brilliant letter, uniting wit and seriousness, returning the (possibly runaway) slave Onesimus to his friends Philemon, Apphia and Archippus, he did not demand that a Christian should free him as a matter of principle – though in this particular case Paul no doubt hoped that the owner would do so, since he asked for Onesimus to be returned to him 'for the sake of the gospel'. To free a slave was regarded as a 'good work'; the Church treasury would be used to finance the manumission of slaves in bad households as also of those who became slaves by being prisoners of war. A Christian master would solemnly affirm his intention to free a slave in the presence of the bishop, a practice which Constantine confirmed by giving the ceremony a legal validity equal to that of formal manumission before a magistrate. In the Church masters and slaves were brethren. Several emancipated slaves rose to be bishops, notably Callistus of Rome in the third century (below, p. 88). Towards the end of the fourth century State legislation began to protect property rights by prohibiting the ordination of slaves without leave or financial compensation to the owner. Whereas under Roman law slaves could not contract a legal marriage, the Church regarded marriages between slaves and free as indissoluble. Protests against the institution of slavery as such came in the fourth century when the Christians were beginning to be in a position to affect social policy. But bequests had by this time made the fourth-century Church a considerable landowner, already dependent on endowments for clergy stipends and therefore in a weak position for initiating economic changes. These protests were too little and too late to revolutionize the economy of the ancient world and only have the historical significance of outlining a programme for the future.

THE GEOGRAPHICAL EXTENSION OF THE CHURCH

Christianity spread with remarkable rapidity in Syria and north-westwards into Asia Minor and Greece. To the north-east, however, it met both the imperial frontier and a lan-

guage barrier: the kingdom of Osrhoene with its capital at
Edessa lay outside the empire until 216 and spoke Syriac,
though educated people at Edessa knew Greek also. During
the second century a Christian community was established
in Edessa. Its most prominent member, Bardesanes, was
intimate with King Abgar IX the Great who was also converted to Christianity. Bardesanes was a cultivated man
whose poetry was of such quality as to achieve almost classical
status in Syriac literature. Before conversion he had been
expert in astrology. A pupil summarized his teaching in a
much plagiarized book, based on extensive comparative
researches, to prove that the divergent religious customs of
the different races invalidate astrological belief but do not,
as pagans (like Celsus) were arguing, establish the truth of
polytheism against Biblical monotheism. He recognized,
however, that not all diversity in worship and not all evils
can be attributed simply to free will. Those facts in the world
which are not attributable to either nature or human freedom
he ascribed to the conflict between angels and demons and
to destiny which, he conceded, had some relative power,
though not as much as the astrologers thought. At this point
a number of Gnostic themes and images began to enter his
poetic vision of the world and, though he vigorously opposed
the Marcionites in Edessa, his own orthodoxy was not
trusted at Antioch. Later Syrian Christians like Ephraem
(306–73) regarded him as a dangerous genius. To combat his
influence an Edessene Christian named Palut was consecrated to be bishop of Edessa by Serapion, bishop of Antioch,
about 200. At first Palut ministered only to a small minority
group; but after Edessa became part of the empire, the
Palutians were able to show that they enjoyed catholic
communion with Antioch and Rome as the followers of
Bardesanes did not.

The third century church at Edessa claimed as its founder
one of the 72 disciples of Jesus named Addai, sent in answer
to a letter written to Jesus by King Abgar the Black (*c.* A.D.
9–46). They could produce Jesus' reply promising Edessa
freedom from conquest. The correspondence between Abgar
and Jesus came to be a popular amulet, inscribed on houses

to avert evil. (The earliest known example comes from fifth century Asia Minor; copies may still be found in twentieth-century Britain.) Incorporation within the empire in 216, and the closer links with Antioch which were thereby fostered, brought in time one important change to the Mesopotamian Christians: though they had an early Syriac version of the separate gospels, they normally used the Gospel Harmony or *Diatessaron* of Tatian. A Greek fragment of this has been found in the Roman fortress at Dura on the Euphrates where also the spade has disclosed the oldest known house-church (below, p. 279). In the fourth or fifth century the *Diatessaron* was ousted by the Peshitta or standard Syriac version, and its text has now to be reconstructed from later adaptations in Arabic, Persian, Latin, Dutch, Italian, and Middle English.

Third-century legends in the *Acts of Thomas* (famous for its wonderful poem, 'The Hymn of the Soul')[1] give probable evidence of the existence of Christians not only in Persia but even in India, perhaps on the Malabar coast.

The main stream of missionary work flowed westwards and the fact that St Paul's eye had been towards Italy and Spain was fateful for the future identification of Christianity with European culture. When the Epistle to the Romans was written there was already a substantial church in Rome, and extension into other Italian cities quickly followed. At Pompeii, destroyed by the eruption of Vesuvius in 79, an inscription has been found in the form of the square:

ROTAS
OPERA
TENET
AREPO
SATOR

The letters can be rearranged to give PATERNOSTER with A and O, and this could conceivably be a Christian crypto-gram;[2] if this is correct, there were Christians in Pompeii before 79. By 250 there were about 100 episcopal sees in Italy.

1. M. R. James, *Apocryphal New Testament*, pp. 364–438.
2. Early examples have recently turned up at Aquincum (Budapest), A.D. 107; at Manchester, A.D. 175; at Coimbra, Portugal, possibly first century.

In Gaul, Britain and Spain the mission advanced more slowly. Christianity in Gaul seems to have begun with Paul's disciple Crescens (ii Tim. iv, 10). In the Rhône Valley in the second century there was a growing community of Greek Christians, having close connexions with Asia Minor, centred on a bishop at Lyons, and a mission-church under a deacon at nearby Vienne. They suffered grievously in 177 under the persecution of Marcus Aurelius, and not long afterwards were subjected to an infiltration by Gnostic teachers, which provoked the great work of bishop Irenaeus of Lyons, 'A Refutation of the knowledge falsely so-called'. Irenaeus preached in Celtic as well as in Greek, so that the evangelization of the native population had begun. By the beginning of the fourth century several bishoprics were established, including Arles, Vaison, Autun, Rouen, Paris, Bordeaux, Trier and Rheims.

How soon Christianity reached Britain is uncertain. Tertullian and Origen speak rhetorically of the gospel's extension even to the distant barbarian island of Britain, but probably the Church had little serious foothold until the middle of the third century. At the Council of Arles (314) three British bishops attended from London, York and either Colchester or Lincoln. British bishops also came to the unhappy council of Ariminum (Rimini) in 359 (below, p. 142); we are told that three of them were too poor to pay their own travelling expenses, but apparently the rest could afford it. The story of St Alban's martyrdom at Verulamium is thickly encrusted with legend, but probably has at least a substratum of truth since his shrine was a place of pilgrimage by the first half of the fifth century. In fact under the protection of Constantius, father of Constantine, Britain did not suffer any more than Gaul in the great persecution. Archaeology has disclosed small basilicas which may be churches at Silchester and Caerwent; a certainly Christian chapel in a wealthy villa of the fourth century has turned up at Lullingstone in Kent.[1] By 400, on the eve of the invasions,

1. The earliest known Christian silver, not later than the fourth century, was found in 1975 buried at the Roman fort, Water Newton, near Peterborough; now in the British Museum.

Roman Britain was a broadly Christian province within the now orthodox Empire, and the faith had penetrated the native population. The earliest surviving British writer was a Christian of this epoch, the monk Pelagius, and he had like-minded friends among the Britons. The gradual Saxon invasions had already begun when St Patrick began his mission in Ireland (perhaps about 432). The heathen Saxons were much resented by the native Britons who did little or nothing about evangelizing them, and retired into Cornwall, Wales and Ireland. St Patrick complained that his Irish labours were undermined by hostile British clergy and had to write a formal protest to the Christian prince Coroticus (possibly Ceretic son of Cunedda, the founder of Cardigan), whose soldiers had carried off his newly baptized converts to be sold as slaves. Not until 597 was the opportunity offered by the Kentish kingdom seized by Pope Gregory the Great, and a beginning was made with the conversion of the Anglo-Saxons (below, p. 256).

Not much evidence survives of the early development of Christianity in Egypt. Papyrus fragments show that in the second century the mission had moved far up the Nile Valley. The character of some Egyptian Christianity appears to have been none too orthodox judged by later standards: surviving fragments of 'The Gospel according to the Egyptians', like many of the apocryphal gospels, tend to the 'Encratite' view that marriage is incompatible with Christian perfection, but is not otherwise heretical. The story, attested by Clement of Alexandria at the end of the second century, that the Alexandrian church was founded by St Mark, the disciple of St Peter (cf. 1 Peter v. 13); may echo the establishment of orthodoxy by a mission from Rome about the middle of the second century, at the time when the Roman church was engaged in a life and death struggle with Marcionites and Valentinians. A papyrus find proves that Irenaeus' refutation of Gnosticism was being read at Oxyrhynchus within a very few years of its publication, which suggests much concern in Egypt for the maintenance of orthodoxy. Not until Clement of Alexandria and Origen is the character of Alexandrian Christianity clear to see.

In Roman Africa, i.e. the coastal strip looking culturally and economically north, towards Europe, with a natural capital at the old Phoenician trading city of Carthage, the first evidence of Christianity comes from the Latin *Acts* of the Martyrs of Scilli near Carthage in the year 180. The origins of the mission must go back much earlier. By 200 Tertullian witnesses not only to the vigour of the Church in Carthage and Africa Proconsularis (North Tunisia) but to the existence of churches far afield in the provinces of Byzacena (South Tunisia), Numidia, and Mauretania (Algeria). And in Tertullian's time the Christian population was very numerous. *Hesterni sumus et vestra omnia implevimus:* 'We are but of yesterday and we have filled all you have – cities, islands, forts, towns, assembly halls, even military camps, tribes, town councils, the palace, senate and forum. We have left you nothing but the temples'.[1] The origins of the first missionaries are unknown. Tertullian looked to Rome as a nearby see of apostolic foundation with which African Christianity had close connexions. But Carthage had much trade with the Levant, and the first missionaries may well have come from there. In 200 there were many African Christians whose first language was Greek, and there were differences of custom between the Greek and the Latin brethren. It was perhaps African missionaries who made the first translations of the Bible into Latin, using vulgar and colloquial usages, and probably making their versions not all at one time or in one place but piecemeal as occasion arose. The many individual efforts were united and became the first Latin Bible, and by 400 it was so firmly established as the Authorized Version that Jerome's Revised Version (the so-called Vulgate) aroused deep opposition.

Apart from St Paul's proposed journey the first evidence of churches in Spain comes from allusions in Irenaeus and Tertullian. Cyprian mentions churches at the chief cities of León, Astorga, Merida and Saragossa. Early in the fourth century a vivid picture of the by then vast extension of the Church and of its contemporary problems of moral laxity is provided by the canons of the Council of Elvira. A leader at

1. Tertullian, *Apol.* 37.

this Council, Ossius or Hosius of Cordova, became Constantine's ecclesiastical adviser.

The Christians themselves wondered at the speed and extent of Church expansion before Constantine. It is hardly surprising that the Church felt itself to be riding on the crest of a wave, and faced the world with that confidence which is a marked feature of the early apologists.

THE DEFENCE OF THE FAITH

It inhered in the nature of the church's existence that from the start it was engaged in debate with critics, and that the formulation of its doctrines was hammered out in an intellectual dialogue, both within the church itself and also with those outside it. Its first critics were orthodox Jews, and for a surprisingly long period the discussion between church and synagogue occupied the attention of Christian thinkers. It is no accident that the most substantial extant work by a second century Christian is the *Dialogue with Trypho the Jew*, written by Justin Martyr about 160. This is the longest example of an extensive genre of literature, principally concerned with the Christian claim to be the universal religion to which the Old Testament prophets had looked forward, and dominated by detailed arguments from particular prophetic texts. Naturally enough, the orthodox Jews resented the church's assumption of its continuity with the past history of the elect people of God, and rejected as sophistry the allegorical interpretations (such as those provided in the *Epistle of Barnabas*) of the Mosaic laws enjoining the observance of circumcision, sabbaths, sacrifices, and food laws. To the orthodox Jews, the Christians were dangerous trimmers, adjusting the unalterable religion revealed to Moses to make it more palatable to Gentile prejudices. In Christian eyes the intense particularity of Judaism was incompatible with its own monotheistic principles: was not their God the God of the Gentiles also? (cf. Rom. iii, 29–30). The Christians regarded the ceremonial legislation of the Mosaic law as a special discipline temporarily imposed for good reasons but not intended to be taken as God's first or

last word; they liked to look back to the patriarchs before
Moses who had no Law to keep other than the moral imperative of the inward conscience, and argued that Moses was
compelled to impose the particular ceremonies of Leviticus
because the Jews were showing a tendency to become
merged with the heathen Canaanites and needed a strict
system to keep them separate and distinct. This need was
now past. In the Sermon on the Mount Justin Martyr saw
an ethic of universal validity, continuous with the highest
aspirations of Judaism, but freed of the shackles of ceremonial
rules peculiar to one race among the hundreds of God's
creation.

The Christian attitude was the more disturbing for their
insistence that, under the new covenant inaugurated by
Jesus the Messiah, a blood relationship to Abraham was of
no importance. The orthodox synagogue tended to regard
all Jews as possessed of faith at least in germ, simply in virtue
of membership of the chosen people, though it could freely
concede that there were many Jews who did not make their
faith effective in practice. For the Christians, on the other
hand, the distinction between belief and unbelief was sharper
and more absolute, and assent required a more profound
decision of allegiance. Although initiation into the church
by baptism was an intensely corporate and social act in relation to the Christian community, the act of faith was understood in a more individualistic way than in Judaism. The
gospel of Christ divided families and disturbed traditional
patterns of social behaviour. It is not surprising that in some
cases the impact of Christianity was to produce emotional
excitement and antinomianism, as in the case of the 'Nico-
laitans' denounced in the Apocalypse of John; and misunderstood Pauline language about freedom from the law
and the inheritance of the sons of the kingdom might easily
make things worse. It was in answer to such dangers of
anarchy that a strongly moralistic emphasis appeared in
Christian writings of the second century, which it is all too
easy to disparage as a falling off from the first vigour of the
apostolic age. Round about A.D. 100 it must have seemed that
new converts of Gentile origin needed no kind of instruction

so urgently as clear moral rules and exhortations to good works.

In spite of the fact that the Christians criticized Judaism for its particularity and exclusiveness, they themselves could not have seemed so much less exclusive to pagan observers. They inherited the Jewish reserve towards the pagan gods and the cult of the emperor. Most of them felt unable in conscience to eat meat that had been offered in sacrifice to idols and then sold in the market. They were withdrawn from society, meeting apart, often in secret, and did not attend public shows and gladiatorial combats provided for the entertainment of the populace. Yet they drew recruits from all groups and classes in imperial society. In pagan eyes eccentric behaviour on religious grounds could be tolerated in the empire provided that it was not morally corrupting or politically dangerous, and provided that the religion was that of a racial group, in which case it could be powerfully defended as an honourable following of ancestral tradition. But in the second century Christianity was widely suspected of secret vice, was normally reserved towards military service in the Roman army, and was conspicuous for its disrespect towards any religious attitudes that could only be defended as ancestral practice. In the time of Marcus Aurelius, the anti-Christian pamphleteer Celsus put the matter succinctly. He cordially disliked and despised the Jews, but declared himself in principle tolerant of their strange religious customs: 'The religion of the Jews may be highly peculiar, but it is at least the custom of their fathers.' The Christians, on the other hand, followed no ancestral tradition, not even that of the Jews whence they had sprung, and were being dangerously successful in encouraging people all over the empire to abandon the old polytheism which was built into the fabric of society by centuries of usage. Although Celsus upheld the polytheistic tradition, he had an uneasy conscience about it and had clearly been touched by the sceptical arguments of the philosophers. But philosophical scepticism tended to reinforce social and religious conservatism. A sceptic like Cicero explicitly held that, since it is impossible to be certain of anything, one ought strictly to continue the age-old traditions and religious customs of antiquity. To abandon them would mean that one had confidence in one's reasons for doing so and in the superiority of alternative policies. Celsus was similarly conservative about tradition and rejected the Christians because they had the wrong prejudices.

It was possible for the Jews to gain greater tolerance than the Christians partly because they were more opposed to any public disparagement of pagan cults. Both Philo and Josephus held that, while the God of the Bible was the only true God, it was wrong to insult the religious feelings of others, and they enjoined courtesy upon their fellow Jews. They were content to ask the imperial government for as much toleration as it accorded to other national religions, but were more interested in the defence of Judaism and its liberty of worship than in any active mission to convert pagans and to make them proselytes. For the Christians, by contrast, the *raison d'être* of the church consisted in its reconciling role for all mankind, including Jew and Gentile alike, religious and even irreligious alike. Like Philo, St Paul disapproved of insulting pagan temples, but he took the lowest view of polytheistic religion. The paradox of the church was that it was a religious revolutionary movement, yet without a conscious political ideology; it aimed at the capture of society throughout all its strata, but was at the same time characteristic for its indifference to the possession of power in this world. Celsus was the first known person to realize that this non-political, quietist, and pacifist community had it in its power to transform the social and political order of the empire. He consciously tried to provide the polytheistic tradition with a coherent set of philosophical and theological principles by which it might withstand the Christian onslaught. It is significant that he could only do this by making large concessions to his Christian opponents and by turning many of the Christian apologists' arguments to his own use. The future lay with the programme first announced by Justin Martyr, by which the Church would make common cause with Platonic metaphysics and Stoic ethics, while rejecting pagan myth and cult as a demonic, superstitious, counterfeit

religion propagated by evil powers and maintained by prejudice and erroneous information about the nature of the
Church.

When pressed for evidence of the supernatural origin
of Christianity, the second century Church sought an
answer principally in the fulfilment by Jesus of Old
Testament prophecy and in the visible evidence of the
universal diffusion of the faith. Sometimes they also appealed,
but with less frequency, to the gospel records of the miracles
of Jesus as evidence of divine power; but this argument played
a very subordinate role even in popular apologetic. Justin
Martyr regarded the fulfilment of ancient prophecy as the
most cogent argument known to him. He found there plenty
of attacks on merely external legalism: God desired mercy,
not sacrifice, and was displeased at the ceremonies of Judaism.
He also found plenty of promises of a great restoration with
a new covenant and the advent of the Messiah. The Old
Testament itself could therefore be taken to supply evidence
both for the rejection of Judaism as a permanently ordained
system and for the universal extension of the Church which,
according to Justin, would occupy the interim between the
ascension of Christ and the final consummation towards
which the world was moving under providence. Much of
the earliest Christian theology consisted in the interpretation
of Old Testament prophecy as foreshadowing the gospel, and
Justin and his contemporaries found 'types' or prefigurations
of Christ's redemption in the Exodus from Egypt, in Joshua
crossing the Jordan to enter the promised land, in Noah
the symbolic figure of a renewed humanity, in the out-
stretched hands of Moses which made possible the defeat of
the Amalekites, and in many others. The importance of
this tradition of Old Testament interpretation may be
gauged from the fact that for many centuries the exposition
of prophecy continued to form the prime content of the
instruction given to catechumens when they were taught
about the person of Christ. The second century Church
knew that their crucified Lord had conquered the powers of
evil; but if they were asked to explain how this was so,
they quoted prophecies of the passion, especially the

suffering servant of Isaiah 53, or the Psalm of dereliction, Ps. 22.

The appeal to the fact of the universal diffusion of the faith within a relatively short time was not quite the simple argument from success that it could be taken to be. It implied a claim that the truth of the gospel was verified in moral experience, attested in the conviction of the apostles and the integrity of the martyrs. If the Resurrection had been a fiction, the argument ran, the apostles would not have risked their lives for it. The faith of a handful of ill-educated fishermen had spread with astonishing rapidity to reach from India to Mauretania, from the Caspian to the utterly barbarous tribes of Britain. The agents of this diffusion had not been great orators or subtle reasoners, and they had had to meet the opposition of prejudiced and angry mobs and of a hostile government. Nevertheless, the churches had expanded with extraordinary and embarrassing speed. When Constantine was converted early in the fourth century, it seemed like the fulfilment of a dream, and to the contemporary historian Eusebius of Caesarea (*c.* 262 – 339) the emperor's faith was an essential step in the diffusion of the gospel throughout the empire, from which it would spread in time to the barbarians beyond. In the first half of the third century there were some who believed that the extension of the Church to become coterminous with the human race was the inward symbolic meaning of the primitive 'mythological' hope of a second coming of Christ. In the view of Melito, bishop of Sardis (about A.D. 160–70), Augustus' establishment of peace was a providential part of the divine preparation for the gospel. The destinies of the Church and Empire were somehow bound up in the mysterious purposes of God. Justin Martyr thought that the Roman armies which destroyed Jerusalem in A.D. 70 were the instruments of judgement on a nation that had rejected the Messiah and failed to discern the new dispensation, now inaugurated, in which the temple sacrifices were abrogated. Likewise Eusebius of Caesarea saw the conversion of Constantine as a divine act, establishing Christianity in the citadel of governmental decision as a means to its further extension.

Nevertheless, the Christian mission was not directed merely at centres of power. It was consciously aimed at the common people, and the ideals of simplicity and humility were never far from the minds of those who had to propagate their faith. The missionaries took it for granted that the gospel corresponded to the needs of mortal men and women, and that they must communicate with ordinary people in direct colloquial language. They wrote hymns and songs for the illiterate to sing, and, in a world that was acutely conscious of rank and class, the separate strata of which were distinguished not only by manner and speech but also by forms of address and clothes, the Christians deliberately set out to treat the poor with dignity and without condescension.

There is no reason to think that the early Christian movement was ever a political revolution *manqué*, or that the history of the Church can be told in terms of bourgeois leaders taking over a proletarian uprising and diverting it into innocuous other-worldly mysticism. Such theories can only be maintained by violent and selective use of evidence. But it is certainly true that this essentially religious movement had deep social and political potentialities, many of which were not fully realized in the Roman imperial period. The old gods of polytheism were essentially local deities venerated by the people of a particular region. Even after the cults of Isis and the Oriental mystery religions had spread from their original homes, there was curiously little sense of universality about their worship. During the second century pagans interpreted these local gods as analogous to provincial governors, administering the world for the supreme power who is too transcendent to be troubled about details of government; and something like monotheism became general among the educated. In the third century this striving after monotheism became attached to the worship of the sun. It is possible, therefore, to speculate that Christianity achieved its success in the empire in part because it answered best to the empire's need for a universal religion with which it could identify itself. There are Christian writers of the fourth century who assume without discussion that 'Roman' and 'Christian' are almost synonymous terms.

But in fact the synthesis of Roman imperialism and Christianity broke down, partly because the Christians were aware that their gospel had to be carried to the hostile barbarians as well, and partly because of a reassertion of the old tradition of a certain detachment and even indifference to the political structure of this transitory world.

In consequence, the Christians inherited a lasting ambivalence in their attitudes to government. If under the direction and control of a believing emperor, should this be regarded as a providential instrument in God's hidden hand for the extending of truth, peace, and justice, through a mutual pact with the Church? And if so, could the government entrust to the officers of the Church the moral education of the people? Alternatively, must the government's necessarily material and this-worldly concerns with defence, the economy, law and order and the repression of social dissidence make its role irredeemably secular, alien from the high purposes of God's otherworldly kingdom? 'The emperors have become Christian, but the devil has not' (as Augustine sharply told his people early in the fifth century).

4
Justin and Irenaeus

JUSTIN MARTYR

THE Gnostic heretics had appealed to the principles of
Platonism to provide a philosophical justification for their
doctrine that the elect soul must be liberated from the evil
inherent in the material realm to escape to its true home and
to enjoy the beatific vision. Their deep pessimism about this
created order was not quite fairly deduced from the text of
Plato, but there was a sufficient plausibility about the argument to make it look impressive. The Gnostic appeal to pagan
philosophy did not tend to encourage the study of philosophy among those who feared Gnosticism as a corrupter
of the truth. Philosophy came to seem like the mother of
heresy. To Irenaeus of Lyons Gnosticism was a ragbag of
heathen speculations with bits taken from different philosophers to dress out a bogus, anti-rational mythology. His
successor as an anti-heretical writer, Hippolytus, whose
mind was a curious mixture of scholarship and foolishness,
wrote a lengthy refutation of the sects based on the presupposition that each sect had corrupted the authentic
gospel by principles drawn from a pagan philosopher; he
incidentally preserved thereby many fragments of classical
philosophers like Heraclitus which would otherwise have
been lost. Tertullian scornfully mocked those who 'advocate
a Stoic or a Platonic or an Aristotelian Christianity'. It was
a Gnostic thesis that faith needs supplementation by philosophical inquiries. 'What has Athens in common with Jerusalem?'

But in the middle of the second century the atmosphere
was very different. Justin Martyr was born early in the
second century in Samaritan territory of Greek parentage,

and as a young man went to Ephesus to study philosophy. He described his quest, in a form which owes something to literary embellishment but may well have a substratum of truth, in his *Dialogue with Trypho*. He began with a Stoic tutor – still at this period the most popular philosophy – but passed on to an Aristotelian teacher, who disillusioned him by an unphilosophical anxiety about his fee; he then went to a Pythagorean, and finally to a Platonist with whom he was well content, principally because of the religious and mystical side of Platonic aspirations. Plato had written in ecstatic language of the soul's vision of God. But while meditating in solitude on the seashore Justin met an old man who refuted the Platonic doctrine of the soul, and proceeded to tell him about the prophets of the Old Testament who foretold the coming of Christ. Justin was converted, but did not understand this to mean the abandonment of his philosophical inquiries, nor even the renunciation of all that he had learnt from Platonism. He regarded Christianity as 'the true philosophy', and accordingly began to wear the recognized costume of a teacher of philosophy (which in this age had something of both the authority and the power to repel which in the modern West has come to be associated with the clerical collar).[1] Justin moved from Ephesus to Rome where soon after the year 151 he addressed an *Apology* for Christianity to the emperor Antoninus Pius. Some years later he reissued this work together with a supplement, commonly called his *Second Apology*, at a critical moment in the fortunes of the Church in Rome when it had been harried by the city prefect, Lollius Urbicus. The *Dialogue with Trypho the Jew* was written after the first *Apology*, probably about 160, but is presented as an account of a discussion which Justin had with Trypho about 135.

Justin vigorously rejected pagan myth and cult as gross superstition infected by evil, but gave the most positive welcome possible to the classical philosophical tradition. The transcendent God of Plato, beyond mortal comprehension, is the God of the Bible. Socrates rightly perceived how corrupt the old religion was, and in consequence was hounded to

1. Christian clergy at this period wore no distinctive dress.

death by the Athenians – a model of integrity for Christian martyrs. Much else in the Platonic tradition is warmly accepted by Justin: Plato rightly taught that the soul has a special kinship to God, that we are responsible for our actions, and that in the world to come there is judgement and justice. Justin thinks Plato made some mistakes, e.g. in holding that the soul possesses a natural and inherent immortality in its own right rather than in dependence on the Creator's will, and in accepting the deterministic myth of transmigration. But in Justin's eyes it is remarkable how much Plato got right: he at least knew that it is very hard to find God without special help, and probably had to exercise reserve in declaring all that he had perceived, on account of the deep prejudices of the polytheistic society in which he lived. How Plato had achieved these profound insights Justin explains on two hypotheses. The first hypothesis was already a conventional apologetic theme in the Greek synagogue, namely, that Plato and the Greek sages had had before them the mysterious allegories of the Pentateuch, which provided them with obscure hints of the truth. The second hypothesis was a development of a Pauline theme, namely, the value and validity of the universal moral conscience, quite independent of any special revelation. (cf. Rom. i–ii.) Where St Paul had argued that all are responsible and ultimately inexcusable, Justin argues that the light that all have is implanted by the divine Reason, the Logos of God who was incarnate in Jesus and who is universally active and present in the highest goodness and intelligence wherever they may be found. Justin strikingly interprets in this sense the parable of the Sower. The divine Sower sowed his good seed throughout his creation. Justin does not make rigid and exclusive claims for divine revelation to the Hebrews so as to invalidate the value of other sources of wisdom. Abraham and Socrates are alike 'Christians before Christ'. But just as the aspirations of the Old Testament prophets found their fulfilment in Christ, so also the correct insights achieved by the Greek philosophers reached their completion in the gospel of Christ who embodies the highest moral ideal. Christ is for Justin the principle of unity and the criterion by which we may judge the truth, scattered like divided seeds among the different schools of philosophy in so far as they have dealt with religion and morals.

Justin's debt to Platonic philosophy is important for his theology in one respect of far-reaching importance. He uses the concept of the divine Logos or Reason both to explain how the transcendent Father of all deals with the inferior, created order of things, and to justify his faith in the revelation made by God through the prophets and in Christ. The divine Logos inspired the prophets, he says, and was present entire in Jesus Christ. This inspiring activity and its culmination in the actual incarnation are special cases of divine immanence. It is implicit in Justin's thesis that the distinction between 'Father' and 'Son' corresponds to the distinction between God transcendent and God immanent. The Son-Logos is necessary to mediate between the supreme Father and the material world. Justin therefore insists that the Logos is 'other than' the Father, derived from the Father in a process which in no way diminishes or divides the being of the Father, but in the manner in which one torch may be lit from another. He is Light of Light.

Justin was well aware of the existence of Gnostic heresies, and wrote a (lost) treatise refuting them. He believed in the free will of man, and was therefore critical of the Gnostic doctrine that salvation depends on a predestination which is indifferent to moral virtue; and his confidence in the power of the argument from fulfilled prophecy set him in radical opposition to Marcion's disparagement of the Old Testament. In criticizing the Gnostic devaluation of the natural and material order Justin stressed that the creation is the work of the supreme God, acting through the Logos as mediator; that in the incarnation the Logos assumed a complete manhood, body, soul, and mind, and Christ 'truly suffered' in his passion; above all, that human destiny hereafter is not a deliverance of an immortal soul from the bondage of the physical frame, but is 'resurrection', which Justin interpreted in the most literal way. Accepting the Apocalypse of John as authoritative and inspired, Justin understood the Christian hope to mean the expectation that

Christ would return to a rebuilt Jerusalem to reign with his
saints for a thousand years.[1]

St Paul's pregnant phrase that Christ came 'in the fullness
of time' has come to bear a theological interpretation of
history. Justin was the first writer to think of the annals of
humanity as a twofold story of sacred and profane history,
with a nodal point in the coming of Christ. The principle,
basic to Justin's attitude, that the Creator has implanted
seeds of truth in many places, not only in the inspired prophetic writings, was taken further by later Christian writers.
Justin himself mentioned prophecies of the end of the world
to be found in the Sibylline Oracles and in an Apocalypse
composed by hellenized Zoroastrians in the name of King
Hystaspes of the Avesta. Likewise Lactantius early in the
fourth century had the same Hystaspes Apocalypse before
him, and found valuable testimonies to Christian truth in
the Sibylline Oracles, large collections of which had been
composed by Jewish versifiers and then adapted to Christian
use. The thirteenth-century author of the *Dies Irae*, to whom
King David and the Sibyl were alike prophets of the final
cosmic catastrophe, was taking up a theme of great antiquity
in Christian history. In the Latin world Dante and the
medieval church were following a lead given by Constantine
the Great himself when they interpreted as a prophecy of
Christ the Sibylline oracle contained in the fourth *Eclogue*
of Virgil. The theorists of inspiration might disagree among
themselves whether these 'profane' prophets were inspired
against their will, like Balaam, or without knowing what they

1. Millenarian belief originated in a fusion of various strands. Babylonian astrology contributed the notion of millennial periods under
the seven planets. Psalm 89.4 ('A day with the Lord is as a thousand
years') provided a key for the interpretation of the seven days of creation in Gen. i; and the Epistle to the Hebrews (iv, 4–9) interpreted the
sabbath as a symbol of heavenly rest. By putting these elements together
it was natural to form the notion, found in Irenaeus and Hippolytus,
that world history will last 6,000 years leading up to a seventh millennium under the reign of Christ. After Clement of Alexandria and
Origen, for whom it was a fundamental error to treat the Apocalypse
as providing any basis for chronological calculations, very few Greek
Fathers accepted the literal millennial hope, but it survived longer in
the West.

were doing, like Caiaphas. But it was enough for the purposes of argument to find in these oracles a valuable testimony to divine truth. Soon similar witnesses to the majesty of Christ were found in writings claiming to be revelations of 'Thrice-greatest Hermes', or in oracles of Apollo himself. The manufacture of such oracular testimonies went on among both opponents and defenders of Christianity. In the third century pagan opponents of Christianity circulated an oracle in which Hecate vouched for the holiness of Christ while deploring the folly of those who worshipped him. Eusebius of Caesarea was glad to find in Plutarch the story that some travellers making a voyage in the time of the emperor Tiberius (and therefore contemporaneous with the time of Christ's birth) had heard a great voice crying 'Great Pan is dead'. By his coming Christ rid the world of evil spirits. But it was long before simple Christians ceased to look for oracles as a source of predictions of the mysterious future. Even Augustine did not deny that the demons had some power to foresee the future, though this predictive power was not (he thought) more supernatural in principle than a physician's prognosis or a weather forecast.

Justin Martyr occupies a central position in the history of Christian thought of the second century. His generous and optimistic approach to the Greek philosophical tradition was taken up by others. His pupil Tatian from Mesopotamia admittedly gave Justin's theses a violently anti-hellenic and polemical edge that would have distressed Justin. But Justin's liberal and eirenic spirit reappeared in a *Plea for the Christians* by one Athenagoras of Athens who addressed his work to Marcus Aurelius and Commodus about 177, and especially in Clement of Alexandria. Justin's more strictly theological achievements exercised an influence upon Theophilus, bishop of Antioch, who wrote a rambling defence of Christianity addressed to a certain Autolycus about 180. Justin also moulded the thinking of Irenaeus, bishop of Lyons.

IRENAEUS

With Irenaeus the shape of Christian theology became stable
and coherent. Apart from fragments two complete works
from his pen have been preserved, though neither survives
in his original Greek: a short *Presentation of the apostolic
preaching*, written to provide a manual of doctrinal essentials for a friend, and five books of *Refutation and overthrow of the knowledge falsely so called* which, even after
the numerous recent discoveries of Gnostic documents, remain an essential and remarkably fairminded source for the
history of the second century sects. Irenaeus directed his
polemic principally against Marcion and Valentinus. His
anti-Marcionite argument followed the lines laid down by
Justin and by other unnamed writers in Asia Minor of the
middle years of the second century from whose works
Irenaeus gives important quotations. He rested his case on
the manifest unity of Old and New Testaments apparent in
the fulfilment of ancient prophecy, and especially stressed
the parallelism between Adam and Christ which he
found in St Paul. The divine plan for the new covenant was a
'recapitulation' of the original creation. In Christ the divine
Word assumed a humanity such as Adam possessed before he
fell. Adam was made in the image and likeness of God. By
sin the likeness became lost, though the image has remained
untouched. By faith in Christ mankind may recover the lost
likeness. Because Irenaeus regarded salvation as a restoration of the condition prevailing in paradise before the Fall,
it was easy for him to accept Justin's terrestrial hopes for the
millennium. Because he believed that in the Fall only the
moral likeness to God was lost, not the basic image, he was
able to regard the Fall in a way very different from the deep
pessimism of the Gnostics. Error came in, he thought, because
mankind is growing to maturity, and in the infancy of the
race it was natural that mistakes were made by the frail and
immature children who were Adam and Eve. God allowed
Adam to fall to quench his pride and to teach him by discipline
and experience. So the history of salvation is a progressive
education, in which God has brought humanity forward

step by step in a long process culminating in the incarnation of the divine Word with a universal gospel diffused throughout the world by the church. Irenaeus' scheme does not begin with the Gnostic question: how a world which is the perfect work of a perfect creator can have gone wrong as the present world obviously has. He grants from the start that there is imperfection in the world, but it is like the blunders made by a growing child, and the purpose of our existence is the making of character by the mastery of difficulties and temptations.

By the manner in which he presents revelation as a gradual process Irenaeus was able to turn the edge of the Marcionite arguments against the moral difficulties of the Old Testament. But the followers of Valentinus raised other difficulties for him. Irenaeus' treatment of the Valentinian theology was the most original and independent part of his work. He had taken the trouble to make himself acquainted with the actual tenets of the sect, and saw clearly that the basic question was that of authority. The Valentinians claimed to be able to supplement the writings of the apostles with secret unwritten traditions and with several additional gospels beside the familiar four of Matthew, Mark, Luke and John. Irenaeus realized that Marcion was right in one thing – that it was necessary to have a canon or fixed list of authoritative writings of the New Testament. Hitherto the dividing line between books accorded the status of being read in the church lectionary and books that were of approved orthodoxy had not been decisively drawn. Irenaeus drew the line, and is the first writer whose New Testament virtually corresponds to the canon that became accepted as traditional.[1] What was original in Irenaeus was not the acceptance of four gospels or of the Acts, Epistles, and Apocalypse, but rather the provision of reasoned statements for accepting these books and not others. The Valentinian appeal to unwritten tradition Irenaeus answered by appealing to the churches of apostolic foundation. If the apostles really had taught the strange fantasies of the Valentinian myths, would they not have told the authoritative teachers to whom they entrusted the churches

1. Irenaeus never quotes from 3 John, James or 2 Peter.

they founded? Would not these teachers have passed on these
doctrines to their successors in the episcopal chairs at these
places? Irenaeus explains that he could vindicate orthodoxy
by appealing to the succession of teachers in any church of
apostolic foundation. He proceeds to quote as an especially
good example the list for Rome which could look back to the
glorious martyrs Peter and Paul. Since the authentic faith is
identical throughout the world, no church disagrees with
any other, and diversity of doctrine is inconceivable; nevertheless, because of its great name the Roman succession provides a striking example, and we are assured that the faithful
throughout the world will necessarily be in agreement with
what is taught there. Accordingly, Irenaeus feels himself
justified in citing the list of only one apostolic foundation,
and in omitting Ephesus, Corinth, and the rest, though they
would prove his point equally well.

Irenaeus perceived that the coherence of Christian doctrine depended upon the tradition of faithful instruction, and
that the Gnostic heresies could only be successfully opposed
if the scattered statements of scripture were drawn together
within a system. But originality was the last thing to be expected of a theologian, he urged. It was essential to keep to
the path laid down by authority in scripture and in the clear
tradition of the apostolic churches which was the best guarantee of resistance to innovation and dangerous speculation.
Heresy was born of the itch for something new. It came of
'curiosity', which meant prying into matters which the
human mind had neither capacity to know nor authority
even to think about. Irenaeus loved to contrast the unchanging monolithic Church of orthodoxy, *semper eadem*, standing
on the rock of apostolic foundation, with the fissiparous sects,
continually changing their systems, at loggerheads with one
another, and possessing a clearly traceable history and development back to the first heretic of all, Simon Magus whom
St Peter had resisted both at Samaria (Acts viii, 9–24) and,
as traditions recorded, at Rome also. Irenaeus' work set out
to provide a history of the variations of Gnostic heresy, and
to compare them with the one true Church, immutable in
time and space, guaranteed in its authenticity by its ability

to trace its succession of authoritative teachers to its founding apostles, and by the unanimous consent of believers throughout the world.

Irenaeus exercised wide influence on the immediately following generation. Both Hippolytus, the learned presbyter of Rome, and Tertullian of Carthage freely drew on his writings; and the interest he aroused may be deduced both from the fragments preserved on papyrus and from the fact that his work was translated into Latin early in the fifth century and then into Armenian in the sixth. But his too literal hope of an earthly millennium made him uncongenial reading in the Greek East (except to Epiphanius of Salamis who transcribed parts of Irenaeus for his vast refutation of the heresies in 374–5), and it is only in the Latin translation that his work as a whole has been preserved. Even there one line of the manuscript tradition lacks the final chapters of the fifth book, in which Irenaeus attacked those who wanted to interpret the millennial hope as symbolic of heaven rather than as an earthly reality.

5

Easter, the Monarchian Controversy,
and Tertullian

EASTER

IRENAEUS had written of the universal Church in idealistic
and almost romantic terms, as if it were a body characterized by complete unanimity and possessing a single mind on
all subjects. It would not have been to his purpose to analyse
and describe the differences in custom and attitude and in
theological expression which were to be discerned. It caused
him great pain when the churches of Asia Minor, whence he
himself had come, became passionately divided about the
status of the Montanist prophecy. Moreover, the churches of
Asia Minor had preserved the most ancient of all methods of
determining the date of Easter: they simply kept it at the
same time as the Jewish passover, on the fourteenth day of
the Jewish month Nisan whenever that might fall. When Easter
was introduced at Rome (*c.* 160) the feast, as at Alexandria,
was celebrated on the Sunday following the Jewish passover,
which for practical purposes could be reckoned as the Sunday
next after the first full moon after the spring equinox. Irenaeus was shocked when, about 190, bishop Victor of Rome
proceeded to make a demand for uniformity in the observance of Easter which the churches of Asia Minor regarded
as autocratic and offensive. Victor apparently believed that
the Roman custom must have been inherited from the instructions of Peter and Paul, and declared that those who
observed the feast on any different day could not be regarded
as Catholic Christians. Irenaeus recalled how some thirty-
five years earlier Polycarp of Smyrna had travelled to Rome
to discuss some divergences of custom with bishop Anicetus:
at that time Rome did not keep Easter annually, but

neither regarded the divergence as a ground for breach of communion, and they parted in amicable disagreement. Despite the scandal which it caused to Irenaeus, Victor's drastic action was not thunder out of a clear sky. There had been sharp controversy in Asia Minor about 170 on the related question whether the Last Supper was the Passover meal. Bishop Melito of Sardis vigorously defended the ancient conservative custom of keeping Easter on 'the fourteenth day' with the Jews. From an Easter sermon by Melito, the full text of which has lately been recovered from three early papyrus codices,[1] it is painfully evident that those who celebrated Easter on the same day as the Jewish passover were not motivated by special friendliness towards Judaism (though perhaps it was the sharp charge of 'Judaising' which led Melito to over-compensate in his oratorical and at times gruesome description of the Jews' sad spiritual condition). Victor of Rome's intervention turned out to be successful in the sense that his view was eventually to prevail. But it was a long time before those who kept Easter on the fourteenth day (nicknamed Quartodecimans) died out. The group still existed in the ninth century despite the vigour with which church councils deplored them. It was impossible in so weighty a practical question for diversity to be allowed, but there can be little doubt that the Quartodecimans were right in thinking that they had preserved the most ancient and apostolic custom. They had become heretics simply by being behind the times.

THE MONARCHIAN CONTROVERSY

Another controversy broke out at Rome during the episcopate of Victor, but Irenaeus took no part in it and may have died before its repercussions came to the notice of the churches in the Rhône valley. This was the so-called 'Monarchian controversy', which originated in a revolt against the Logos theology of Justin and the apologists. Justin had boldly spoken of the divine Logos as 'another God' beside the

1. This sermon became so popular that later it was translated into Latin, Coptic, Syriac, and Georgian.

Father, qualified by the gloss 'other, I mean, in number, not in will'. In arguing against hellenized Jews who held that the divine Logos is distinct from God only in the refined sense in which one can distinguish in thought between sun and sunlight, Justin had urged that the analogy of one torch lit from another was a much more satisfactory picture because it did justice to the independence (later theology, from Origen onwards, would have used the technical term *hypostasis*) of the Logos. Such language was disturbing. One of the central issues in the conflict with Gnosticism had been the question whether there is more than one ultimate first principle. The orthodox had insisted that there is no first principle other than God the Creator, no coequal devil, no coeternal matter, but a single *monarchia*. Justin's language appeared to prejudice this affirmation and to be insufficiently protected against the accusation of ditheism. Theophilus of Antioch, whose language had been gratefully borrowed by Irenaeus, spoke more cautiously of God's Reason and Wisdom as like two hands put forth for the work of creation. Theophilus was the first to use the term Triad in relation to God, but it is clear from his analogy of the hands that this plurality is secondary to a more ultimate unity. In Irenaeus the Son and the Spirit have successive missions in the divine plan of redemption, and it is in the working out of this plan that the Triad is revealed.

The Monarchian critics of the Logos theology had two courses open to them. Either they could say that God who created the world was so incarnate in Jesus that there is no difference to be discerned between the 'Son' and the 'Father' (unless 'Son' is a name for the physical body or humanity of Christ and 'Father' a name for the divine Spirit within); or they could say that Jesus was a man like other men, differentiated in being indwelt by the Spirit of God to an absolute and unique degree. The latter view might claim a wide basis of support in the synoptic gospels, but had to meet serious objections that had already been stated by Justin Martyr. Justin insisted that Christ was not a mere man but was also God; at his birth he had been worshipped by the Magi, and there could be no question of a holy life being rewarded by elevation to divine rank. The gospel story how the Lord 'grew in wisdom' was understood by Justin to mean that his knowledge was always appropriate to the stage of growth reached. He was baptized, not because he needed to be, but for our sakes. He was truly born of the Virgin Mary, and his virgin birth is differentiated from all pagan analogies by the absence of any divine paternity.

The force of these arguments advanced by Justin was bound to become overwhelming as St John's gospel established its authority throughout the Church in the second half of the second century. But the field was still open for the former alternative according to which the Father and the Son are one and the same, the distinction being merely one of nomenclature to describe different aspects of the same personal being. This was the view propagated early in the third century at Rome by a certain Sabellius, of whose biography and thought so little is actually known that it is paradoxical to find the name of this obscure figure as a constant label attached to this type of theology, at least in the Greek East. In the West the polemical label for it was usually 'Patripassianism', i.e. the doctrine that the Father suffers. In modern books the same doctrine is often entitled Modalism, because according to this view Father, Son, and Spirit are modes of the same being, perhaps temporary and successive roles adopted for the purpose of the divine plan of redemption, but in no way corresponding to anything in the ultimate nature of the Godhead, since the three titles are purely adjectival.

At Rome the controversy became heated under Victor's successor Zephyrinus (198–217). Sabellius represented one extreme in the Roman community. The opposite extreme was defended by Hippolytus, for whom it was essential to say that the Father and the Logos are two distinct 'persons' or *prosopa*. (Hippolytus applied the title 'Son' only to the incarnate, not to the pre-existent Lord.) Between them, as a man of the middle way, stood a deacon named Callistus, who, if Hippolytus is to be believed, had been in youth a slave to a wealthy Christian in the imperial household, for whom he had administered a bank that attracted large deposits from

members of the church. But the young Callistus found himself in financial embarrassment and was held responsible
for embezzlement by his master. By the intercession of
members of the church he was released by his master from
humiliating punishment, and gained credit by a stupid prank
in the Jewish synagogue for which he was arraigned before
the city prefect and sent to the mines of Sardinia. Together
with other confessors he was released at the time when
Marcia, the emperor Commodus' concubine, successfully
interceded for the Christians, and under bishop Zephyrinus
was put in charge of a new cemetery on the Appian Way
near the place called Catacumbas (above, p. 56). Callistus'
role in the doctrinal debate was not intended to look very
honourable in the account given by Hippolytus, but probably much must be set down to the distrust and dislike that
Hippolytus felt towards him. According to Hippolytus
Callistus distinguished his position from the unacceptable
views of Sabellius by acknowledging a real differentiation
between the Father and the Son; but the difference was that
the 'Father' was the name for the divine Spirit indwelling
the 'Son' who is the human body of Jesus. Callistus publicly denounced Hippolytus' view as sheer ditheism. In 217,
to Hippolytus' horror, Callistus succeeded Zephyrinus as
bishop of Rome. Hippolytus felt unable to be in communion
with such a man, and thought his worst suspicions confirmed
when Callistus proceeded to explain that, since the church
was prefigured by Noah's ark in which there were both clean
and unclean beasts, it was proper for the church to grant
reconciliation to those who had fallen into any sin after
baptism. Callistus also recognized unions between upper
class women and men of inferior social status, whose marriage
was possible only subject to grave penalties under Roman
law. The recognition of monogamous concubinage is important evidence of the social position of Roman Christians at
this time, but it would be going beyond the evidence to
assume that there was more than a single such case. Hippolytus had separated from Callistus' communion in 217, and it
may have been for his own independent congregation that
he wrote the church order, the *Apostolic Tradition,* containing

valuable evidence on the early development of the liturgy (below p. 262). Perhaps also it was his own group which commissioned a statue on the base of which his principal works were recorded. The lower half of the statue was recovered in 1551 and now stands in the Vatican Library.

The Monarchian controversy was not ended by the unsatisfying formulas proposed by Callistus, and in one form or another continued to disturb the church throughout the third century. It was the need to combat Monarchianism which led Tertullian in Africa to write his tract against Praxeas, a Monarchian from Asia Minor who also offended Tertullian by his vehement hostility to Montanism, and who had been influential in preventing the Roman church from granting any degree of recognition to the New Prophecy. In Tertullian's view Praxeas accomplished two bits of the devil's business: he 'expelled the Paraclete and crucified the Father'. Tertullian follows the line suggested by Irenaeus in seeing the threeness of Father, Son, and Spirit as a plurality revealed in the working out of the divine plan in history.[1] 'All three', he says, 'are one (*unus*).' But Tertullian felt that it must be possible to answer the question 'Three what?' or even 'One what?' He therefore proposed to say that God is 'one substance consisting in three persons'. The precise meaning of the Latin words *substantia* and *persona* is not easy to determine in Tertullian's usage. He was a well educated orator rather than a meticulous philosopher, and it is probably a mistake to try to interpret his terminology within a rigorous Aristotelian framework. He had been influenced by Stoicism with its doctrine that the immaterial is simply the non-existent, and was prepared to explain that God in all three 'Persons' is 'Spirit', which he seems to have interpreted as an invisible and intangible but not ultimately immaterial vital force. He therefore imported into the philosophical use of *substantia* a materialistic overtone. At the back of his mind there is always the Greek term *ousia*, 'being'. Likewise his term *persona* was probably suggested by the

1. The Greek word for this divine plan was *oikonomia*, or economy; whence this doctrine of God is sometimes labelled by the shorthand jargon 'economic Trinitarianism'.

Greek word *prosopon,* which Hippolytus applied to the Father and the Son. Hippolytus and Tertullian were contemporaries, and there is no means of discovering whether one influenced the other and which had the priority. In Tertullian *substantia* could be used in the sense of character or nature. Speaking of Christ he could say that he is 'one person' uniting 'two substances', divine and human, which retain their distinctness of being and even of activity while being constituted as a single *persona.*

In his tract against Praxeas Tertullian determined the terminology of Latin theology for the future. He was the first Christian to write in Latin (though he had equal facility in Greek, and published some of his works in that language for the many Christians in North Africa who were Greek-speaking). Hippolytus was the last Western theologian to write in Greek. Until the beginning of the third century the Roman church had consisted principally of the Greek-speaking population of the city. In the third century, as the church's mission penetrated the upper classes, the proportion of Latin-speaking Christians in Rome began to outweigh the Greeks. In the middle of the third century the Roman presbyter Novatian wrote in confident, well composed Latin a tract *On the Trinity* which summarized the doctrine of Tertullian, but purged it of both Stoic materialism and Montanist enthusiasm. The cool temper in which Novatian wrote is evidence that the heated debates at Rome of which Hippolytus gave a vivid account had now become a thing of the past.

TERTULLIAN

North Africa was a province of great importance to the empire as one of its principal sources of grain and, in the West, Carthage had come to rank second only to Rome itself. The old Punic and Berber population was still strong in the countryside, but the cities together with the landowners and administrative classes were Roman. A substantial proportion of the population spoke Greek (as late as the last quarter of the fourth century A.D. there was a Greek bishop of the important city of Hippo who spoke Latin with difficulty and embarrassment; below p. 218). They came of immigrant stock either from the East or from South Italy and Sicily. How Christianity reached this region is not clear, but it is probable that there was a vigorous movement of missionary activity about the middle of the second century. In 180, twelve Christians of Scilli suffered martyrdom at Carthage. There was more trouble in 202 when under the emperor Septimius Severus sharp persecution broke out at Carthage. In the amphitheatre at Carthage there died Perpetua and Felicitas, the extant account of whose martyrdom incorporates a priceless document, viz. Perpetua's diary of her imprisonment. But Tertullian's numerous writings reveal little of the public and external history of the North African church. They compensate for that by disclosing much of its internal discussion and above all by their revelation of Tertullian himself: brilliant, exasperating, sarcastic, and intolerant, yet intensely vigorous and incisive in argument, delighting in logical tricks and with an advocate's love of a clever sophistry if it will make the adversary look foolish, but a powerful writer of splendid, torrential prose. In his *Apology* of about 197 he makes not a merely defensive reply to popular or philosophical objections but a militant and trenchant attack on the corruption, irrationality, and political injustice of polytheistic society. Every page is written with the joy of inflicting discomfort on his adversaries for their error and unreasonableness, but in such a manner as to embarrass his own friends and supporters.

Some of Tertullian's most interesting writing is concerned with the proper behaviour for a Christian in a society pervaded by pagan customs. Tertullian demanded that Christians should keep themselves wholly unspotted from the world's idolatrous corruption. They must keep away from the cruel public shows; but that would be self-evident. Tertullian's most stringent demands for purity forbid his fellow Christians to serve in the army, or in the civil service, or even in schools. A Christian may not even earn his living in an occupation producing anything that might indirectly minister to idolatry. Tertullian's conception of the Christian life is first and foremost as a battle with the devil. This led him to oppose the least compromise with 'idolatry', even in what might seem the most innocuous forms of merely conventional habit, and also to conceive of the intellectual task of the Christian thinker as a conflict with diabolical forces. Because he understood his intellectual role in this way he had no hesitation about using arguments that were fallacious if only they would gain him the victory over his immediate adversary. If he could outmanoeuvre the devil by dialectical subtlety, so much the better. Moreover, he was indifferent to public approval. He was never happier than when advocating the cause of a tiny rigorist minority, and his friends might have predicted that he would take up the Montanist prophecy with its fiercely puritan ethic. For a considerable time his advocacy of Montanism was conducted from within the catholic Church, but as it became clear that the Church was not going to grant recognition to the New Prophecy Tertullian passed outside the Church, condemning it as unspiritual, institutionalized and compromised by worldliness. Tertullian was appalled when an authority in the catholic Church, whom he does not name but describes as 'bishop of bishops' and a veritable 'pontifex maximus', issued an edict declaring that the Church had power to grant remission even in the gravest sins after baptism such as adultery or apostasy. It is possible that he was alluding to Callistus of Rome; but perhaps the authority was the bishop of Carthage.

In spite of the fact that he ended his days outside the Church, Tertullian continued to exercise strong influence on later Western theology. Jerome relates an anecdote that Cyprian called him simply 'the master' and used to study his writings every day. Many turns of phrase and terminology from the tract against Praxeas came to form a permanent part of the Western vocabulary for discussing the doctrines of the Trinity and of the person of Christ, and were to be echoed in documents like the fifth-century Tome of Pope Leo the Great which came to enjoy high authority. In the fiery zeal of his moral essays there is an intense ethical seriousness and passion which go far to reward the reader who can be patient with his tortuous arguments and his merciless impaling of opponents. In some passages, usually in anti-Gnostic contexts, he writes scornfully of the power of philosophers to instruct anyone in truth and cries in tones of defiance 'I believe because it is absurd'. But in fact Tertullian was a well educated man with a considerable amateur knowledge of philosophical debate, and his estimate of the 'natural man' apart from grace was not pessimistic. He believed that, although humanity had inherited a flawed nature, the image of God had only been obscured, not annihilated, and that many traces of original righteousness and goodness were to be discerned. He saw an intuitive feeling after the truth in the unthinking interjections of ordinary people ('Good God') which perhaps betrayed an unconscious recognition of divine truth. The gospel he saw as a stripping away of the prejudices of pagan custom, setting the soul free to attain a natural fulfilment corresponding to the Creator's intention. He did not always write with a Kierkegaardian delight in paradox.

These more conciliatory aspects of Tertullian's mind were shared by another African writer, Minucius Felix. Between 200 and 245 he composed a subtle and charming dialogue in which a Christian named Octavius defends monotheism and belief in the resurrection against the criticisms of a polytheist named Caecilius as they walk along the seashore at Ostia. Minucius was no independent thinker, but a refined stylist and an intelligent compiler. He drew freely on Plato, Virgil, Seneca, Cicero, Fronto (tutor of the emperor Marcus Aurelius), and especially Tertullian. Modern argument whether Minucius used Tertullian or if the debt was the other way round must be decided in favour of Tertullian's priority. Minucius presented Tertullian's arguments in a less militant manner, more suited to the taste of a fastidious literary public. He dropped the trenchant, uncompromising paradoxes and the coarse vehemence of his master. He preferred to ease his cultured friends into the kingdom rather than to dangle them over the pit. He even took tact and restraint so far as to say hardly a word about Christ and nothing whatever about the Bible and the sacraments. Minucius is more attractive and sensitive than Tertullian; but undeniably less exciting to read.

6

Clement of Alexandria and Origen

CLEMENT OF ALEXANDRIA

THE history of the church in Egypt is veiled in mist before
the sudden emergence of Clement of Alexandria in the last
decade of the second century. His biography is almost unknown except as it may be deduced from his writings, which
(apart from fragmentary quotations in later writers) consist
of an exposition of the gospel story of the rich young ruler,
some occasional notes on Valentinian Gnosticism and on
biblical exegesis, and the substantial trilogy – the *Exhortation
to Conversion* (*Protrepticus*), the *Tutor* (*Paedagogus*), and the
Miscellanies (*Stromateis*) which he never completed. The
Protrepticus stands in the tradition of apologetic writing, with
an attacking note criticizing the superstition, crudity, and
eroticism of pagan cults and myths, and observing that the
great philosophers, despite their realization of the corruption
of paganism, had failed to break with it. The *Paedagogus* is a
guide to ethics and etiquette for a Christian moving in a
cultivated society. Clement intended that the third volume
of his trilogy should be entitled the 'Teacher', and that it
should contain a systematic exposition of Christian doctrine.
Clement never wrote the intended study. He felt that high
matters of theology should be treated with reverence as
being concerned with divine mysteries, and it would be
dangerous to put into writing a full and extended statement
for all to read. Instead, therefore, he decided to write a work
of a very different character. Several pagan writers of this
age published miscellaneous collections of antiquarian and
philosophical interest, the form being deliberately unsyste-
matic so that the subject would entirely change after a few
pages. An extant Latin example of the second century is the

Attic Nights of Aulus Gellius, and similar works were produced by Plutarch, Aelian, and Athenaeus. Clement decided to use this form partly no doubt because of contemporary literary fashion, but mainly because the style particularly suited his purpose, which was to suggest rather than to prescribe, to throw out exploratory hints for the reader to investigate and consider at leisure rather than to tell all that was in his heart and so cast his pearls promiscuously before unworthy and swinish readers. The content of the *Stromateis* may certainly be taken to consist of as much dogmatic statement as Clement felt it safe to make, but the matter is wrapped in a deliberately misty and allusive style that prefers to put things in the form of a poetic reminiscence rather than in plain and straightforward prose. The style, however, was more than a mere literary form adopted for tactical reasons; it corresponded in some degree to Clement's view of the very nature of theology that he should seek to express it in terms which suggested a reality transcending the verbal symbol. Religious language, he felt, is akin to poetry. A certain diffidence is proper to it.

Clement was not born at Alexandria. He had come there after various travels in the course of which he had learnt from a number of different Christian teachers. The main attraction at Alexandria was a certain Pantaenus, a convert to Christianity from Stoicism who is reported (credibly) to have visited India. Clement says that Pantaenus had the outstanding merit of combining high intelligence with fidelity to the apostolic tradition – not a common phenomenon in second-century Alexandria where the influence of Valentinian Gnosticism was certainly very powerful. As Christianity penetrated the well educated society of Alexandria, the choice for the convert seemed too often to be between clever, eloquently defended heresy on the one side and a dim, obscurantist orthodoxy on the other. It was one of Clement's principal achievements to render this dilemma unreal and irrelevant, and Pantaenus seems to have helped him to discover the right way. At Alexandria Clement found a church afraid and on the defensive against Greek philosophy and pagan literature. Gnosticism had made philosophy suspect; and pagan religion so permeated classical literature that it was not easy to disentangle a literary education from an acceptance of pagan values and polytheistic myth. The method of the *Stromateis*, written with very positive convictions about the truth contained in Greek philosophy and the value of classical poetry, enabled Clement to present his position to the fearful Christian reader in such a way as to diminish any anxieties. He saw that philosophy, so far from giving support to Gnosticism, provided a rational method for its destruction; the Gnostics talked much of a higher reason, but did not in fact exercise it. So the *Stromateis* move from statements pressing the need for the study of philosophy to statements attacking the Gnostic heretics, and at the same time provide an acute and well constructed interpretation of Biblical themes in language and categories familiar to the educated Greek world. Apologetic motifs addressed to the pagan outsider mingle with a defence of the true faith against Gnostic perversions of it. At one moment Clement will be explaining that Plato plagiarized Moses and the prophets without making proper acknowledgements; at the next that Greek philosophy, like the Law of Moses according to St Paul, was given as a tutor to bring the Greeks to Christ and as a restraint on sin; and at the next that Gnostic doctrines of love and freedom ignore the fact that no serious ethic can dispense with giving a place to rules, or that Gnosticism places far too wide a gulf between God and the world and far too narrow a gulf between God and the soul. Moreover, Clement was sensitive to the difficulty that educated Greeks felt when confronted by the simple and popular style of the scriptures. In one passage, by a *tour de force,* he presents a summary of the moral teaching of the Sermon on the Mount translated into the language of Neopythagorean gnomic wisdom. Yet he felt it necessary to reassure any anxious Christian readers that, although the form of expression was not scriptural and there was no invocation of Biblical texts, yet the content of teaching would be found on examination to correspond with the New Testament.

Clement found it hard to use the word 'orthodox' without a half-ironic apology. He was not sure that he was perfectly happy to be associated with those commonly so entitled. Yet he knew himself to be a committed defender of the apostolic tradition, which he believed to include a 'true knowledge' quite opposed to the false 'knowledge' offered by the sects. The 'true gnostic' was not afraid of philosophy; he could use it for his purposes, to understand what he had come to believe within the church, and to refute any adulteration. The higher life of the spirit is for Clement a moral and spiritual ascent. It was characteristic of the Gnostic heretics that they were little interested in virtue or in training of character. Clement's true gnostic knows that spiritual insight is given to the pure in heart, to those humble enough to walk with God as a child with his father, to those whose motive for ethical action passes beyond fear of punishment or hope of reward to a love of the good for its own sake. It is an ascent from faith through knowledge to the beatific vision beyond this life, when the redeemed are one with God in a 'deification' symbolized by the holy of holies in the Mosaic tabernacle, or by Moses' entrance into the darkness on Sinai. The ground of this possibility of mystical union is the image of God implanted by creation.

The central principle of Clement's thinking is the doctrine of Creation. This is the ground of Redemption. Moreover, because God had implanted the good seeds of truth in all his rational creatures, Clement was confident that there is much to be learnt from Platonic metaphysics, and from Stoic ethics, and from Aristotelian logic. All truth and goodness, wherever found, come from the Creator. On the same ground Clement opposed the Gnostics who disparaged the created order by making matter wholly alien from the supreme God, with ethical consequences leading either to rabid asceticism or to antinomian eroticism. In a long review of the Christian sex ethic Clement vigorously opposed the Gnostic thesis that sex is either irrelevant to or incompatible with the higher spiritual life. While affirming all respect for individual vocations to celibacy, he dismisses any suggestion that marriage is an inherently inferior spiritual status. On the same principles he rejected demands that all Christians ought to be teetotallers or vegetarians; it was for him a matter of individual conscience, not of universal prohibition. But Clement was very far from a naturalistic hedonism when writing of delight in the goodness of the created world. The good things of the material order were, he directed, to be used with gratitude but also with detachment, on the conditions given by the Creator and with restraint.

Clement wrote a special discourse to help Christians puzzled about the right use of their money and troubled especially by the absolute command of the Lord to the rich young ruler, 'If you would be perfect, sell all you have . . .' On a rapid reading it might seem as if Clement were merely a compromiser trying to wriggle out of the plain meaning of a commandment. But a fairer reading of his tract shows that he did not see the gospel ethic as imposing legalistic obligations but rather as a statement of God's highest purpose for those who follow him to the utmost. What really matters is the use rather than the accident of possession. Accordingly Clement laid down a guide for the wealthy converts of the Alexandrian church, which imposed a most strenuous standard of frugality and self-discipline. Clement passionately opposed any luxury or ostentation, and much that he protested to be lawful he regarded as highly inexpedient.

The exposition of the saying to the rich young ruler and several passages in the *Paedagogus* and *Stromateis* show Clement acting as a spiritual director. It lay in the nature of his view of the Christian life as a progress towards the likeness of God in Christ that he saw it both as a dynamic advance in the comprehension of the nature of Christian doctrine and also as a process of education in which the aspirant would make mistakes calling for penitence. The church he described as a 'school', with many grades and differing abilities among its pupils, where all the elect were equal, but some were 'more elect' than others. Accordingly Clement could take a view of the church which allowed room for the restoration of the lapsed and at the same time held the highest demands before all Christians. The seventh book of the *Stromateis* (the last that he lived to complete, since the so-called eighth book consists of scattered notes on logic probably found among his papers after his death) portrays the spiritual ideal of the true gnostic in terms which blend the high aspirations of St Paul (Philippians iii) with Platonic language about the soul's assimilation to God and Stoic ideals of passionlessness. It seems to have been from St Paul rather than from the Platonists that he had learnt to regard the knowledge of God as a dynamic advance rather than a static possession. He once declared that if the true gnostic were required to choose between eternal salvation and the knowledge of God, he would unhesitatingly choose the latter.

Because Clement understood the spiritual life as a never-ending progress, he did not think that the process of divine education came to an end with death. His sense of indebtedness to Justin and Irenaeus was not so strong as to make him look kindly on their all too literal belief in a physical resurrection to participate in Christ's reign for a thousand years on earth. For the sinner there is burning fire, destructive not of the image of God but of the wood, hay and stubble of sins. None in this life can achieve such holiness that he will not need to be purified by the wise fire so that he may be fitted for the presence of God.

Clement's personal reticence allowed him to reveal little of himself, but his personal ideals are clear to see. In cultural background and in temperament he could hardly be further removed from the militant zeal of Tertullian. Yet in between the lines of urbane dinner-party conversation reflected in his pages there is to be discerned a moral passion in no way cooler than Tertullian's. Clement is equally reticent about the external life of the church to which he belongs. He never mentions the contemporary bishop of Alexandria, Demetrius, and relatively little can be deduced from his text which helps to explain the institutional development of the community. Like Justin Martyr, he did his chief work as a layman, working as an independent teacher of 'the Christian philosophy', instructing pupils in grammar, rhetoric and etiquette as well as in specifically religious matters. An uncertain scrap of evidence suggests that he may have been ordained presbyter before his death soon after 215. If he was ordained, the fact of his ordination may reasonably be interpreted as the expression of a desire on the part of the bishop of Alexandria to bring lay teachers like Clement under rather closer control.

ORIGEN (184–254)

Origen stands out as a giant among the early Christian thinkers. Although he never names Clement in his writings, he had certainly read him with attention and in many respects continued Clement's work. One of his own early works was entitled *Stromateis;* the few surviving fragments suggest that it resembled Clement's Miscellanies, trying to interpret Christian concepts in language familiar to the Platonic tradition, and mingling philosophical discussion with expositions of biblical cruxes (like the dissension between St Peter and St Paul at Antioch which Origen interpreted as edifying play-acting). But the temper of Origen's mind was very different from Clement's. Throughout Clement's works there is a note of cheerfulness and open-eyed enjoyment of the Creator's mercies. In Origen there is a sterner austerity, a steely determination of the will to renounce not merely all that is evil but also natural goods if they are an obstacle to the attainment of higher ends. Origen knew his way about the classics of Greek poetry, but was little disposed to display the fact. Perhaps he was a little afraid of beauty of form and expression as a dangerous snare that might entrap or distract him. Perhaps it was only that he had no time for such trifles. He worked to a rigorous programme, studying the great philosophers, but above all the scriptures, of which his memory could recall almost any text at will. The excellence of his memory was a source of some natural pride to him, and in consequence he occasionally did not trouble to verify his references and made trivial mistakes.

Pagan literature was for Origen an indissoluble part of the tradition of pagan society, to which as a member of the persecuted church he felt himself to be implacably opposed. Family memory may have played some part in imparting this feeling to him. When he was eighteen years old, in 202 during the persecution of Septimius Severus, his father Leonides died a martyr's death. Origen always writes as

a member of a martyr church, and his attitude towards
pagan philosophy and culture is less sympathetic than Clement's, passing at times into an ice-cold disparagement. For
Clement Plato enjoyed high authority. In Origen's eyes he
enjoyed none whatever. Origen recognized, of course, that
Plato had said many wise things, and that his dialogues
contain much that is true. But with Origen one feels that he
believed it to be true almost despite Plato, not because of
him. He differs from Clement in that he has not the least
desire to claim the protection of a great philosophical name
for some principle that is important to Christians. Yet, quite
unconsciously, Origen is inwardly less critical of Platonism
than Clement, and proposes a system that incorporates a
larger proportion of Platonic assumptions than is apparent
in Clement's writings. He was completely at home in the
arguments of the Greek philosophical schools, and could
move with the familiarity of a master among the different
positions of Stoic, Epicurean, Platonist, and Aristotelian,
using whatever he needed to make his point, but never identifying himself with any one school. Like Justin and Clement
before him, he ungrudgingly welcomes the help of Stoic
arguments about ethical questions and about providence,
and is very sympathetic to the Platonic doctrine of the soul
as being 'akin' to God, but obliged to live in a material world
which is not its true home. Only there could be no question
of Plato being actually inspired to discover divine truth.
For Origen the only source of revelation was the Bible, and
he devoted many hours of each day to prayer and study,
strenuously forcing himself to almost unending toil, and
living with little sleep and food. He desired with all his heart
to be a man of the Church, defending its doctrines against
all adversaries, Jewish, heretical, or pagan.

Early in his career Origen discovered from disputations
with Jews that it was essential for Christians to argue with
synagogue representatives on the basis of a Biblical text
recognized by both sides. The Church used the Septuagint
translation. The Greek synagogues were now using more
literal versions by Symmachus, Theodotion, and especially
Aquila, a Gentile who, after becoming a Christian for a

time, became a proselyte to Judaism and about 140 produced a version which took literalism to fanatical lengths. Moreover, in Christian usage there was a tendency, especially in collections of excerpts of Messianic prophecies, for some texts to suffer slight alteration to make them better adapted for their purpose. Justin Martyr believed that the words 'The Lord reigned from the tree' were part of the true text of Psalm 96 and explained their absence from Jewish copies of the Septuagint on the hypothesis that Jewish controversialists had omitted them. In this situation Origen saw how imperative it was to discover the accurate text of the Old Testament, if Christians were not to be faulted on their facts by Rabbinic disputants. He therefore compiled a vast synopsis of the Old Testament versions entitled the *Hexapla*. He placed in parallel columns the Hebrew, a transliteration of the Hebrew text in Greek characters (perhaps to help with the vocalization of the consonantal text, perhaps derived from churches that may have followed the old synagogue custom of reading the Hebrew text before expounding it in Greek), and the four main Greek versions. For the Psalms two more translations were added; one of them Origen found in a jar in the Jordan valley, perhaps in some find analogous to that of the Dead Sea Scrolls. The central purpose of the *Hexapla* was to ensure the accuracy of the Septuagint, which was the accepted version used in all the Greek churches. Origen added supplements to the Septuagint text mainly from Theodotion's version, and marked with an obelus (to indicate hesitation about their authority) passages in the Septuagint diverging from the Hebrew text. These divergences could be considerable. For example, the Greek book of Daniel included the History of Susanna, for which the Hebrew had nothing to correspond. Origen did not doubt that Susanna was a true part of the book of Daniel, since it was contained in both the Septuagint and Theodotion. Moreover, the story showed up the Jewish elders in an unhappy light, so that the synagogue had an obvious motive for suppressing it.

Origen's view, however, was correctly challenged on the point in a dramatic correspondence with an older Christian scholar, Julius Africanus. In his time Africanus was a figure of considerable interest. A native of Jerusalem (Aelia) he had travelled widely. He once visited the court of King Abgar IX the Great at Edessa, where he met Bardesanes (above, p. 61) and went out hunting with him and the crown prince. He visited Ararat in search of Noah's Ark. He had seen the Dead Sea and Jacob's terebinth in Palestine. About 220 he settled at Emmaus (renamed Nicopolis) in Palestine, whence in 222 he travelled to Rome on an embassy for his city. At Rome he so impressed the emperor Alexander Severus (222–35) by his erudition that the emperor entrusted him with the building of his library at the Pantheon in Rome. His learning was that of a typical antiquarian. He compiled a chronicle of world history, placing the incarnation in the 5500th year after the creation. He also wrote a voluminous miscellany, similar in content to Pliny's *Natural History*; the extant fragments include curious lore about veterinary medicine, military tactics, rhetoric, the textual criticism of Homer, and magic. Africanus was the first Christian whose writings were not all concerned with his faith. Africanus' attitude to the Bible was likewise antiquarian in character. He harmonized the gospel genealogies, and noticed that the History of Susanna contains an atrocious Greek pun. He once attended a theological disputation during which Origen appealed to the History of Susanna, and afterwards wrote to Origen a fatherly rebuke for failing to notice that the pun, being only possible in Greek, proves the History of Susanna to be an addition to the original book of Daniel. Origen testily replied that the pun could have been introduced by the translators, but that did not prove that there was no Hebrew original. One could not suppose that the Lord, who had given all to redeem his church, would allow it to err in such a weighty matter. Here at least Origen's attitude to the Septuagint was strongly conservative. He felt bound by the fact that its canon was accepted by the churches. But Origen conceded that since the synagogue, together with a number of churches, did not accept the authority and canonicity of those books or parts of books which were to be found only in the Septuagint and not in the Hebrew. it was impossible to use these books in a controversy about doctrine.

The defence of orthodoxy against heresy occupied much of Origen's attention. He saw that an answer to Gnosticism could not be made piecemeal by taking particular points in isolation, but only by providing a coherent and all-embracing view of the nature of Christian doctrine, within which the central Gnostic questions (the problem of evil, the place of matter in the divine purpose, free will, divine justice) could find an answer by being seen in a wider and deeper perspective. It was to provide this broad interpretation of Christian theology that Origen wrote his controversial work *On First Principles*. It was translated into Latin at the end of the fourth century by Rufinus of Aquileia, who frankly explained that he had altered some passages to bring them into conformity with more orthodox opinions expressed in Origen's other writings. Jerome, however, published an exact version of the principal passages which Rufinus had thus mitigated and qualified, so that it is still possible to discover the original meaning of the work.

According to Origen's speculative system, God created not this material world in the first instance, but a realm of spiritual beings endowed with reason and free will and dependent upon the Creator. To explain the Fall Origen took an idea from Philo of Alexandria; he suggested that the spiritual beings became 'sated' with the adoration of God, and fell by neglect, gradually cooling in their love and turning away from God to what is inferior. The material world was brought into being as a consequence of this Fall, not, as the heretics said, as the result of an accident, but as an expression of the direct purpose of the Creator himself, whose goodness is manifest in its beauty and order. So the material world is not a disastrous mistake in which humanity is involved by a cruel chance, but a realm created under the will of the supreme God and expressing his goodness, justice, and redemptive purpose, which is not to make souls comfortable but to educate, to train, and to remake them so that they turn back towards their Maker without whom they are less than themselves. Origen saw that the 'problem' of evil lies in its apparent purposelessness. For a solution he looked both to Irenaeus' idea that the world is intended to make strenuous demands on us who are called to overcome the difficulties confronting us, and also to the Platonic tradition that evil is a privation of goodness and that responsibility for the disorder lies in the misuse of free will. The material world is for Origen temporary and provisional, and life in it is a short period in a much longer life of the soul, which exists before being united to the body and will continue hereafter. The process of redemption is therefore gradual; the atonement is going on all the time and, since it is God's way not to use force but to respect freedom, the work of restoration to a correspondence with the divine intention is a slow and painful ascent.

One soul had never turned away from God when the rest fell. This soul was chosen to be united to the divine Logos in a union as close as that of human body and soul, united like white-hot iron in the fire; even the body derived from Mary was also caught up into the union that constituted the one incarnate Lord. But to discern the presence of God in the Son of Man is a grace. Christ means different things to different people in accordance with their spiritual progress. We may begin with him as Son of Man but learn, as we go on, to understand him more deeply. Christ is 'all things to all men', answering to individual need and aspiration which change as faith matures into knowledge and as moral insight becomes more sensitive.

It is axiomatic for Origen that all revelation is conditioned by the capacity of the recipient. The incarnation is of necessity a divine incognito: sinful man could not bear the direct splendour. The Church preaches a gospel which, though absolute within the possibilities of this life, is relative in comparison with the truth that shall be revealed hereafter. We see through a glass, darkly. In the life to come our understanding will transcend what we know now by at least as much as the New Testament transcends the Old. And the soul's ascent in comprehension will continue after the death of this physical frame. Because at death none is sinless and fit for the presence of the divine holiness and love, there will be a purging 'fire', purifying the soul of all dross. All language about heaven and hell is expressed in figurative symbols:

for Origen there is no measuring of hell's temperature. The truth within the symbolic language is that there is divine punishment. But the crucial question is the purpose of this punishment. Origen will never allow that a remedial purpose is not present in 'the wrath of God' (which, as he never tires of explaining, is not an emotional reaction in God).

Origen was convinced that the symbols of early Christian eschatology – heaven, hell, resurrection, the Second Coming of Christ – were not to be rejected merely because literalistic believers understood them in a crude and prosaic way. It was, he thought, the opposite error of Gnosticism to reinterpret all these symbols to refer exclusively to inward psychological experience here and now. Origen himself had much inner sympathy with this view, and could explain hell, for example, as meaning a complete disintegration of the soul in utter un-relatedness. But he wanted to find a way of interpreting the symbols in a sense 'worthy of the divine greatness' which maintained the essential meaning of the church's tradition. His quest for a *via media* may often have ended in a rather confused use of language, and in the eyes of the orthodox his reinterpretations sounded alarmingly heretical. But he felt himself justified by St Paul's discussion in 1 Corinthians xv, where the apostle implicitly rejected the notion that 'resurrection' is a purely inward psychological or mystical experience, but also criticizes the notion that the resurrection of the body means a literal resuscitation of this present physical frame.

Origen's language about the last things became a stimulus to some fanciful speculations in the sixth century. Some enthusiastic monks in Palestine then claimed his authority for the view that the resurrection body will be spherical. (Plato had explained that the sphere is the perfect shape.) There is no clear evidence that Origen himself ever said this.

Origen believed that the devil was a fallen angel, and that the demonic powers were not created evil by God. They fell by neglect of God and by pride which prevented immediate repentance. But evil powers have retained freedom and reason. No being is totally depraved, or it would cease to be in any sense responsible and rational, and one could feel only pity for its unfortunate condition. Therefore even Satan himself retains some vestige of power to acknowledge the truth; even he can repent at the very last. The atonement is incomplete until all are brought to redemption, and God is all in all. But this universalist hope is not a comfortable belief in a naturalistic process that will come to pass whatever happens. Freedom is an inalienable possession of rational beings, and the divine love treats each individual with sovereign respect. Indeed, because freedom is inalienable, Origen has to allow that the redeemed may once again neglect to love God, so that there is a speculative possibility of an unending cycle of fall and redemption repeated again and again. Origen ends with a question. He cannot know, because he cannot believe either that freedom is lost or that love can fail.

Controversy with Gnosticism also forced Origen to an extended examination of the right principles for interpreting the Bible. Against literalists, such as Marcion, he vindicated the claims of allegory to a place in Christian exegesis. Parts of the Bible might look like merely ceremonial laws or ancient tribal traditions, but beneath the veil of law, history, and even geography Origen could discern timeless truth. Philo had pointed the way for him here, and Origen took over many of his basic principles of interpretation. But for Origen the key to the unity of the Bible, linking Old and New Testaments, is the person of Christ. Difficulties, to which the Marcionites liked to point, were understood by Origen as providential signposts to the necessity of a spiritual interpretation. That the four evangelists did not intend simply to give a dry and factual record of events was demonstrated by their differing accounts of Christ cleansing the Temple; the differences cannot be reconciled at the literal and historical level, but are entirely explicable when the spiritual purposes of the evangelists are taken into account. Accordingly, Origen concludes that the prime purpose of scripture is to convey spiritual truth, and that the narrative of historical events is secondary to this. Most passages of scripture have two, or three, or very occasionally even four levels of meaning. Besides the literal meaning the text may also contain

teaching about the Church as a society, or about the
individual soul's relation to God. In this respect Origen's
doctrine of various levels of meaning became profoundly
influential in both East and West. His homilies on the Pentateuch and Joshua were long read in Rufinus' Latin
translation and deeply influenced Gregory the Great. He
also exercised great influence through the medium of
Jerome, who made much of Origen's biblical exegesis his
own.

Origen's attitude to the literal sense of scripture was criticized by his contemporaries and by unfriendly readers in
the fourth century. He believed that only very few passages
in the Bible have no literal sense but only a spiritual meaning.
But it was not clear that he seriously regarded the literal
sense as being important in itself. It was almost accidental,
theologically peripheral, that the Bible contained much true
history. The soul within the body of scripture was the important thing. For Origen it was in line with the entire principle
of revelation and redemption that humanity is educated
to rise from the letter to the spirit, from the world of sense to
the immaterial realm, from the Son of Man to the Son of
God. But the theologian to whom the unity of divine and
human elements in scripture is analogous to the union of
divine and human in Christ cannot have been a thinker to
whom the literal and historical sense was completely irrelevant. In fact Origen's doctrine of prayer and his personal
'mysticism' are always rooted in an attachment to scripture.
He once remarks that 'even at the very highest climax of
contemplation we do not for a moment forget the incarnation'. So also in prayer the spiritual ascent of the soul finds
its foothold in the ladder of biblical meditation. 'Daily we
read the scriptures and experience dryness of soul until God
grants food to satisfy the soul's hunger.' So by grace the soul
is lifted above earthly concerns and rejoices in God alone,
looking into the inward mirror which reflects the glory of
the Lord and is transformed as the light of the glory of God
makes its mark. In such prayer, Origen adds, there is no
need for spoken petitions; for the soul is brought into a sense
of union with Christ, the immanent 'world-soul', and is

enabled to accept with thankfulness whatever burdens and difficulties it has to bear.

Origen regarded the exposition of scripture as his primary task, and the majority of his voluminous works consists of biblical commentaries and sermons on particular books; the commentaries were conceived on so vast a scale that none has been transmitted in complete form. When Rufinus of Aquileia came to translate Origen's *Commentary on Romans* he found it necessary to remould the work and to make a drastically abbreviating paraphrase; as early as Rufinus' time, some individual books of this Commentary were already lost, and he was forced to fill some gaps on his own account. 'Who', asked Jerome (in his pro-Origenist period), 'could ever read all that Origen wrote?' Because of his ceaseless toil he was nicknamed 'Adamantius'. His exacting and ascetic standards did not always endear him to other Christians, and he confessed that he often found himself the object of envy, malice, and even hatred. The story, told by Eusebius of Caesarea on hearsay evidence, that in the enthusiasm of youth Origen castrated himself to ensure chastity, could be true, since a few cases of such extreme acts of asceticism certainly occurred in the early Church. But when Origen himself expounded Matt. xix, 12 ('there are some who have made themselves eunuchs for the kingdom of heaven's sake') he strongly deplored any literal interpretation of the words. Perhaps Eusebius was uncritically reporting malicious gossip retailed by Origen's enemies, of whom there were many.

Origen found it difficult to be on good terms with Demetrius, bishop of Alexandria. He thought Demetrius a worldly, power-hungry prelate consumed with pride in his own self-importance, enjoying the honour of presiding over a wealthy community in a great city. Demetrius was anxious to bring order and episcopal control to the church in Egypt which in the second century seems to have enjoyed a rare degree of anarchy. It would be easy for assertions of episcopal authority to appear autocratic. Origen's friends felt that in Demetrius' attitude to Origen there was an element of envy. Origen was frequently being invited to visit other churches to take part in some public disputation or to help in unravelling some knotty problem of theology. A recent papyrus find has recovered the transcript, taken down by two shorthand writers, of a discussion probably in Transjordan where Origen was invited by a synod of bishops to confute the Monarchian opinions of a certain bishop Heraclides. His fame became so great that he once had the honour of being summoned to Antioch to converse with Mamaea,[1] mother of the emperor Alexander Severus, who had many Christians in his household and is reported (unhappily by an unreliable historical source)[2] to have included statues of Apollonius of Tyana, Abraham, Orpheus, and Christ in his private chapel.

About 229 Origen was invited to Athens to help the church there to answer a troublesome Valentinian heretic named Candidus. On his way to Greece he passed through Palestine where he had many admirers, and at Caesarea he accepted ordination to the presbyterate. At Athens Candidus argued that the orthodox could not object to the Valentinian doctrine of predestination to salvation or reprobation when they themselves held that the devil lay beyond hope of redemption. Origen replied that even the devil could be saved. When reports of the ordination at Caesarea and of the disputation at Athens reached Alexandria, there was an explosion of wrath against Origen. Demetrius complained to the bishop of Rome, and together with a synod of Egyptian bishops condemned Origen. Origen defended himself, regretting that deep truths had been disclosed to those unworthy to comprehend them, and adding that he would not wish to speak evil of the devil any more than of the bishops who condemned him. Thereafter he had to make his home at Caesarea in Palestine, until his death about 254 at Tyre (where his tomb was still to be seen by the Crusaders in the twelfth century).

In 235 Alexander Severus was succeeded by the emperor Maximin, who disliked the favour shown to Christians in the imperial household, and for a short period there was

---

1. Hippolytus addressed to Mamaea a discourse on the resurrection, lost except for nine quotations preserved in later writers.

2. The *Augustan History*, a group of historical novels written c. 350–400.

an unpleasant persecution which, unlike most of the earlier persecutions where the decisive factor was the attitude of the local governor, seems to have been inspired by the emperor's personal decision. Origen left Caesarea for a time in company with a friend and wealthy patron, named Ambrose, who paid for the stenographers that recorded Origen's sermons. It was to Ambrose that he addressed his *Exhortation to Martyrdom* – a plea that Christians like Ambrose with a position in society should resist every temptation to compromise. To Ambrose he likewise dedicated his treatise *On Prayer,* which sought to answer the deterministic philosophy of those who believed that prayer made no difference. In 248 Ambrose persuaded Origen to compose his one major essay in the vindication of Christianity against pagan criticism, the *contra Celsum.* The reply to Celsus is a loosely constructed work in which the arguments are presented in association with successive quotations from Celsus' attack. In consequence it is possible to hear both sides of the debate, and for the modern reader the work remains one of the most fascinating among early Christian writings. The conflict between Celsus and Origen was the more intense because Origen himself was, like Celsus, a Platonist, so that both parties to the dispute shared the same philosophical presuppositions. Origen saw clearly that the issue at stake went far deeper than the arguments of popular apologetic from miracles, fulfilled prophecies and the miraculous growth of the church, towards which Origen himself was in part reserved. The crucial question in Origen's eyes was whether, within a Platonic metaphysic, it is possible to speak of freedom in God or whether 'God' is only another name for the impersonal process of the cosmos rolling on its everlasting way. Because Celsus thought in the latter way, he was a religious conservative, shocked and alarmed by the new and potentially revolutionary forces released by Christianity. Origen regarded the idea of freedom as an emphasis that was especially characteristic of Christian philosophy: it meant the possibility of change, of moral conversion, of spontaneity and creativity, and of critical detachment towards accepted conventions and traditions.

How far Origen won a fair hearing for Christianity among the pagan intelligentsia is very unclear. Porphyry, the pupil and biographer of the philosopher Plotinus, had certainly read some of Origen's work, and could not forgive Origen's disrespectful attitude to Plato and to the classics of Greek literature, which for Porphyry were inspired authorities. Probably Origen lost some of his potential influence by his cold and critical comments on the philosophers. But there were others to whom his words were golden. He attracted many pupils, and the most distinguished of them, a young nobleman named Gregory, published an extant panegyric hailing him, according to the convention of the age, as a master of religious and philosophical education. Gregory had been a student at the law school at Berytus (Beirut) and was converted to Christianity by hearing Origen. He left Origen's lecture room to undertake pioneer missionary work in Pontus in Asia Minor, where a century later the peasants told wonderful tales of his exorcisms – he became known as the 'wonder-worker', Thaumaturgus, and achieved great popularity as a saint. Origen's influence was also profound among the churches of Palestine and Asia Minor in the century after his death. Eusebius of Caesarea, the church historian, looked back on Origen as the supreme saint and highest intelligence in the catalogue of heroes in his history; and no Greek commentator on scripture could escape his influence. Even Epiphanius of Salamis in Cyprus (below, p. 184), who regarded Origen as a heretic who had corrupted Christianity with the poison of Greek culture, admitted that there was excellent stuff in his Bible commentaries. As the monastic movement developed in the fourth century, there were many ascetics who found in Origen's spirituality a theological basis for their personal aspirations. Yet he had many critics. About 300 a Lycian bishop, Methodius, attacked his spiritualizing doctrine of the resurrection. His most extreme enemies (Epiphanius, Jerome in his later period, and the emperor Justinian) explained the mixture of orthodoxy and heresy in his writings by the hypothesis that his real intentions were heretical, but that he had introduced orthodox ideas to confuse the simple. Origen's sympathizers and friends knew that he desired nothing so much as to be a loyal member of the church.

DIONYSIUS OF ALEXANDRIA AND PAUL OF SAMOSATA

Origen died about 254, but his spirit lived on in theological discussion. Shortly after his death there was a sharp reaction against his interpretation of the doctrine of the Trinity, both among the churches in Libya and at Antioch in Syria.

Origen had been deeply opposed to Monarchianism, either in its 'modalist' form that Father, Son, and Spirit are mere names which do not correspond to any distinctions within the Godhead, or in its 'dynamic' form that Christ was a holy man and wise teacher filled to a unique degree with the Spirit of God. For Origen Christ is the pre-existent Logos, the mediator through whom Christians are taught to pray to the Father. That this is no heresy Origen proved by appealing to the tradition of the church that the great prayer or 'anaphora' of the eucharist is addressed to the Father through the Son. Therefore a distinction of some kind must be affirmed. Origen explained that while the Father and the Son are one in power and will, they are two distinct realities – they differ, he said, in *hypostasis*. They are distinct as archetype and flawless image. This is reconciled with monotheism by allowing that the Son is in some sense subordinate to the Father, as a lower level of 'being' within the Godhead. Origen did not think that the divine Logos belonged to the created order. The Son is begotten, not made, and his generation is eternal, not in time. Yet he is the mediator between the Supreme Father and this created world, as a high priest between God and man, representing each to the other.

From 247 to about 264 the see of Alexandria was held by a pupil of Origen named Dionysius. Though not uncritical of Origen's spirit, he was horrified when he met believers in an earthly millennium – the encounter led Dionysius to a penetrating critique of the grammar and style of the Apocalypse designed to prove that it cannot have been written by the author of St John's Gospel. In 259 Dionysius' help was invoked in a dispute among the churches in Libya between adherents of the Logos-theology and some modalist Monarchians. Dionysius did not consider his words very carefully. He vehemently attacked the modalist standpoint. He even affirmed that the Son and the Father were as different as a boat and a boatman and denied that they were 'of one substance' (*homoousios*). The Libyans appealed to Dionysius of Rome, whose rebuke to his Alexandrian namesake stressed the unity of God and condemned 'those who divide the divine monarchy into three separate hypostases and three deities'. The correspondence is the first indication of a gulf, which soon became a yawning chasm, between East and West. The Origenist theology looked like tritheism to the West. The Western doctrine was perilously near 'Sabellianism' in the eyes of the East. (cf. below, p. 138.)

The dominance of Origenism throughout the East in the period 260–300 is illustrated by the crisis over Paul of Samosata, who became bishop of Antioch in Syria in 260. He had no respect for Origen; he spoke slightingly of the Logos-theology and was reserved towards the doctrine of three distinct *hypostases*; he did not understand language about the pre-existence of the Word. For Paul, God and his Word or Wisdom are one (*homoousios*) without differentiation, and to affirm the pre-existence of the Son is to profess two Sons, two Christs; Jesus is a uniquely inspired man.

Paul's doctrine is akin to the primitive Jewish-Christian idea of the person of Christ. His native air is Syrian rather than Greek. But to the contemporary Church his doctrine seemed plain heresy. According to the bishops who in 268 condemned Paul at a synod in Antioch, orthodoxy teaches that Christ differs from the prophets not in degree but in kind, since the prophets were only inspired 'from without', whereas the divine Logos was present 'substantially' in the body born of Mary and indeed took the place of the human soul.

The bishops found it easier to condemn Paul than to expel him, and he remained in full possession of the church with his enthusiastic supporters ('waving their handkerchiefs and applauding', as the angry bishops complain).

In 260 the emperor Valerian was taken prisoner in battle with the Persian emperor Shahpuhr I, and the collapse of Roman power in the East was exploited by the princes of Palmyra on the edge of the Syrian desert, who succeeded in gaining control of all the Eastern provinces of the empire until 272 when the Palmyrene kingdom was crushed by Aurelian. Paul enjoyed the confidence of the Palmyra government, and even combined the tenure of his see with high civil office. But Aurelian's victory settled Paul's fate. The impotent bishops appealed to the pagan emperor who decided that the legal right to the church building should be assigned 'to those to whom the bishops of Italy and Rome should communicate in writing'. It was the first time that an ecclesiastical dispute had to be settled by the secular power. The thorny problem of the relation between Church and State is beginning to emerge as a complicating factor in the internal doctrinal debates of the Church.

7

Church, State and Society in the Third Century

THE PAGAN REVIVAL AND THE PERSECUTION OF DECIUS

By the third century Christianity was widely disseminated in society throughout the empire. As the church grew there was a narrow intellectual revival of paganism, which probably owed much of its impetus to conscious or unconscious reaction against the challenge presented by the Christian attack. The criticism of Christianity by the Platonist Celsus (probably about 177–80) is much more than a negative statement that Christianity is vulgar and its doctrine of a divine intervention in history incompatible with Platonic axioms. Celsus also felt it necessary to provide a theological justification of polytheistic practice; he was thrown on to the defensive, and was even ready to concede to the Christian critics that in certain respects there could be some substance to their case. In the third century Stoicism ceased effectively to exist as an independent philosophical school; it is one of the puzzles about the history of Stoicism that Marcus Aurelius was its last representative. The likeliest explanation is that the distinctively Stoic theses on the ethical side were taken over by the Church, while Plotinus (205–70) claimed to offer a philosophical synthesis in which Stoic ethics and Aristotelian logic were found a place within a broad Platonic metaphysic. Plotinus must have known about Christianity. He had been a pupil of the mysterious teacher, Ammonius Saccas, at Alexandria, in whose lecture room Origen had also studied philosophy a few years before him. Plotinus certainly knew much about Gnosticism, and wrote a special treatise (*Enneads* II, 9) to combat Gnostic infiltration into the circle of his own disciples. Plotinus' biographer Porphyry

(232–305) became an implacable and formidable opponent
of Christianity, with which he probably had some direct
contact in his youth. His numerous writings on religious
questions betray a strange mixture of sceptical rationalism
and superstitious credulity towards the polytheistic tradition
of the past, and strongly suggest a deep inner insecurity.
He was once dissuaded from suicide by Plotinus' personal
intervention.

Porphyry was a man of great learning, though his attitude towards scholarship was more than a little pedantic.
He turned his scholarly equipment against the Church not
only in a special treatise in fifteen books, but also in a chronicle of world history designed to refute Julius Africanus
(above, p. 103) and other Christian chronographers who cal-
culated that Biblical monotheism was the oldest religion of
humanity.

As the defenders of paganism were thrown back on to the
defensive, it was natural that a certain prickliness should
appear in their attitude. But it is characteristic of the changed
situation of the Church in society in the third century that,
whereas earlier persecution usually depended on local factors,
the personal attitude of the emperor himself now became
increasingly decisive in determining the Church's fortunes.

The friendliness shown to the Church by Alexander
Severus (above p. 110) was so marked as to provoke sharp
hostility from his successor Maximin in 235. The emperor
Philip the Arab (244–9) was also sympathetic, and was
popularly rumoured to be a believer. But if so his faith
affected neither his private life nor his public policy, apart
from ensuring toleration for the Church; and on 21 April
247 he and his wife took a leading part in the cultic celebrations of Rome's millennium. His coins, proudly proclaiming
ROMA AETERNA, advertised the greatness of Rome's
thousand-year achievement under the smile of the old gods.
The violent Gothic invasions beginning in 248, coinciding
with successive rebellions and mutinies, made many wonder
whether heaven was indeed so propitious now as in the past.
Writing in 248 Origen observed that popular hostility to the
Church was rising sharply. The Christians had abstained

from participating in the celebrations and in 249 the Alexandrian mob staged an anti-Christian pogrom. In 250 the new emperor Decius (249–51) ordered a systematic persecution, requiring that everyone should possess a certificate (*libellus*) that he had sacrificed to the gods before special commissioners. The sands of Egypt have preserved several of these certificates. They were a deliberate attempt to catch people, and were the gravest attack hitherto suffered by the Church. Especially among property-owners the number of apostates was immense, and in Africa, if not in the East, the Church treated as 'lapsed' not only those who had sacrificed but also those who had been able to buy certificates from friendly commissioners.

CYPRIAN

Cyprian of Carthage and Dionysius of Alexandria went into hiding and controlled their flocks by secret correspondence. The bishops of Rome, Antioch and Jerusalem were martyred, and the see of Rome had to remain vacant from January 250 until March 251, when competing factions elected two rival candidates, Cornelius and Novatian. At Carthage Cyprian's immediate problem was to assert his authority over the church. By his flight he had lost caste, but more serious still was the way in which his position was being flouted by the 'confessors', i.e. Christians in prison, who were believed to be uniquely possessed by the Spirit (Mark xiii, 11) and therefore to have the power of the keys. Cyprian issued a statement *On the Lapsed* in which he denied that any human being had power to remit apostasy, holding that the guilty must be left for God's judgement; but as his position improved with the return of peace in 251 he moved forward to the view that the power of the keys even in such grave matters was vested in the bishop who might act on the confessors' advice. To avoid penitents being treated severely by one bishop and leniently by another, the African bishops met in council and agreed on a common policy which they also notified to Rome 'lest our numbers should not seem enough'.

The Carthaginian opposition to Cyprian went so far as to elevate a rival bishop, and Cyprian replied with an impassioned tract *On the Unity of the Church*: the Church cannot, of its very nature, be divided; for Christ signified that unity is of its very essence when he first entrusted to Peter alone that power of the keys which he later entrusted to all the apostles. They were of equal rank and honour with Peter, but he gave it to Peter first to show that the Church cannot be other than one. The focus of unity is the bishop. To forsake him is to forsake the Church, and 'he cannot have God for his Father who has not the Church for his mother'.

The problems of the lapsed and of division in the Church also troubled Rome. There the learned presbyter Novatian was advocate of the traditional view that to those guilty of murder, adultery and apostasy the Church had no power to grant remission but only to intercede for divine mercy at the Last Judgement. The less austere presbyter Cornelius held the view that the bishop could remit even grave sins. This split of 251 highlighted the conflict between the primitive conception of the Church as a society of saints and the now growing view (which Callistus had advocated) that it should be a school for sinners. The immense numbers of the Christians made it inevitable that Cornelius' policy should win, and he was elected bishop of Rome by a majority, Novatian only by a minority. After embarrassing hesitations Cyprian ended in communion with Cornelius rather than with Novatian. In 254 the supporters of Novatian in Rome and Africa slipped away as it became clear that Novatian had failed to obtain recognition elsewhere,[1] and many applied for re-admission to communion. Cyprian held that baptism given outside the sphere of the Spirit-filled community was no baptism, and that the schismatics could not be recognized at all: 'For how can he who lacks the Spirit confer the Spirit's gifts?' At Rome, however, the new bishop Stephen (254–6), held that by tradition baptism in water in the name

1. Substantial Novatianist communities appear in Asia Minor and especially at Constantinople in the fourth and fifth centuries, but the sect gradually withered away; at Rome itself the remnants were suppressed about 400.

of the Trinity was valid wherever given, and that those baptized outside the Church should not be rebaptized but reconciled, like penitents within the Church, by the laying on of hands. According to Stephen the sacrament is not the church's, but Christ's, and depends upon the correctness not of the minister but of the form. The controversy between Rome and Carthage on this fundamental divergence in sacramental theology reached white heat, with Stephen denouncing Cyprian as Antichrist. His attack is also notable as being the first occasion when the bishop of Rome is known to have appealed to the text 'Thou art Peter . . .' in order to affirm his primatial position as Peter's successor. Cyprian did not share Stephen's view on this point either: for him all bishops are in theory equal just as the apostles were equal. Each bishop is answerable to God alone. The controversy was settled by the death of Stephen in 256 and by Cyprian's martyrdom in the persecution of Valerian on 14 September 258. Dionysius of Alexandria intervened with an eirenicon, and Rome and Carthage reluctantly agreed to differ. Fifty-five years later the Donatist crisis at last made it possible for Rome to persuade the bishops of Carthage into abandoning Cyprianic sacramental theology.

The persecutions of the fifties of the third century were serious, especially perhaps that of Valerian which forbade meetings for worship and picked out the bishops and senior clergy for execution (a model which Diocletian was to follow). But the distracted empire was fighting for its life against the invading barbarians, and in consequence the persecutions were neither continuous nor systematic enough to do permanent damage. Their worst legacy was their by-product of internal divisions. In 260–61 the emperor Gallienus granted toleration by edict and in reply to petitions from bishops restored confiscated churches and cemeteries. Attacks were now to be by the pen, not the sword. Except for a passing moment in 274–5 when Aurelian fostered the worship of the Sun-god as a comprehensive monotheism which could embrace all the cults of the empire, the Church enjoyed undisturbed peace until 303. Even provincial governors who were Christians were silently excused participation in sacrifices. In Spain collaboration went so far that by 300 some Christians were happily combining church membership with municipal priesthoods.

THE GREAT PERSECUTION AND ITS CONSEQUENCES

Diocletian, emperor from 284 until his abdication in 305, carried through a major remodelling of the empire after the fearful crisis of the third century; defence, currency, taxation and prices were all reorganized. The empire was divided between two Augusti who had each an assistant Caesar. Diocletian and his Caesar Galerius ruled the empire east of the Adriatic, while the West was ruled by Maximian and his Caesar Constantius (father of Constantine). From about 300 the question of loyalty in the army was becoming an issue, and Galerius urged the necessity of coercing the Christians. His headquarters were at Nicomedia where he was much influenced by one Hierocles, governor of Bithynia, a Neoplatonist bitterly hostile to Christianity. At a solemn sacrifice attended by Diocletian and Galerius, the augurs found that they could not discern the usual signs on the livers of the sacrificial animals – some Christians present had crossed themselves. Diocletian consulted the oracle of Apollo at Miletus; the god replied that false oracles were being caused by the Christians. On 23 February 303 the Christian cathedral opposite the imperial palace at Nicomedia was dismantled and next day an edict was posted declaring that all churches were to be destroyed, all Bibles and liturgical books surrendered, sacred vessels confiscated, and all meetings for worship forbidden. A few months later a second edict (apparently confined to the East) ordered the arrest of the clergy, but the prisons would not accommodate so many and in the autumn an amnesty was granted on condition of sacrifice. Not until 304 were all citizens of the Empire required to sacrifice on pain of death, but this also was in practice limited to the East.

The persecution did not strike everywhere with equal ferocity. In Gaul, Britain and Spain, Constantius did not go beyond destroying some churches; no one was executed. When he died at York on 25 July 306 the soldiers proclaimed his son Constantine as emperor. Constantine, like his father, worshipped the Unconquered Sun; but there was Christian influence in his household since he had a half-sister named Anastasia (*anastasis*=resurrection). At the crisis of his career in the war of 312 to gain sole power in the West, Constantine invoked the mighty aid of the Christian God and was not disappointed. His rise to power in 306 made it certain that persecution would not affect provinces under his control.

In the East where Christians were far more numerous, the story was quite different. Diocletian wanted to avoid bloodshed; but in 304 he retired from public life, emerging in 305 only to announce his abdication and permanent retirement to Split in Dalmatia, and Galerius' now unrestrained fanaticism, abetted by his Caesar Maximin Daia, produced a minor blood-bath. The intensity of Galerius' feeling is shown by the edict he issued on 30 April 311 when he was dying in great pain. He explains that he had tried to persuade the Christians to return to the religion of their forefathers, but 'very many persisted in their determination,' and he now grants them toleration and the right of assembly in return for which they are begged to pray for his health and for the defence of the State. Galerius' death did not end the troubles. In 312 inspired pagan petitions poured in to Maximin Daia asking him to suppress the 'novelty' of the disloyal Christians.[1] But Maximin soon fell in civil war against Licinius and out of the welter of war and intrigue in 311–12 two figures emerged as supreme, Constantine in the West and Licinius in the East. In February 313 at Milan they agreed on a policy of religious freedom for all, Christians and pagans alike, and on the restoration of all property, whether belonging to individual Christians or to churches as corporations.

The worst legacy of the persecution was once again schism. As in modern times the Christians differed among themselves about the point at which resistance to the State must

1. See the inscription from Arycanda in Lycia (found in 1892), translated in Stevenson, *A New Eusebius*, p. 297.

be absolute. In the East sacrifice was regarded as apostasy, not the surrender of sacred books and church plate. But in the West opinion was divided, passion ran high, and in consequence, although persecution was briefer and left most western provinces unaffected, the scars were more serious than in the East. Mensurius, bishop of Carthage, cooperated with the authorities in holding no public worship; though he gave up no sacred books, he was able to satisfy the friendly police with heretical volumes. His policy was to lie quiet until the storm passed over. Likewise bishop Marcellinus of Rome surrendered the sacred books. But in Numidia especially, the surrender of the scriptures or indeed of any books which the police were ready to accept as such (one bishop handed in medical treatises) was regarded as apostasy. To think otherwise was to derogate from the glory of those who had died rather than surrender, since it implied that they had been overdoing it. Mensurius found himself the target of bitter criticism. He regarded those who refused any cooperation with the police as merely provocative; his archdeacon Caecilian actually picketed the local prison to prevent food being taken to the 'confessors' there who were denouncing their bishop and all his works. This deep division led to the fanatical Donatist schism when Mensurius died and Caecilian was hastily consecrated his successor by three country bishops, one of whom was generally believed to have surrendered the scriptures to the police. This consecration raised anew Cyprian's question whether one who (by apostasy or schism) had lost the Spirit could confer the Spirit's gifts. The Numidian bishops proceeded to consecrate another bishop of Carthage, one Majorinus, of the household of a difficult lady named Lucilla who had a long-standing feud with Caecilian. Before the persecution she had made a practice of producing, during the commemoration of the departed at the eucharist, the bone of a martyr not recognized by the ecclesiastical authorities; she lavished kisses on it so ostentatiously that she was rebuked by archdeacon Caecilian. The resulting enmity between Lucilla and Caecilian shows how the genuine issues of principle on which the schism took its rise were bedevilled by private resentments.

As bishop of Carthage Caecilian was only able to survive because of the powerful support of Constantine and because he enjoyed ecclesiastical communion with Rome and the churches north of the Mediterranean, granted in 313 on condition that Caecilian abandoned the Cyprianic sacramental theology. Donatus (Majorinus' successor) appealed. This was referred by Constantine to a Council at Arles (1 August 314), which he constituted a court of appeal for reviewing the Roman decision. The bishops at Arles naturally upheld the previous findings. Thenceforth the Donatists became increasingly intransigent, determined to keep the purity of the church unstained by any communion with the compromised and compromising Catholics. The schism completely dominated African church life for the next century, and survived until both Donatist and Catholic were swept away by Islam (below, p. 225).

In Egypt there was also schism: the issue turned not on the surrender of books but on the possibility of submission to the edict forbidding meetings for worship. Bishop Peter of Alexandria fled the country; when the metropolitan of the Thebaid, Melitius of Lycopolis, arrived at Alexandria he was scandalized by this absence of worship and pastoral care, and proceeded to ordain two (one perhaps the future heresiarch Arius) to look after the Alexandrian church. Peter's hasty return and Melitius' arrest averted a crisis, and the schism, though long-lived, never became large; but it was serious enough to demand the attention of the Council of Nicaea and to cause acute embarrassment to Athanasius when he became bishop of Alexandria in 328 (below, p. 134). Arius himself very soon left the Melitians and was reconciled to Peter's successors, becoming a trusted and popular presbyter at Alexandria with an immense following both among the young women and among the dockers for whom he wrote theological sea-shanties. Not until about 318–20 were there signs that Arius' orthodoxy was highly questionable. He could not believe that the incarnate Son was one with the transcendent First Cause of creation. 'The Son who is tempted, suffers, and dies, however exalted he may be, is not to be equal to the immutable Father beyond pain and death: if he is other than the Father, he is inferior.'

8

Constantine and the Council of Nicaea

THE conversion of Constantine marks a turning-point
in the history of the Church and of Europe. It meant
much more than the end of persecution. The sovereign auto-
crat was inevitably and immediately involved in the development of the church, and conversely the Church became more
and more implicated in high political decisions. It is characteristic that the Western attitude towards the conversion
of Constantine and its consequences has generally been
more ambivalent than the Eastern. In the West there has
been a sharper consciousness of the double-sidedness of his
benefits to the Church. But if his conversion should not be
interpreted as an inward experience of grace, neither was it
a cynical act of Machiavellian cunning. It was a military
matter. His comprehension of Christian doctrine was never
very clear, but he was sure that victory in battle lay in the
gift of the God of the Christians. In 312 with inferior forces
and against all prudence he made a rapid invasion of Italy
and attacked his rival Maxentius in Rome. Instead of remaining secure behind Aurelian's walls, Maxentius chose to
come out and fight with the Tiber behind him. It was such
unaccountable folly that Constantine's victory at the Milvian
Bridge (312) seemed a signal manifestation of celestial
favour. The Roman senate erected in his honour the Arch
that stands today by the Colosseum, depicting the drowning
of Maxentius' troops and proclaiming in its inscription
that Constantine won 'by the prompting of the deity'.
The deity to whom they referred was the Unconquered
Sun.

The Christians believed the one God whom they worshipped had given Constantine victory. Lactantius, the

Latin apologist who taught rhetoric at Nicomedia in Asia
Minor, tells of a dream granted to Constantine directing
him to put the 'Chi-Rho' monogram ☧ on his shields and
standards as a talisman of victory. The sign, which appears
on Constantine's coins from 315, was a monogram of the
name of Christ. Late fourth-century writers called it the
'labarum'. Its name and shape might suggest an echo of the
double-axe (*labrys*) which was an ancient cult-symbol of
Zeus. But that its meaning was universally understood to be
Christian is shown by the fact that under Julian it was abolished. Perhaps Constantine decided to make the Christian
monogram his military standard even prior to 312. Before a
battle against invading barbarians (he told Eusebius of
Caesarea many years later) he had seen the cross athwart the
midday sun inscribed with the words 'By this conquer'.
The occasion may have been during his campaign against
the Franks near Autun in 311; a contemporary pagan orator
mentions a vision of the Sun-god on the eve of his victory on
this occasion.

In other words, Constantine was not aware of any mutual
exclusiveness between Christianity and his faith in the Unconquered Sun. The transition from solar monotheism (the
most popular form of contemporary paganism) to Christianity was not difficult. In Old Testament prophecy Christ
was entitled 'the sun of righteousness'. Clement of Alexandria (*c.* A.D. 200) speaks of Christ driving his chariot across
the sky like the Sun-god. A tomb mosaic recently found at
Rome, probably made early in the fourth century, depicts
Christ as the Sun-god mounting the heavens with his chariot.
Tertullian says that many pagans imagined the Christians
worshipped the sun because they met on Sundays and prayed
towards the East. Moreover, early in the fourth century
there begins in the West (where first and by whom is not
known) the celebration of 25 December, the birthday of the
Sun-god at the winter solstice, as the date for the nativity of
Christ. How easy it was for Christianity and solar religion
to become entangled at the popular level is strikingly illustrated by a mid-fifth century sermon of Pope Leo the Great,
rebuking his over-cautious flock for paying reverence to the

Sun on the steps of St Peter's before turning their back on it to worship inside the westward-facing basilica.[1]

If Constantine's coins long continued to be engraved with the symbolic representation of the Sun, his letters from 313 onwards leave no doubt that he regarded himself as a Christian whose imperial duty it was to keep a united Church. He was not baptized until he lay dying in 337, but this implies no doubt about his Christian belief. It was common at this time (and continued so until about A.D. 400) to postpone baptism to the end of one's life, especially if one's duty as an official included torture and execution of criminals. Part of the reason for postponement lay in the seriousness with which the responsibilities of baptism were taken. Constantine favoured Christianity among the many religions of his subjects, but did not make it the official or 'established' religion of the empire.

When in obedience to a divinely granted dream he decided to found a new capital for the eastern half of the empire at the magnificent strategic site of Byzantium on the Bosphorus, he intended it to be a 'New Rome', providing it with two noble churches dedicated to the Apostles and to Peace (Irene).[2] But he also placed in the forum a statue of the Sungod bearing his own features, and even found room for a statue of the mother-goddess Cybele.[3] The 'genius' of the city he solemnly invoked with a celebration conducted by Christian clergy on 11 May 330.

Constantine's benefactions to the Church were on a large scale. The ravages of persecution he made good by financing

1. Conversely, under Julian some found it easy to revert from Christianity to solar monotheism. The bishop of Troy apostatized without fear for his integrity because even as a bishop he had secretly continued to pray to the sun.

2. Both churches were rebuilt under Justinian in the sixth century. The church of the Apostles was destroyed by the Turks in the fifteenth century, but Justinian's church of Irene remains, adorned with splendid (iconoclast) decoration. The old church of St Sophia (of Christ the divine Wisdom) was built not by Constantine but by his son Constantius (below, p. 143); this church perished by fire in the Nika riot of 15 January 532, leaving the ground free for Justinian's masterpiece.

3. She was represented, however, in an attitude of prayer which provoked pagan wrath.

new copies of the Bible and by building churches, especially the basilicas in Rome at the traditional shrines of St Peter and St Paul and in the Holy Land at Bethlehem and the Holy Sepulchre. The palace of his second wife Fausta, formerly the property of the Lateran family, he gave to the bishops of Rome as an episcopal residence (which it remained until 1308). He even assigned a fixed proportion of provincial revenues to church charity, so large that even when cut to a third at its restoration after the suspension under Julian's pagan revival, it was reckoned generous. Constantine also endeavoured to express Christian ideals in some of his laws, protecting children, slaves, peasants and prisoners. An edict of 316 directs that criminals may not be branded on the face 'because man is made in God's image'.

A law of Constantine of 321 closed law courts 'on the venerable day of the sun' except for the pious purpose of freeing slaves, and deprecated Sunday labour except where necessary on farms. An inscription found near Zagreb records that Constantine changed the old custom of working for seven days and holding a market-day every eighth, directing farmers to hold their market-day each Sunday. This is the earliest evidence for the process by which Sunday became not merely the day on which Christians met for worship but also a day of rest, and it is noteworthy that in both law and inscription Constantine's stated motive for introducing this custom is respect for the sun.

The Christian practice of commemorating the Lord's resurrection on the first day of the week was already traditional before St Paul wrote 1 Corinthians. The Church derived the habit of worship on one day in seven from Judaism, not from Mithraic sun-cult, and they chose Sunday as the day when the Lord rose again. But popular astrology from the first century A.D. onwards was spreading the idea that each of the seven planets (among which the ancients included the sun and moon) presided over a day. To the Roman poets Tibullus and Ovid Saturn's day was inauspicious for work and travel. Gentile Christians of the second century (Ignatius, Justin, Clement of Alexandria and Tertullian) saw rich symbolism in the coincidence of the Lord's day with

the day of light and sun. Accordingly the institution of the
week, unknown to the classical age, was gradually diffused
by popular astrology and derived a little additional impetus
from the spread of Christianity. The Church tried to replace
the pagan names for the days by numerical terms, and in the
Greek East succeeded, but in the less Christianized West the
planetary names could not be eliminated and now survive in
all West European languages except Portuguese.

By 321 Constantine's faith had become a political factor.
His eastern colleague Licinius (with whom he had agreed on
religious toleration in 313) was a pagan, and as suspicion of
each other's intentions rose Constantine tried to enlist
Christian support in the East. He succeeded in encircling
Licinius by making alliance with the Armenians who had
recently become Christians. When Licinius harried Christians near the Armenian frontier and prohibited synods,
Constantine had an excuse for a crusading war culminating
in a victory on the Bosphorus in September 324 which left
him sole ruler.

Constantine's move to the East brought him to the centre
of gravity of the empire. He also desired to visit the Holy
Land and expressed a wish to be baptized in Jordan. But
his expectation of the Christian East was sadly disappointed.
Just as the Donatist controversy in Africa had distressed him
in the West, so now he found that the Greek churches had
just become involved in sharp dissension, originating in an
abstruse disagreement between bishop Alexander of Alexandria and his presbyter Arius. It had started as a local
quarrel. But Arius had invoked weighty support outside
Egypt, and now Alexander of Alexandria was being opposed
by important bishops like the learned historian, Eusebius of
Palestinian Caesarea, and his powerful namesake Eusebius
bishop of Nicomedia, the imperial residence in Bithynia.
The Greek episcopate was split into two parties, with feeling
running high. Constantine at once abandoned his proposed
pilgrimage; he sent his ecclesiastical adviser, Hosius, bishop
of Cordova, on a mission of reconciliation and inquiry, and
decided to call a vast council of bishops at Ancyra (Ankara)
after Easter 325.

On arrival at Alexandria Hosius sided with Alexander against Arius, and then went to Antioch in Syria to inquire into the support which Arius had been receiving from Eusebius of Caesarea and others. At a council of Antioch, where Hosius presided, Eusebius was excommunicated – subject to confirmation by the great council already called for Ancyra. It was a clear attempt to prejudge the issue, and Constantine reacted at once by transferring the council from Ancyra (Ankara) to Nicaea (Iznik) near Nicomedia so that he could personally control the proceedings.

The Council of Nicaea, soon to be reckoned the first 'ecumenical' or world council because of the range of representation there, was attended by about 220 bishops, almost all Greek. Only four or five came from the Latin West apart from Hosius of Cordova and two Roman presbyters sent by Pope Silvester. Nevertheless, it was a notable event for the church and was felt to be so at the time. At the solemn opening on 20 May 325 Constantine urged the bishops to achieve unity and peace. He quickly made it clear that he deplored the censure of Eusebius of Caesarea and declared full support for his doctrines. But Eusebius' vindication did not mean that his friend Arius was to be upheld. The creed proposed for adoption by the council was sharply anti-Arian in its affirmation that the Son is 'of one substance with the Father'. Its concluding anathema condemned the propositions that the Son is metaphysically or morally inferior to the Father and belongs to the created order. Astonishingly enough, after the strong partisanship apparent before the council, 218 out of 220 bishops signed the creed, a unanimity that must certainly have gratified the anxious emperor. It is, however, clear that the crucial terms of the creed were not understood in a precisely identical sense by all the signatories. 'Of one substance' (*homoousios*) affirmed identity. It declared that the Father and the Son are 'the same'. But this was ambiguous. To some it meant a personal or specific identity; to many others it meant a much broader, generic identity. The happy accident of this ambiguity enabled Constantine to secure the assent of everyone except two Libyan bishops, whose objections seem to have been less to the creed than to the sixth canon which subjected them to Alexandrian control.

Besides the doctrinal question the council of Nicaea brought Syria into line with Egypt and Rome in calculating the date of Easter, made arrangements for the reconciliation of the dissident Melitians in Egypt (above, p. 124), and issued twenty canons mainly regulating discipline. Hitherto individual bishops had been remarkably free in their actions, and churches had been little controlled in electing them. The Nicene code of canon law forbade ambitious bishops moving from one see to another, directed that a bishop should be consecrated by all the bishops of his province if possible and in no case by less than three, and placed a power of veto in the hands of the bishop of the provincial metropolis. This last rule accelerated the process which concentrated authority increasingly in the hands of metropolitans. Three bishops (Rome, Alexandria and Antioch) had traditionally exercised a measure of jurisdiction beyond the frontiers of their province, Alexandria controlling upper Egypt and Libya, and Rome the churches of southern Italy. These rights were recognized as a modification of the metropolitan system, though their nature and limits are not defined. A significant canon declared that special honour attaches to the see of Jerusalem, though without prejudice to the metropolitan rights of Caesarea. These pregnant words marked a crucial step towards the fifth-century creation of the patriarchate of Jerusalem, gradually achieved in face of bitter opposition from Caesarea.

The Nicene canons throw much light, therefore, on the developing organization and 'power structure' of the church. By 325 the Greek churches at least were accustomed to an organization based on the secular provincial system, and the unit normally conformed to that of the State. But what court of appeal could stand above a provincial council? Unlike the West, the East had no single see of unquestioned pre-eminence, but only great cities like Alexandria and Antioch and (from 330) Constantinople. The one Greek city with sacred sites of the first importance was Jerusalem, whose bishops showed a strong awareness that they presided over the mother-church of Christendom; but it never became a major centre of power in the Church. Not until the fifth century, in face of passionate opposition from Alexandria, could the see of Constantinople establish in the East a position comparable with that of Rome in the West. But for the Latin bishops the Western prestige of Rome simplified the problem. In 342/3 the Latin bishops at Serdica sensibly ruled that the court of appeal from a provincial synod should be judges appointed by the Pope. Even so the Serdican bishops had to pass a special resolution deploring individual bishops who brought the church into disrepute by continual visits to the court (especially when they petitioned the emperor not for some charitable purpose but to obtain some secular promotion for their friends or themselves). In fact, as the fourth century advanced, it became increasingly the tendency for the final decisions about church policy to be taken by the emperor, and the group in the church which at any given time swayed the course of events was very often that which succeeded in obtaining the imperial ear.

9

The Arian Controversy after the Council of Nicaea

IT was the misfortune of the fourth-century church that it became engrossed in a theological controversy at the same time as it was working out its institutional organization. The doctrinal disagreements quickly became inextricably associated with matters of order, discipline, and authority. Above all they became bound up with the gradually growing tension between the Greek East and the Latin West. During the first half of the century the Arian leaders in the East were able to use this tension to build a considerable united front among the Greek churches, and they had the support of a tolerant emperor, first Constantius II (337–61) and then Valens (364–78). Moreover, the manner in which Arianism was finally overcome in the East was such as to ensure that even after the controversy was over the tension between East and West was continued. How this came about will be clear from the story.

The Arian controversy after the council of Nicaea may be divided into three stages; the first down to the death of Constantine (22 May 337), the second from the accession of the sons of Constantine to the death of Constantius II (361), and the third from the accession of Julian to the suppression of Arianism under Theodosius I (381).

FROM NICAEA (325) TO THE DEATH OF CONSTANTINE (337)

During the period while Constantine was alive the Nicene creed remained unquestioned as the criterion of true faith. Nevertheless, the friends of Arius were able to recover much of the ground that they lost in the summer of 325. This recovery was mainly the achievement of their brilliant leader, Eusebius of Nicomedia, who by virtue of his position in proximity to the court was well placed to get things done. It was especially to him that Arius had appealed for help against bishop Alexander of Alexandria in the sharp negotiations before the council of Nicaea. At Nicaea in 325 he had signed the creed without gloss or explanation, but it was evident to everybody that he had not meant the same by it as, say, Hosius of Cordova or Alexander of Alexandria. A month or so after Nicaea he made a momentary slip: he received Arius to communion at Nicomedia when Arius' status was under review, and was at once sent into exile by the incensed Constantine. But before long he was back, and concentrated his able mind on ways of undermining the position of the chief opponents of Arian theology.

The three principal bishops at whom Eusebius of Nicomedia directed his attack were all men who made no secret of their regret at his existence, and who thought it an intolerable weakness in Constantine's policy of comprehension, perhaps even in the wording of the Nicene creed, that Eusebius and his party should be allowed to continue in office.

The first to fall was the bishop of Antioch, Eustace, a violent critic of Origen's theology who made it easy for the Eusebians to eliminate him: he spoke disrespectfully of Constantine's mother Helena when she was visiting the Holy Land on pilgrimage in 326. A synod at Antioch deposed him, and Constantine sent him to an exile from which he never returned.

The second to fall was harder for Eusebius to dislodge. Athanasius had succeeded to the bishopric of Alexandria on Alexander's death in April 328, and his mind was dedicated to the defence of his church and to the absolute exclusion of heresy and schism. Soon after his election he received a letter from Constantine saying that Arius himself had now signed the Nicene creed (with a few private glosses), and should be restored to communion at Alexandria. Athanasius refused and, when summoned to the emperor, so impressed Constantine by his qualities that the demand was not pressed.

Unhappily he had trivial local troubles in Egypt which led to his downfall. The schismatic Melitians had been reconciled by the decisions of Nicaea, but this did not prevent them being very tiresome. Athanasius dealt with them so roughly that they complained of his violent methods. The charges brought by these dissident Copts (recently found papyrus letters show that there was substance in their accusations) were quickly exploited by Eusebius of Nicomedia. The process culminated in a synod at Tyre in August 335 at which the Eusebian party were able to secure Athanasius' formal excommunication and deposition for acts unworthy of a Christian bishop. Athanasius petitioned Constantine. But Eusebius of Nicomedia clinched the issue by producing testimony that in a rash moment Athanasius had threatened to call a dock strike at Alexandria, stopping the vital corn supply to Constantinople, if the emperor failed to support him. Constantine angrily exiled him to Trier, the seat of the prefecture in Gaul. At no stage was there any doctrinal charge against Athanasius.

The third to fall was the bishop of Ancyra, Marcellus. He had long carried on a pamphlet war against the theological tradition of Origen with its strong emphasis on the independence of Father, Son, and Spirit as 'three hypostases'. To Marcellus the unity of God was prior to all plurality: in himself God is one, and he is only 'three' in a relative sense because of his activity in creation and redemption. Marcellus wanted a strictly Biblical theology, based on texts, not on Plato or Origen; and he found an excellent proof-text for his position in the words of St Paul that 'the Son shall at the last deliver up the kingdom to the Father and God will be all in all', showing that any distinction between Son and Father is only temporary and relative to the created order. Politically Marcellus was not a powerful figure and therefore did not attract the fire of the Eusebians until 335–6. But in 335, immediately after the turbulent council of Tyre which condemned Athanasius, Constantine instructed all the bishops in the East to attend the dedication of his new church of the Holy Sepulchre at Jerusalem, and planned that, in celebration of the thirtieth anniversary of his elevation as emperor, the ceremonies should include a splendid reconciliation of all those Arians who had come to submit since the Council of Nicaea. Marcellus declined to soil his conscience by attending, and was at once accused of disrespect to the emperor as well as of heresy. At a council at Constantinople early in 336 he was deposed. The now usual exile followed.

It was at about this time that Arius died. It is significant of the course of events that the precise circumstances and date are shrouded in mist. He had been left out in the cold, almost forgotten. At length, sick and old, he had pleaded with Constantine to allow him the benefit of the sacraments before he died, sadly complaining that his powerful friends like Eusebius of Nicomedia could no longer be bothered to do anything for him. It was charitably arranged that he should be formally restored at Constantinople. Some twenty years later Athanasius began to circulate a dramatic story that, in response to the prayers of the local bishop that he might be spared pollution, Arius was struck dead in the manner of Judas Iscariot on the eve of his restoration. Perhaps the heretic's death came before the intended act of peace. Perhaps Athanasius' story is untrue and he died shriven. It does not matter to the history, because Arius had ceased to matter. He had long been discarded by both sides, and, as he himself painfully realized, he had become negligible.

Shortly before his death at Pentecost 337 Constantine was baptized by Eusebius of Nicomedia. He lay in state in the white robe of a neophyte, and was buried at his own capital of Constantinople in the church of the Apostles. With his removal from the scene the Arian controversy at once took a sharper turn.

THE CHURCH UNDER THE SONS OF CONSTANTINE

The second period of the Arian controversy coincides with the reign of Constantius (337–61), and is marked by political and ecclesiastical confusion. Constantine had intended that the empire of which he had been sole ruler since 324 should once again be governed by a tetrarchy such as Diocletian had instituted. He proposed to divide the *imperium* between his three sons and his nephew. But the army declined to be governed by any but the sons of Constantine. All other male relatives were killed, except two small boys, Gallus and Julian, sons of Constantine's half-brother. After this blood-bath the three sons of Constantine divided the empire between them: Constantine II took the western provinces, Constantius II the eastern, while the youngest, Constans, took Italy and North Africa. Relations between the brothers were not easy. In 340 war between Constantine II and Constans ended in the death of Constantine II, and Constans remained sole ruler of all the western provinces until he was himself murdered by the rebel Magnentius in 350.

These political disturbances had immediate effects on the course of church politics. During the summer of 337 the exiled bishops, Athanasius, Marcellus and others, tried to return to their sees. But Constantius in the East was favourable to Eusebius of Nicomedia who at about this time decided to move to the see of Constantinople which had displaced Nicomedia as the effective capital. Accordingly the returning exiles had a hostile reception, and were forced to withdraw to the West. In 340 Athanasius and Marcellus, as persecuted refugees, were welcomed to communion at Rome by bishop Julius (337–52). This welcome in itself added fuel to the flames. It was a grave matter for Rome to accept clergy formally excommunicated by Greek synods. Athanasius and Marcellus held that these synodical judgements were invalid since their accusers were heretics, but the proposition did not seem self-evident at the time in the East. The alternative argument was to affirm that Rome had a canonical right to act as a court of appeal. In the Greek East such a claim was much less self-evident.

On 6 January 341 ninety-seven Greek bishops gathered with the emperor Constantius at Antioch for the dedication of the new cathedral begun by Constantine. They sat in synod to deplore the growing bitterness of the situation. They disowned the accusation that they were Arians ('for how should bishops be followers of a presbyter?') or that they wanted to abandon the Nicene creed, of which their only criticism was its insufficiency to exclude manifest heretics like Marcellus. As for the claim of Rome to act as a court of appeal, the Greeks retorted that it was a new thing for a western synod to judge eastern decisions; that they held the Roman church in high honour for its tradition of apostolic doctrine, yet it was from the Greek East that the apostles had gone to Rome – or was it on the ground of the secular dignity of the city that Julius assumed superiority? The theological acumen of Rome would have impressed the Greeks more if Julius had not naïvely accepted Marcellus to communion on the basis of no severer doctrinal test than the simple Roman baptismal creed. In the eyes of the Greek theologians Marcellus denied the distinctness of the Father and Son and used the Nicene affirmation of their identity to conceal his Sabellian heresy. The council of Antioch concluded by drawing up a creed to supplement Nicaea, all the crucial clauses of which were directed against Marcellus. This is the earliest creed to include the affirmation that Christ's 'kingdom shall have no end', a proposition that Marcellus was held to deny.

The Antioch manifesto of 341 illustrates the full gravity and complexity of the controversy. It was no longer an abstract and remote dispute about the theses of a slightly neurotic popular preacher in Alexandria. The Arian controversy had developed into an imminent split between East and West. The East resented the Roman claim to a superior jurisdiction, for which they could see no justification. The Greeks also looked down on the intellectual capacities of the Latins, and suspected their theology of naïve Sabellianism. On the other side, the West distrusted the Greeks for being so clever, and for using language which when translated into Latin sounded uncommonly like tritheism, since 'three *hypostases*' came into Latin as 'three *substantiae*'. (Cf. above, p. 114). The fact that the Eastern church policy was dominated by Eusebius of Nicomedia (now of Constantinople) made it natural for Rome to assume that the Greek bishops were supporting Arianism; and so long as Eusebius remained influential, all Greek disclaimers of Arianism looked implausible.

The Eastern leaders might have held out for a long time against the Western demands if the circumstances had not changed. But in the winter of 341–2 Eusebius of Constantinople died; the succession at Constantinople became a matter of heated partisanship and ended with two rival bishops (Paul and Macedonius) who alternately ousted one another for several years to come. Accordingly, the Eusebian party was left without a leader, and at the capital see there was a power vacuum. Imperial politics also weakened the eastern position. After 340 Constans was sole ruler of the western provinces, and began to put pressure on Constantius to make his Greek bishops more amenable.

The exchanges of 340–41 clearly threatened a schism of the first magnitude. The emperors urgently called a council of both East and West to meet in 342/3 at Serdica (Sofia in Bulgaria). The synod split into two camps which roundly cursed one another, and the threat of schism was realized. The separated councils did not entirely waste their time in hurling anathemas. The Greeks also produced a creed with an anti-Arian anathema and a well constructed Easter table. The Latins issued a set of canons chiefly designed to impose discipline on individualistic and over-ambitious bishops. The Western canons included the rule that the bishop of Rome could appoint judges to hear appeals by bishops under censure in their own province, and deplored the diminution in the social standing and authority of bishops resulting from a tendency for unimportant towns to desire the status of a bishopric. Unhappily the Western council also published a naïve theological manifesto to justify their decision to admit Marcellus of Ancyra to communion. They explained that it was a supplementary interpretation of the Nicene creed which in no way replaced that authoritative document. They also denounced two bishops from the Danube region, Valens of Mursa (Esseg) and Ursacius of Singidunum (Belgrade), who had joined the Greek bishops. But the cover given to Sabellianism by this manifesto was large and generous. Athanasius regretted its publication, and at the time it did nothing to promote Eastern respect for Western theology.

After the deadlock at Serdica reunion was achieved, under the strongest imperial pressure, only by painful and unacknowledged sacrifices on either side. The East agreed to take back Athanasius at Alexandria, while the West silently dropped the cause of Marcellus of Ancyra. Athanasius re-entered Alexandria in 346 to an enthusiastic welcome, and for the next ten years enjoyed his longest single period of uninterrupted possession of his see. The tacit agreement on reunion was only a truce, however. In 350 Constans fell before the usurper Magnentius in Gaul. Constantius refused to recognize Magnentius, and bloody civil war followed in which the decisive victory was won by Constantius at Mursa. In a chapel near the battle none prayed more fervently for Constantius' victory than the Arian bishop of Mursa, Valens, and from this time onwards Valens became a potent adviser of the emperor in church matters. Valens was vehemently opposed to Athanasius, and Constantius was now sole emperor.

Athanasius' periods of exile had enabled him to build up solid and entrenched support in the West. It was clear to Constantius that the West was the citadel which must be brought to condemn Athanasius, and the process would not be very difficult since many Western bishops had only the haziest idea of what the controversy was really about.[1] At successive synods summoned at Arles (353) and Milan (355) Constantius extracted from pliant bishops a condemnation of Athanasius. Exile was imposed on the few who refused – Lucifer of Calaris (Sardinia), Eusebius of Vercellae, Dionysius of Milan (who was replaced by the safe Arian Auxentius), Hilary of Poitiers, and above all the bishop of Rome, Liberius, who had succeeded Julius in 352.

Not until the submission of the West was secure did the storm finally break on Athanasius in Egypt, though it had long been clear to him what was coming, and he made good preparations. In February 356 it took a military force to oust him and to install an Arian successor, named George,

1. How hazy is shown by the declaration of Hilary of Poitiers that he had been a bishop for many years before he had even heard of the Nicene creed.

who conspicuously failed to endear himself to the Alexandrians (below, p. 155). Athanasius fled to the desert – to the monks with whom he always stood in the closest sympathy – and successfully evaded all attempts to find him. From his hiding-place he poured out vitriolic pamphlets against Constantius and his Arian advisers, painting a lurid picture of the sufferings being endured by the orthodox under the current regime. It is some measure of the almost monolithic support he now enjoyed in Egypt that he was never betrayed to the vigilant authorities.

George of Alexandria was a radical Arian. During 357 the great see of Antioch also fell into the hands of a likeminded radical, Eudoxius. The occupation of these crucially important sees by extreme Arians caused great alarm in the Greek East. The language of these men was unmarked by concessions to religious devotion or doctrinal tradition. Their approach to religion was influenced by a clever Antiochene layman, Aetius, expert in logic. He used to argue relentlessly that the principles both of monotheism and of divine impassibility could only be consistently maintained if one frankly asserted that the Son is not merely distinct from the Father but actually belongs to the created order; that all derived being is substantially dissimilar from the underived First Cause; in short, that the Son's essence is unlike (*anomoios*) the Father's. This position, quickly labelled Anomoean or 'dissimilarian', was opposed not merely to the Nicene formula that the essence of the Father and the Son is identical (*homoousios*), but also to the predominant formula of the great majority of Greek bishops that the Son's essence is 'like' the Father's (*homoiousios*) as a perfect image resembles its archetype. This *homoiousios* formula seemed to possess the attractions that it affirmed the highest degree of resemblance short of that 'identity of essence' which, under the umbrella of the Nicene creed, could give dangerous protection to 'Sabellians' like Marcellus of Ancyra.

The enthusiastic advocacy of Dissimilarian theology by Eudoxius of Antioch caused consternation among those many bishops who belonged to the 'central' conservative tradition represented by the *homoiousios* formula that the

Son's essence is like the Father's. Their leader in 357–8 was Basil, bishop of Ancyra (Marcellus' successor), an ascetic to whom Eudoxius and George of Alexandria appeared irreligious men bent on the shipwreck of the church. Basil knew his way about the imperial court and forthwith hastened to Constantius at Sirmium (Mitrovica in Yugoslavia). He successfully persuaded Constantius that *homoiousios* was the only formula capable of maintaining both unity in the church and the true faith. For a time Basil of Ancyra succeeded in holding the emperor's confidence and in ousting the Arianizing Valens of Mursa, who had effectively dominated Constantius' mind on church questions for the preceding six years. Only a few months previously Valens had had his supreme triumph in gaining the submission of none other than Hosius of Cordova, the veteran of Nicaea, to a creed which deplored both the Nicene 'identity of essence' and Basil of Ancyra's 'likeness of essence' as unscriptural formulas which disturbed the faithful and made assertions beyond human knowledge. But Valens had failed to gain the assent of the exiled Liberius of Rome to this creed. Liberius, however, felt no comparable objections to the doctrine of Basil of Ancyra; and on his assent to Basil's formula (which enhanced Basil's authority) Constantius allowed him to return to Rome in 358.

For a year Valens of Mursa and Basil of Ancyra competed for the emperor's favour. Valens wanted to say no more than the Son is 'like' the Father, without using the troublesome word 'essence' (*ousia*). Basil saw that so vague a formula left the gate open to an Arian flood, and insisted that one must affirm the Son's essential likeness to the Father. In 359 Constantius decided to hold a grand universal council of East and West, divided for convenience into two parts, the West to meet in Italy at Rimini, the East at Seleucia (Silifke) near the south coast of Asia Minor. The division was fatal to Basil's cause. Valens was able to bring the Western representatives to an abject surrender to Constantius' will, and once the West had failed to stand firm for its tradition it was easy work for Eudoxius of Antioch and George of Alexandria to crush altogether Basil's hope of retaining the emperor's support. In 360 Eudoxius was translated from Antioch to Constantinople; and at a council there, gathered to celebrate the dedication of the new church of Holy Wisdom, Sancta Sophia, a creed was formally promulgated that the Son is 'like' the Father without further qualification. As Jerome wrote of the council of Rimini, 'the world groaned to find itself Arian'.

To all outward appearance the confused intrigues of 357–60 had ended in an almost complete victory for Arianism. The extreme Arian Aetius, who could not conscientiously bring himself to say that the Son was even 'like' the Father, was exiled, but he was of no real consequence. The agony of 360 was the crushing defeat of Basil of Ancyra and his friends, many of whom were deposed from their sees and exiled. Yet the consistent, overruling objective of Constantius' church policy was to find a formula on which the largest possible number could agree. Constantius was persuaded by Valens of Mursa that the right recipe for a united church throughout the empire was an imprecise and broad definition. The emperor was convinced by plentiful evidence that the old Nicene formula of 325, with which his father had had extraordinary success, was a cause of sharp disputes and not at all conducive to peace. It seemed sensible, therefore, to propose for everyone's assent a simpler creed which avoided unscriptural words, which did not make assertions about matters God had not thought fit to reveal, and which was sufficiently wide to comprehend everybody but the intransigent extremists on either side.

There were, however, difficulties about this policy, inherent in its nature. Constantius wanted the vague formula of 'likeness' because it seemed politically expedient for the welfare of the empire. The dissensions of the Christians were not a matter to be regarded with amused indifference or sad resignation. They were a political and social problem which the government had the strongest interest in settling. The interest of the State demanded a compromise, affirming enough to escape being merely negative, but not so much as to adopt a clear-cut position. Unfortunately the policy of compromise presupposed that the Arian theology of

Eudoxius and his friends was a tolerable form of Christianity, and this was a proposition to which Basil of Ancyra, to say nothing of Athanasius, could not agree. Accordingly Constantius was forced into persecuting those who were unwilling to tolerate Arianism. They happened to believe that it was fundamentally false, and their conscience made them prefer exile or even martyrdom rather than bend their will to a course of political expediency.

These considerations help to explain why it was only at this stage of the Arian controversy that the really serious and hard thinking began to be done. Those who rejected the Arian theology had to show with reasoned arguments that the 'orthodox' alternative was true. Paradoxically this was a matter to which relatively little attention had been paid before the fifties of the fourth century. The controversy, it is true, had not simply consisted of shouting rival anathemas and slogans. In 344 the Eastern leaders had produced a long and sober statement of their theology, intended to instruct the West about the underlying issues. On the Nicene side Athanasius produced a number of tracts, especially from about 350 onwards, full of theological explanations of the anti-Arian case. Even so it was not until the late fifties that the thinking became strenuous, partly under the impulse of Basil of Ancyra. At Rome the conversion of the Neoplatonist Marius Victorinus brought into the controversy on the Nicene side an acute philosophical mind. In 360 Athanasius realized that Basil of Ancyra and he were basically fighting for the same cause, and held out a proposal of an alliance even if Basil and his friends retained their scruples about the keyword of the Nicene formula, 'identical in essence' (*homoousios*): 'Those who accept the Nicene creed but have doubts about the term *homoousios* must not be treated as enemies; we discuss the matter with them as brothers with brothers; they mean the same as we, and dispute only about the word.' The eirenic words introduce Athanasius' longest and best discussion of the meaning of the Nicene formula. The rapprochement, though the kiss of death for the party of Basil of Ancyra, was to contribute much to the ultimate defeat of Arianism. But the hour of triumph had to wait twenty years until there was an emperor in the East ready to carry it through.

FROM JULIAN TO THEODOSIUS I (361—81)

The third and final stage of the Arian controversy, from Julian (361) to Theodosius' suppression of Arianism in the East (380–81), is marked by the appearance of new men and fresh problems cutting across the old issues. When Athanasius died in 373 he was perhaps the last survivor of those who had been present at Nicaea in 325. In the last fifteen years of his life he was called to play a different role – no longer the intransigent zealot but the elder statesman whose authority had been vastly enhanced by his record of unbending firmness. He found himself consulted by the rising men of the new generation and, although his vocabulary belonged to an older way of speaking, his answers in reply to their questions were esteemed by them as decisive encyclicals.

Throughout the period the attitude of the emperor was again of the first importance. Under Julian's pagan revival (below, p. 155) all parties were tolerated, since Julian hoped the different factions would simply consume one another, once the restraint of government coercion had been removed. But Julian's reign was short. He was succeeded in 363 by Jovian, who favoured Athanasius and the Nicene cause, but reigned for too short a time for his church policy to take firm shape. After a few months he died and was succeeded by the tolerant Valentinian I who restored the division of the empire, taking the Western provinces himself and entrusting the East to his brother Valens. From 364 to 378 the Greek half of the empire was ruled by Valens, whose wife quickly influenced him in favour of the Arian Eudoxius, bishop of Constantinople until 370, and then in favour of his more moderate but still Arian successor, bishop Demophilus (retired 380). Those who refused communion with Eudoxius and Demophilus were subjected to sporadic persecution.[1] But

---

1. The repressive persecution was discredited by an atrocity in 370, when a deputation of clergy protesting against Demophilus' appointment was burnt to death.

the government policy of a comprehensive church that included Arianism was becoming increasingly out of touch with the main movement of religious life and thought. The tide was running in the direction of the Nicene cause.

During the sixties and seventies three new problems were being thrust into the debate in the East. Two concerned the doctrine of the Trinity; the third concerned the person of Christ.

First, there were theologians who affirmed with the Nicene creed the Son's identity of essence with the Father, but held that the Holy Spirit was not within the supreme Godhead but at the summit of the created, angelic order. In 357–8 Athanasius argued in his *Letters to Serapion* that this was an indefensible half-way house; but Macedonius of Constantinople led a group which denied the divinity of the Holy Spirit and rested their case partly on two or three Biblical texts and partly on the absence of any declaration on the subject in the Nicene creed of 325 which had merely said 'And we believe in the Holy Spirit', without any further explanation. The orthodox labelled them 'fighters against the Spirit', Pneumatomachi, or Macedonians.

Secondly, there was a terminological muddle. The only natural Greek word for expressing the distinctness of the Son from the Father (in opposition to the 'Sabellianism' of Marcellus of Ancyra) was *hypostasis,* which meant that which exists in its own right. The anti-Sabellian tradition stemming from Origen had spoken of three *hypostases* as a formal safeguard against the notion that Father, Son and Spirit are merely adjectival terms describing different attributes of one God. But the pluralistic language of 'three *hypostases*' had been disliked by Marcellus of Ancyra and Eustace of Antioch; and Athanasius himself consistently avoided the expression before the sixties. In the circle of Basil of Ancyra, however, some had been urging that the formula 'three *hypostases*' should be combined with the assertion of one essence (*ousia*), and that the words *hypostasis* and *ousia* should be distinguished as the particular and the general or common.

This terminological question was far from being a remote and academic matter. At Antioch-on-the-Orontes in Syria it became the subject of a painful dispute. By the summer of 362 Antioch had acquired no less than three rival bishops. First, there was a small group of Nicene believers led by a presbyter Paulinus, faithful to the memory of their exiled bishop Eustace and holding in high regard the writings of his friend Marcellus of Ancyra. Early in 362 Paulinus received episcopal orders from a fanatical anti-Arian, Lucifer of Calaris in Sardinia (above, p. 140), who had been exiled to Egypt by Constantius (355) but was liberated by Julian. Secondly, there was bishop Meletius, a 'dark horse' who had been appointed to Antioch in 360 on Eudoxius' translation to the greater see of Constantinople, but was then discovered by Eudoxius and his friends to be much opposed to Arianism, and a friend of Basil of Ancyra. They quickly replaced him by a safe Arian bishop named Euzoius. In 362–3, therefore, the burning question at Antioch was whether the two anti-Arian congregations could unite. Both accepted the Nicene creed. But the fact that both Meletius and Paulinus were bishops made union difficult, since it was axiomatic that there could not be two lawful bishops of one city. Both men had a past that gave grounds for mutual distrust. The suspicion was sharpened by Paulinus' insistence that Father, Son and Spirit are one *hypostasis*, while Meletius affirmed three *hypostases*.

In the summer of 362 Athanasius called a statesmanlike little council at Alexandria which tried to sort out the confusion. Athanasius recognized that orthodoxy is a matter of intention, not of formulas. He saw that the Meletian group intended no unorthodoxy in speaking of three *hypostases*, and that they were strongly opposed to the Arianism of Eudoxius. Nevertheless, he held communion with Paulinus as the true bishop of Antioch, and Rome followed his example. Since Paulinus was widely (and with some reason) suspected of holding Sabellian opinions akin to those of Marcellus of Ancyra, it was with Meletius that the future lay. The past made it natural and intelligible that Athanasius (and Rome) should recognize Paulinus; but the consequence was unfortunate, and Meletius achieved only posthumous admission to communion with the see of Rome.

The third new problem to emerge in the sixties was more difficult. It was raised by one of Athanasius' oldest friends and supporters, Apollinaris of Laodicea in Syria. In an extreme anti-Arian reaction he asserted that Christ's human nature differed from that of other men in one all-important respect: the divine Word or Logos replaced the natural mind. For only so could one avoid thinking of Christ as a dual personality. Apollinaris had a high sacramental theology, a sharp mind, and a pungent pen. But he could not obscure the fact that he was denying the completeness and the genuineness of Christ's humanity. He was asserting that only by a sacrifice of the highest element of human nature was it possible for God and man to be united to form one person, a single nature (*physis*) of which the divine Word is the active subject. His views provoked a storm which broke in force after Athanasius' death (373).

The mantle of Athanasius passed to the 'Cappadocian Fathers' – to Basil of Caesarea, his friend Gregory whose father (not he) was bishop of Nazianzus, and Basil's younger brother Gregory, who became bishop of Nyssa. Their social and educational background made them natural leaders, and they were in the forefront in giving encouragement and organization to the growing monastic movement of the time. When Basil was elected bishop of Caesarea (Kayseri), metropolis of Cappadocia, in 370, he set about building a solid Nicene party in the episcopate of Asia Minor. Whenever a neighbouring see fell vacant, he tried to arrange the election of an orthodox candidate.[1] His letters paint a vivid portrait of his difficulties in recreating confidence where, as a result of the legacy of past controversy, each bishop seemed to suspect all his colleagues of heresy. He found it impossible at first to put anything doctrinal into writing, for fear of the

1. In 372 the government divided Cappadocia into two provinces, which left him as metropolitan of a small area. He vainly tried to re-assert jurisdiction over the lost territory, and it was in these efforts that he unwisely consecrated his friend Gregory of Nazianzus to be bishop of a little town, Sasima, at a road junction in the lost area. Gregory reluctantly submitted to consecration, but never visited Sasima. Basil's consecration of his brother to Nyssa was also part of the plan to fill the Cappadocian sees with reliable men.

way in which written documents could be exploited by enemies, especially under the government of Valens. On the other hand, Basil's reserve in upholding Nicene theology meant that he himself was distrusted by those who believed that he ought to have been proclaiming the truth loud and clear, whatever the cost might be. At Epiphany 372 Valens attended church at Caesarea with his court. Basil disappointed zealots who vainly hoped for a dramatic scene at which their bishop would refuse communion to the Arianizing emperor. By 375 Basil's position was sufficiently secure to allow more outspoken statements. His book *On the Holy Spirit* continued from the point where Athanasius' *Letters to Serapion* stopped, and marked a decisive step forwards in the debate about the doctrine of the Trinity. The essence of Basil's argument was an appeal to liturgical and sacramental tradition in baptism and the doxology, by which he was able to turn the edge of his opponents' refusal to go beyond the letter of Scripture and the Nicene creed of 325.

Basil and the two Gregories were united in their Trinitarian terminology. They affirmed 'three *hypostases* in one essence'. In the painful schism at Antioch, therefore, they naturally supported the claims of Meletius. Basil pleaded repeatedly with Alexandria and Rome that Meletius, not Paulinus, should be recognized; but when he died (1 January 379) he had met with nothing but frustration, and the replies from Rome to his letters seemed uncomprehending and arrogant.

In August 378 the emperor Valens died at the battle of Adrianople against the Goths, and the situation of the Greek churches was soon transformed by the advent of Theodosius from the West. Theodosius had been carefully instructed. He sent advance warning to the Greek world that the terms of ecclesiastical recognition were to be acceptance of the Nicene creed and communion with Pope Damasus and bishop Peter (Athanasius' successor) of Alexandria. This implied among other things the automatic recognition of Paulinus of Antioch. But after arriving at Constantinople (November 380), Theodosius' attitude was soon changed by better information. He saw that the one man capable of rallying the Greek bishops to a united front was Meletius of Antioch, and that Paulinus must be tacitly abandoned.

In May 381 Theodosius summoned a large 'ecumenical' council to Constantinople, and it is a sign of the sea-change in his understanding of the problems that he made Meletius its president. No representatives came from Rome. The new bishop of Alexandria, Timothy, arrived reluctantly and late. The council had to decide about the succession at Constantinople, where the Arian Demophilus had withdrawn before the Theodosian wind of change. At first the council appointed Gregory of Nazianzus to be bishop of Constantinople, and it seemed a suitable appointment: he was an eloquent preacher and an intelligent defender of the Nicene cause. But during the council Meletius died, and when Gregory advocated the recognition of Paulinus as his successor at Antioch on the ground that it would conciliate the West, a storm followed to which Gregory was unequal. Technical objections were brought against the validity of Gregory's own translation from Sasima to Constantinople; had not the Nicene canons forbidden translations? Gregory retired in distress to Cappadocia, where he wrote a self-pitying autobiography in iambic verse. The council then had to decide the succession for both Antioch and Constantinople. For Antioch they chose one of Meletius' clergy, Flavian. For Constantinople they chose a distinguished government official, Nectarius, who was so free of past association with any party in the controversy that he had not even been baptized, and was consecrated bishop immediately after baptism. It was not without precedent for an upper-class layman to be promoted bishop without passing through the diaconate and presbyterate; but such sudden preferments were disliked by the clergy and had been deplored by synods.

The council reaffirmed the Nicene faith in the sense that it reasserted the Nicene keyword 'identical in essence' (*homoousios*). But the actual creed promulgated by the council was differently worded from that of Nicaea, and had a cautiously worded article concerning the Holy Spirit. This reflected the argument of Basil of Caesarea that in the liturgy the Holy Spirit is worshipped and glorified together with the Father and the Son, and that the difference between the Son and the Spirit is to be seen in that while the Son is '*begotten* of the Father,' the Holy Spirit '*proceeds* from the Father'. Although the council condemned Apollinarianism and Macedonianism, it wrote no clauses into its creed which the Apollinarians and Macedonians could not accept.

Finally the council agreed on a fateful canon: 'the bishop of Constantinople shall have rank after the bishop of Rome because it is New Rome'. This canon was resented both at Alexandria, long regarded as the second city of the empire, and at Rome because, although it conceded that Rome was the first see of Christendom, it implied that Roman primacy depended on the city's secular standing.

The West fought a long struggle against this canon, against Nectarius' appointment, and against the council's refusal to recognize Paulinus of Antioch. But the doctrinal decisions of the council marked the end of the Arian attempt to capture the church of the empire. Arianism lived on among the Goths, who had been converted by Arian missionaries – especially by Ulfila (*c.* 311–83), translator of the Gothic Bible, himself a Visigoth[1] who had been consecrated as missionary bishop in 341 by Eusebius of Nicomedia (below, p. 249). But within the empire Arianism died unloved and unlamented. The surviving fragments of the Arian historian Philostorgius, who wrote an apology for Arianism about 425, show how the movement which had begun as a bold endeavour to reformulate Christian doctrine in a way more palatable to the educated public of A.D. 320, sadly ended in the superstitious repetition of antiquated slogans.

1. Racially Ulfila was partly of Greek stock; his maternal grandparents had been taken prisoner in the third-century Gothic raids on Cappadocia. Prisoners were one of the ways in which Christianity penetrated the Northern barbarian tribes.

10

The Conflict of Paganism and Christianity in the Fourth Century

PAGANISM[1] was far from being moribund when Constantine was converted to Christianity, and probably remained the religion of the majority in the empire until well into the second half of the fourth century. It had never been difficult for the Christians to argue that the ancient myths of the gods were unedifying and that pagan cult was sodden in super-stition and black magic. Many educated and enlightened pagans thought so too. But it was hard for the church to overcome the inertia of social habit. The old polytheism was somehow built into the fabric of society, and to challenge it could sound dangerously like revolution and a loosening of the bonds of custom and morality. This conservative attitude was not merely found among the half-educated. People of high education and rank upheld the old religion, often helped by symbolist reinterpretations of the myths in cosmic or psychological terms, and they participated in the traditional cultic acts on the principle that these rites were received ways of keeping the unseen powers friendly, and in any event one could hardly be too careful. Official Roman religion was not of a character to evoke religious emotion as

1. The term 'paganus' to describe a non-Christian first appears in two Latin inscriptions of the early fourth century. It remained a collo-quialism, and did not penetrate Bible or liturgy. In secular usage it had two meanings (1) 'rustic', and (2) 'civilian' as opposed to military. Orosius (below, p. 225) writing in 417 thought the Christian usage explained by the fact that the countryside was still heathen after the towns had become Christian. But this was not the situation as early as 300. Therefore the correct explanation is probably that the 'pagans' were those who had not by baptism become soldiers of Christ and so were non-combatants in the conflict with evil powers. In the East the Christian word for a non-Christian was 'Hellene'.

distinct from patriotism, and for excitement devotees were more likely to turn to the Oriental mystery cults of Isis, Mithras, Attis, Cybele, and the Syrian goddess, all of which were diffused throughout the empire from the Euphrates to Hadrian's wall in Britain (north of which it was alleged that there dwelt only venomous things). Between the various pagan cults there were no sharp frontiers, and a worshipper of Isis was not precluded by loyalty to her from initiation into the mysteries of Attis or Mithras. All would take part in the imperial cult as a patriotic act.

From the time of Justin Martyr and Clement of Alexandria the Christian programme had been to accept and uphold the positive value of the best Greek philosophy and of the peace-keeping Roman government, but to be vehemently opposed to pagan cult and myth. Even if at first Constantine found it hard to distinguish solar monotheism from Christianity, his episcopal advisers must quickly have told him that Christians did not regard the sun as the dwelling-place of the Deity. Towards the last years of Constantine's reign, there was some discouragement of pagan cult to the extent that a few temples were destroyed in the Greek East (where Christianity was fairly strong), but nothing was done to molest the ancient official ceremonies of Rome. Constantine retained the title *pontifex maximus* and, 'provided that superstitious rites were avoided', did not object to the continuance of the custom of dedicating temples in the emperor's honour. Under Constantine's sons there was a more decisive move against paganism. Sacrifices were forbidden, and a number of unimportant temples destroyed. In general it was mainly the Oriental mystery religions which directly suffered.

About 346 a converted senator, Firmicus Maternus, who in 335, before his conversion, had composed a remarkable Latin encyclopedia of astrological information, wrote a vigorous tract especially attacking the Oriental mystery cults but extending his scorn also to the Vestal cult at Rome and the domestic shrines of household gods. He concluded with an urgent request to the emperors for a root and branch suppression of paganism. Perhaps the work was intended as a justification of the intended policy of the emperors. When

Constantius visited Rome in 357 he ordered the removal of the Altar of Victory from the Senate House at least while he was present. Since the usurper Magnentius in 351 (above, p. 140) had tried to gain support against Constantius by appealing not only to dissident Nicene bishops like Athanasius but also to the pagan Roman aristocracy, Constantius may have regarded the Altar as tainted by sacrifices that were not only superstitious but also treasonable. It is certain that before Constantius' death (361) there were Christians in the Roman senate and in high office. In 359 the prefect of Rome, Junius Bassus, was baptized on his deathbed and buried in a sarcophagus decorated with exquisitely cut scenes from the gospels. At Rome in 354 a professional calligrapher, Dionysius Philocalus, helped to publish an almanac containing lists of emperors, consuls, city prefects and bishops of Rome, an Easter table from 312 to 410, some astrological lore, and two important calendars, viz. the ecclesiastical calendar of the Roman church, and the official city calendar in which the old Roman holidays are recorded without the addition of any Christian festivals. The contents of this almanac, with its quiet juxtaposition of the old and the new without fusion, are symbolic of the gradual transition from pagan to Christian taking place in high Roman society during the second half of the fourth century.

The movement of gradual permeation was sharply arrested by the crisis of Julian's pagan revival (361–3). Julian had been educated by Christian tutors with liberal sympathies who imparted to him an excellent knowledge of Homer and the Greek classics. In adolescence, living in a country palace in Cappadocia, he turned to theological studies, was baptized, and even became a 'reader' in the church. But at the age of eighteen he began to desire more freedom than Constantius thought it safe to grant a prince. He also wished to know more of paganism not from old books but from direct contact with its contemporary apologists. At Ephesus in 350–51 he came under the spell-binding influence of a neoplatonic philosopher named Maximus whose magical abilities were such that by burning incense and reciting the proper charm he could make an image of

Hecate smile and kindle the torch in her hands into flame. By 351 the fascinated Julian had secretly abandoned Christianity, and his inward estrangement from Constantius became a smouldering resentment after Constantius had executed his elder brother Gallus (354) for being party to a treasonable conspiracy. Nominated 'Caesar' in 355, he was sent to the Rhine frontier to repel German raids. When the army acclaimed him as 'Augustus' in February 360, the tension with Constantius led Julian to move eastwards to attack, and the civil war was only arrested by Constantius' death of fever (3 November 361).

Julian's accession as emperor had immediate consequences for the Church. As lately as Epiphany 360 he had been attending church services in Gaul, perhaps with an eye to his need for Christian support in the coming struggle with Constantius, perhaps to please his Christian wife Helena, who died childless in 360. In 361 he threw off all secrecy about his support for the old religion and his renunciation of Christianity. Throughout the empire pagan hopes revived. When the news of Constantius' death reached Alexandria, the Arian bishop George[1] (above, p. 141), who had only a minority following among the Christians and who had enraged the pagan mob by expressing regret at the existence of the temple dedicated to the city's Genius, was torn limb from limb on 24 December 361. Julian's reaction to the lynching was mild. He gently reproved the Alexandrians for taking matters into their own hands, and showed a livelier interest in acquiring rare treasures from George's distinguished library. At first Julian's formal policy was to reopen and repair the temples, to declare toleration for all, and to oppose Christianity not by force or even argument so much as by ridicule. He was determined to avoid making 'the Galileans' into martyrs. Even Julian, however, had to repress zealous Christians in Syria and Asia Minor whose robust methods with his newly built temples and images extended to insult and destruction. At a succession of cities in the Greek East there were incidents of this kind resulting

1. An Arian account of his martyrdom became mixed up with the life of the soldier-saint, George of Lydda, who became patron of England.

from the Christian populace's reaction against the pagan revival. When a pagan worshipper carelessly left midnight candles burning before the statue of Apollo in the great temple at Daphne by Antioch-on-the-Orontes in Syria, which resulted in the building's total destruction by fire, Julian held the Christians responsible for the disaster and as a reprisal ordered the cathedral at Antioch to be closed. The clashes between Julian and Christians in the East added a few names to the church calendar of martyrs.

In 363 Julian decided to gain the good will of the Jews. He was already planning a campaign against the Persians, modelled on the Oriental conquests of Alexander the Great whose soul he believed to be reincarnate in himself. The Jewish population along his route would be numerous. Moreover, although Julian had little but contempt for Judaism, he was well aware that a proposal to restore sacrifices in a rebuilt temple at Jerusalem would touch the Christians at a tender spot. The plan for rebuilding the temple was apparently coupled with a political, quasi-Zionist proposal for the creation of a territorial area in Palestine administered by the Jewish patriarch. The rebuilding project, however, was abandoned after an earth tremor. Since Julian's plans included the abolition of financial support for the patriarchate from the Jews of the dispersion, perhaps the enthusiasm of the Palestinian Jews themselves was lukewarm. The alliance, however, between the apostate emperor and Judaism had unhappy consequences for the Jews, who were remembered to have cooperated with the anti-Christian government in a way that was all too reminiscent of early persecutions.

To encourage paganism Julian discriminated against Christians in making appointments to high office in the civil administration and army. Apostasy became a particular recommendation for preferment, and a number of nominal Christians availed themselves of the chance. Feeling it to be insufferable that Christians should teach the pagan classics without believing in the myths of the gods, he issued a formal edict excluding Christians from the teaching profession, a decision which was regarded as folly by pagans like

Ammianus the historian and was resented by cultivated Christians like Gregory of Nazianzus who understood and loved the classical literary tradition fully as well as Julian. Perhaps as an ironic *jeu d'esprit* at this time, Apollinaris of Laodicea published a version of the Pentateuch cast in hexameters and of the gospels and epistles in the form of Platonic dialogues. Julian travelled round the Greek East preaching the gospel of polytheism to Christian city councillors with passionate fervour and without the least sense of reserve or dignity; his behaviour provoked ridicule to which he did not know how to reply. Of Cappadocia he complained that the province was so predominantly Christian that the few who wished to offer pagan sacrifices no longer knew how to do it. At one Mesopotamian town he visited, the pagan council was so over-anxious to please that the air became foggy with the clouds of incense, and Julian felt that the ritual was amateurish and overdone.

Taking seriously his position as *pontifex maximus*, Julian set about the reorganization of paganism. He saw that it could only meet the Christian attack by modelling itself on its hated opponents. His friend Sallustius composed a short (extant) catechism of pagan dogma. High priests, nominated by Julian, were to fulfil the function of Christian metropolitans. There was to be a system of stipends for priests who would preach sermons and organize works of charity for the poor: 'No Jew is ever seen begging, and the impious Galileans support not merely their own poor but ours as well.' The standing and moral character of the pagan priests also had to be sharply raised. Like the Christian clergy, they were required to keep away from obscene shows, taverns, and all disreputable employment. Within the temples the priests would be expected to exercise authority. Following Christian custom, they were not to allow high officials to be preceded into temples by soldiers, and should remind dignitaries that the moment they entered a temple they were only private citizens. Julian's personal practice was to offer sacrifices every day. Before important decisions he consulted augurers and soothsayers, a considerable corps of which attended on him during his Persian expedition.

The ardour with which Julian devoted himself to the reconstruction of paganism was regarded by many who were not Christians with a detachment and incomprehension that saddened the emperor's heart. The execution of animals for his sacrifices was on so large a scale as to affect the economics of the meat market in some areas. The highly strung emperor could only ascribe the lack of sympathy he received to the 'corrupting folly' of the Christians. Yet even pagans who felt that Julian was ridiculous in taking soothsaying so seriously were sincere in support of the attempt to preserve the threatened past. Julian's friend Libanius was a man of more aesthetic than religious feeling and sensitivity; but he was appalled by the vandalism which destroyed beautiful temples and idols.

Julian completely identified himself with his religious cause. To both Christian and pagan he personified the polytheistic tradition, the revival of which stood or fell with his endeavours. The Persian campaign, guided by the emperor's diviners and soothsayers, was to be the vindication of the old gods as the true givers of military success. The campaign was foolishly conducted without proper attention to lines of communication or the risk of encirclement. On 26 June 363 in a desperate mêlée Julian was fatally wounded by a lance in his side. How it happened nobody was sure, and different accounts circulated from the start. But the most widespread opinion was that the lance belonged to an incompetent or disaffected soldier in Julian's army, or to an auxiliary Saracen. A story already circulating in the bazaars of Nisibis when Julian's corpse was carried there was that the emperor had thrown away his life almost suicidally when he realized that the army's position was hopeless. Five years later Libanius attributed responsibility to the Christians. Certainly the Christians did nothing whatever to conceal their jubilation at the apostate's fall, and this very obvious absence of regret made it natural that they should have been credited with a deliberate act of homicide, which some of the more zealous among them would unhesitatingly have defended as an act of justifiable resistance to the tyranny of Antichrist. But among the numerous contemporary accounts it is only Libanius who suggests that 'probably' a Christian killed Julian; and even he proposes it as no more than a likely hypothesis. The pagan historian Ammianus Marcellinus regarded it as simply a tragic accident caused by carelessness. According to a member of Julian's pagan bodyguard the mishap was caused by an envious evil spirit.

Of the dying emperor's last words there were also divergent accounts and an early crop of legends. One early fifth-century source gives the quite plausible story that Julian flung blood from his wound up at the sun-god with the bitter words 'Be satisfied'. Theodoret of Cyrus, writing in 450, is the first to attest the famous but implausible version that as he threw his blood in the air he cried 'Galilean, you have conquered'.

Although the collapse of Julian's pagan revival was a bitter blow to the adherents of the old polytheism, his voice did not cease to speak after his death. His letters and religious discourses continued to circulate widely. More than fifty years after his death Cyril of Alexandria felt it necessary to write a long answer to Julian's tract 'Against the Galileans'. In pagan memory Julian remained the ideal saint. In his memorial oration (about the end of 365) the orator Libanius claimed that Julian had been received to divine rank in heaven and that devout souls were already being granted answers to the prayers which they addressed to him.

11

Church, State and Society from Julian to Theodosius

ALTHOUGH no one, whether pagan or Christian, conceived of a society that did not require some religious form, it was generally understood in antiquity that religious conviction could not be compelled, and the strong passions roused under Constantius and Julian had left their mark. The policy of Valentinian I, Western emperor 364–75 and a Christian, was one of toleration strictly enforced. Arian bishops in the West like Auxentius of Milan (355–74), who were now a small minority, were protected from interference. Valentinian feared black magic and discouraged Manichaeism (below, p. 169), but did not impede official pagan ceremonies at Rome, Eleusis, or elsewhere. An edict forbidding the African Donatists to rebaptize converts from the Catholic Church can only have been ineffective. It was probably intended to enforce the policy of religious neutrality.

In one local church controversy State intervention was required in the interests of public order. At Rome, during the enforced absence of Pope Liberius in exile 355–8, two factions had come into being which broke into bitter conflict on Liberius' death (366). The rival parties each elected a bishop, Ursinus and Damasus, and the partisanship flared into an ugly riot in a church where 137 lost their lives. With the support of the city prefect Damasus won possession of the papal throne, but at a fearful price in public discredit to his church. His morally weak position was not improved when he was formally accused before a new and unsympathetic city prefect with responsibility for homicide, and could be rescued from the humiliation only when rich friends obtained the emperor's personal intervention on his behalf. Damasus compensated for his weakness in temporal power and moral authority by stressing the exalted spiritual dignity of his office as St Peter's successor. Above all, he did notable work for the aesthetic and liturgical enrichment of the city churches, employing the calligrapher Dionysius Philocalus (above, p. 154) to adorn the shrines of martyrs and popes with epigrams, and encouraging a prodigious scholar from Dalmatia, Jerome, to produce a revised version of the Latin Bible, which (very gradually) ousted the old translation and became the commonly accepted version (*Vulgate*). But something of Damasus' unsympathetic and uncomprehending attitude towards the ecumenical efforts of Basil of Caesarea (above, p. 149) may be attributed to the weakness in his position at home which put him permanently on the defensive and made him appear to Basil blind and arrogant.

There were those in Roman society, both pagan and Christian, who credited Damasus with deep worldly ambitions for high society. The opulence of papal entertainments was said to surpass imperial hospitality. The rich aristocrat, Praetextatus, who was priest in the cults of numerous deities, used to say waggishly to Damasus, 'Make me bishop of Rome and I will become a Christian.' Damasus' Christian critics maliciously called him 'the ladies' ear-tickler'.

A more charitable view of Damasus is possible. He did as much as any fourth-century Pope to make it natural for the great upper-class families of Rome to turn to Christianity without feeling that they were doing something disreputable and un-Roman. The ladies were converted first, but the men long tended to remain pagan. Like the intellectuals of the Greek East, of whom the orator Libanius was the best contemporary representative, their attachment to the past was aesthetic and antiquarian. To their elegant and disillusioned scepticism Julian's fervour would have been almost as embarrassing as that of the most strenuous Christian evangelist. The bonds of class and wealth were stronger to them than the divisiveness caused by religious differences. One pagan aristocrat used to listen in delight to his little granddaughter singing Christian hymns. The religion of these men expressed a sad conservatism *á la recherche du temps perdu*; it was an idealization of the glory of Rome, with a private mysticism especially fed on speculative Neoplatonic exegesis of Cicero's *Scipio's Dream* and the sixth book of Virgil's *Aeneid* (the descent to the underworld). The Christians learnt to interpret the same texts in a way that fitted them into the Christian scheme; and they also found in Virgil's fourth *Eclogue* a messianic prophecy (above, p. 78). About 360 a great Roman lady, Proba, whose husband had been prefect of Rome in 351, even wrote versified Biblical history in the form of a Virgilian cento, producing, it must be said, an alarmingly sub-Christian theology in the process.

It was the achievement of Damasus to fuse the old Roman civic and imperial pride with Christianity. Constantine had in one sense begun the fusion when he built the noble basilicas to St Peter and St Paul on the shrines associated with the apostles since at least 160–70. Recent excavations under St Peter's have disclosed a pagan necropolis of the second century A.D., in the middle of which there stood a monument in honour of St Peter built in that decade. Whether this monument marked the actual grave is quite uncertain; but the builders of the monument probably believed that it did, and it is a real possibility (unhappily not more) that they were right. A Roman writer of 200 named Gaius mentions both this monument on the Vatican hill and one for St Paul on the road to Ostia, i.e. at the present site of St Paul's-without-the-walls. The Roman church also possessed a third shrine by the third milestone on the Appian Way where both St Peter and St Paul were commemorated together on 29 June (a date which happens to coincide with a festival of Romulus in the pagan city calendar since Augustus' time). The origin of this joint shrine on the Appian Way and its relation to the two separate shrines on the Vatican and the road to Ostia are highly problematic. The two most favoured explanations are either that the joint shrine on the Appian way was once a rival claimant to the separate shrines, or that relics were temporarily moved from the separate shrines to the Appian way, perhaps during the persecution of Valerian in 258 (since the calendar of 354, above, p. 154, associates 29 June 258 with the joint shrine); but the ancient evidence preserves no record of any such translation. In the time of Pope Damasus the festival on 29 June was marked by a procession from St Peter's to St Paul's and on to a final celebration at the joint shrine on the Appian Way. Probably because the lengthy ceremonies were exhausting, the visit to the Appian Way was dropped before 400; before long the celebration at St Paul's was postponed to 30 June and by 600 was far better attended by visiting tourists than by the local Romans.

The rich adornment which Damasus lavished on martyrs' shrines and the stress on the founding apostles asserted a claim that the real glory of Rome was not pagan but Christian. In one epigram which reflects East-West tension during the Arian controversy, Damasus remarked that 'although the East sent the apostles, yet because of the merit of their martyrdom Rome has acquired a superior right to claim them as citizens'. Under the potent patronage of the apostles who were intimate with Christ, the city could be assured of security and of a more lasting grandeur than the old gods had conferred. Like his predecessor Liberius, Damasus speaks self-consciously of Rome as 'the apostolic see'.

Damasus was not the initiator of a quite new social development. In the third century Origen had commented with asperity that in great cities bishops were being cultivated socially by 'ladies of wealth and refinement'. After Constantine the social status of high clergy quickly advanced. It became less common for an emancipated slave like Callistus of Rome to become bishop, less uncommon for a man like Cyprian, of (probably) senatorial rank, to find his way into holy orders. Constantine invested bishops with magistrates' powers of proving wills and arbitrating in disputes. As early as 313 he may have conferred the exalted secular rank of Illustrious on high clergy. The Council of Arles in 314 addressed the bishop of Rome by the title 'most glorious'[1] which in secular usage was enjoyed by very distinguished persons

1. 'Gloriosissime papa'. The Latin *papa* or Greek *pappas* was a respectful, affectionate title that a child would use to his father. Christians used it for any bishop to whom they stood in a filial relation. Fifth-century African bishops addressed their own primate of Carthage as 'papa', and the Pope as 'bishop' only. Rome's exclusive claims to *papa* began in the sixth century. A ninth-century pope was hurt when addressed as 'brother'.

with precedence second only to the imperial family. As bishops acquired a social rank, so they also acquired the corresponding insignia. These insignia were to continue in the Church long after they had ceased to be customary in secular use. It was in this way that bishops came to have staff, mitre, and probably also pallium. The custom of kissing a bishop's hand is first attested in the fourth century. The ring was not general before the seventh century, and a pectoral cross was not specifically episcopal before the thirteenth.

From the time of Cyprian onwards bishops began to be addressed as abstractions ('your holiness', etc.) through appropriation of the contemporary usage of polite society. The model of ceremonial at the imperial court even came to influence some of the external forms of eucharistic worship such as the use of candles: it was the proper way in which the King of Kings should be honoured. But in the West the clergy did not wear distinct dress, even when officiating at services. In a remarkable letter of 428 Pope Celestine I rebuked clergy in southern Gaul for disturbing innovations in this respect. Western 'vestments' originated simply in the ordinary secular costume of antiquity, preserved by conservatism in churches after it had been abandoned elsewhere.

There were naturally plenty of voices to express doubts about the beneficial effect of worldly favour upon the Church. At the end of the fourth century John Chrysostom deplored the fact that as patriarch of Constantinople the court protocol accorded him precedence before the highest state officials. The pagan historian Ammianus, after narrating the story of Damasus' election at Rome with sardonic detachment, contrasts the high style of bishops in great cities with the frugal life of the country bishops. It was of course impossible for the bishops of great cities to act in a manner that was above criticism. It was a material cause of the unpopularity of John Chrysostom at Constantinople that so many were offended by his ascetic refusal to give lavish hospitality (below, p. 187). In the time of Pope Gregory the Great a Dalmatian metropolitan justified the opulence of his private entertainments by pointing to the number he had thereby reconciled to the church and to the precedent of

Abraham's hospitality to the angels, a defence which earned him a scorching rebuke from the ascetic Gregory. Did he think that the lower he sank the more fish he would catch?

The Church did not take long to discover that under the Christian emperors it might in some respects enjoy less freedom and self-determination than under pagan governments. Imperial influence on certain important episcopal appointments began to appear even under Constantine. Originally a bishop was freely elected by his people, and the voice of the laity was substantially more than a mere assent or testimony to fitness. But the liberty of a local congregation was not absolute, since the man they elected had to receive recognition from other neighbouring churches. The bishops who came from the other churches to consecrate the candidate by prayer and laying on of hands gradually came to be more important than the local congregation. If a local church was divided, external recognition would decide the issue. In the canons of Nicaea (325) a power of veto was placed in the hands of the metropolitan. By 381 there appear clear beginnings of the concentration of power at a yet higher level than that of the metropolitan, namely in the 'patriarchs' of the East, at Alexandria, Antioch and Constantinople, to which distinguished company Jerusalem succeeded in elevating itself during the fifth century. Part of the unpopularity suffered by fifth-century patriarchs of Constantinople (John Chrysostom and Nestorius) was caused by the desire of metropolitans in Asia Minor to retain their old independence. Apart from the see of Constantinople, for which the emperors naturally liked to propose acceptable candidates, episcopal appointments in the Greek churches were generally left free of State intervention.

It is usual to contrast the Western, dualistic attitude to the relation of Church and State with the Eastern attitude as more readily acknowledging the authority of the emperor in spiritual matters. The contrast is not so simple. It was essential to the Eastern theory that the emperor should be orthodox. If he was not (as in the Arian and Iconoclastic controversies), then resistance would be passionate. The term 'Caesaropapism' is not a useful or illuminating word for broad generalizations about the political theory of the Greek East. So Western a writer as Pope Leo the Great can tell the orthodox Greek emperor that he is invested not only with *imperium* but with a priestly office (*sacerdotium*) and that by the Holy Spirit he is preserved from all doctrinal error. Both Pope Gelasius and Pope Gregory the Great recognized the authority of the emperor in temporal matters. The difference between East and West lies more in that the Byzantine world did not think of itself as two 'societies', sacred and secular, but as a single society in harmony with the emperor as the earthly counterpart of the divine Monarch. The balance of this theory could be seriously upset by State domination of the Church; the more dualistic Western theory could produce ecclesiastical domination over lay society. But it is in the West, especially in Merovingian Gaul in the sixth century, not in the Greek East, that we find emerging a regular system of royal nomination of bishops. Again, it is characteristic that coronation services came from Byzantium to the West under Charlemagne.

The pagan emperors had equated polytheism with good citizenship. Not long passed before, under the Christian emperors, to be a heretic or an infidel was to be suspected of being less than fully loyal to the empire. How quickly the conclusion was drawn that the emperor would specially favour his Christian subjects may be seen in an inscription recording a petition addressed to Constantine in 325 by a Phrygian town asking for special tax privileges on the simple ground that the inhabitants were Christian to a man. In Palestine, likewise, the people of Maiuma, the port area of Gaza, underwent a mass conversion to Christianity and were duly rewarded with city status, independent of pagan Gaza, which they retained until Julian.

Gradually the imposition of disabilities on dissenters came to occupy a substantial place in imperial legislation. From the synod of Arles (314) onwards it was assumed that bishops deposed by church councils would be exiled by the civil power to prevent them stirring up trouble. The main architect in the West of the concept of an orthodox empire from which religious error would be excluded (or would at least reduce its holder to the status of a second-class citizen) was Ambrose of Milan.

Ambrose was in many respects a typical figure of the social and political situation in the last quarter of the fourth century. The son of the praetorian prefect at Trier, he had embarked on a legal and administrative career, rising speedily to the rank of provincial governor at Milan. In 374, on the death of the Arian Auxentius, he was chosen bishop by overwhelming popular acclamation, even though he had not yet been baptized. Baptized by a non-Arian senior priest, a week later he was ordained to the episcopate. He quickly came to exercise a progressive influence upon the religious policy of the Western emperors Gratian, Valentinian II, and Theodosius. In 382 Gratian removed the Altar of Victory from the Senate House (leaving untouched, however, the statue of Victoria which Christian senators could happily treat as an angel).[1] The wealthy pagan aristocracy, led by Symmachus, had to suffer the slight until Gratian's death (he was murdered in 383); but in 384 Symmachus addressed an eloquent plea to the youthful new emperor Valentinian II, asking for the restoration of the Altar as a symbol of all that had made Rome great and for a positive policy of toleration, since 'it is not possible by only one road to attain to so great a mystery'. Ambrose wrote a reply that successfully stayed Valentinian's hand. In 385 Ambrose mobilized the populace at Milan to resist the demand of Valentinian I's widow Justina that one of the Milanese churches be handed over to the use of the Arian Goths in the army, an act that in Ambrose's eyes would have meant the profanation of a consecrated building. In 388 a synagogue at Callinicus on the Euphrates was burnt by Christian zealots, and Theodosius ordered the local bishop to make restitution in full from church funds. By a dramatic refusal to proceed with the eucharistic liturgy until Theodosius yielded, Ambrose persuaded the emperor (against his better judgement) to revoke the restitution order. More creditable to Ambrose was his bold

1. The fourth-century mosaic floor of the church at Aquileia has a splendid example of a winged Victoria beside a basket of eucharistic loaves.

excommunication of Theodosius in 390 for a hot-tempered decision to massacre thousands of citizens in the circus at Thessalonica after they had killed a barbarian army commander. Ambrose required the emperor to accept public penance before restoration to communion, and thereby enforced the point that the concern of the church extends to actions contrary to natural law and repugnant to humanity, not merely to its own private interests.

It is natural to assume some connexion between the ascendancy decisively established by Ambrose over Theodosius in 390 and the succession of edicts against paganism which began to flow from the imperial chancery from 391 onwards. In the East there had been a wave of temple-smashing under an anti-pagan prefect, Cynegius, 384–8, who had occasionally seen to it that the zealous monks were unmolested in their demolitions by providing military units to keep the angry peasants at bay. The great temple of Serapis at Alexandria was dismantled in 391 under the direction of bishop Theophilus of Alexandria. The temple of the city's Genius, which George had regretted (p. 155), became a tavern. Theodosius did not order these incidents, but it must have been tacitly understood that no grave penalties were likely to be inflicted. Special directions were given that the most beautiful temples containing artistic masterpieces were not to be damaged. Aesthetic claims were weak, however, before fierce moral disapproval. Several temples were transformed into churches in the course of the fifth century, like the richly endowed shrine of the goddess Ma at Comana in Cappadocia. Where the habit of popular attachment to a holy place was too great to break, it was sometimes possible for the church to disinfect the old site and to invest it with some Christian significance. Theophilus' successor at Alexandria, Cyril (below, p. 194), replaced the cult of Isis at Menuthis by installing there relics of the popular Egyptian saints, Cyrus and John. At Athens the Parthenon was preserved by becoming eventually a church of St Mary.

In rural districts the country folk were deeply attached to old pagan customs, especially those associated with birth, marriage, and death. In the Western provinces the pastoral problem for centuries was to stamp out pagan superstitions among the peasants on the land. But in the towns, even in such Christian citadels as Syria and Asia Minor, clandestine rites, including occasional sacrifices, continued to be practised as late as at least the seventh century.

In the Theodosian legislation against heretical sects the Manichees were the most severely handled. They were followers of the Syriac-speaking Babylonian Mani (216–76) who had founded on an Iranian Zervanite basis a dualistic religion of the Gnostic type. He blended elements drawn from Zoroastrianism, Buddhism and Gnostic forms of Christianity, in an explicit attempt to provide a universal religion valid for both East and West. The Manichee myth of a primeval conflict between light and darkness explained why the world of contemporary experience was a mixture of good and evil, and provided a rationale for an ascetic morality, by the pursuit of which the Elect were destined to gain release for the particles of divine light imprisoned within their bodies. An inferior order of Hearers was expected only to keep simple moral rules; they were encouraged to hope for reincarnation as Elect with the prospect of deliverance from the treadmill of transmigration. The secretive ceremonies made the Manichees suspected of moral enormity and black magic. As early as 297 Diocletian issued a violent edict against them. Valentinian I made their property liable to confiscation, and Theodosius imposed further penalties, which had the effect of driving the community underground in some places. Although Augustine could live quietly as a Manichee Hearer in Africa, he found the community lying low when he moved to Rome in 383. In the middle of the fifth century an inquisition unearthed a movement of secret Manichaeism that had deeply infiltrated among members of the Roman church (below, p. 243).

The feeling of hostility towards the Manichees in the 380s led to one tragedy. About 380 in Spain an influential layman named Priscillian, whose ascetic life had been influenced by theosophical dualist speculations, was denounced as a Manichee. His friends were nevertheless able to install him as bishop of Avila in 381. After four years' hard work his enemies secured his condemnation by a synod at Bordeaux. When Priscillian appealed to the Western emperor Maximus (who had succeeded after Gratian's murder, 383), a charge of witchcraft was brought against him on which, despite protests from bishop Martin of Tours, the prefect executed him. The prosecution of one bishop by another on a capital charge aroused high feeling, and Priscillian's accusers were excommunicated by Ambrose of Milan and Pope Siricius (Damasus' successor).

For the Jews the Theodosian laws appear slightly to have improved their position. The relations of church and synagogue during the fourth century were an unhappy story, especially after the alliance of the Jews with the apostate Julian which was criticized by Christian preachers as a worship of the golden calf. But the policy of the Christian emperors towards Judaism was far from being consistently hostile and repressive. When times were normal, the Jews could practise their religion unhindered. The Jewish patriarchs enjoyed the high social rank of 'Illustrious' until 429 (when the office was abolished), and their disciplinary decisions regarding members of their own race were supported and enforced by the empire. In law synagogues were protected for freedom of worship. When one was burnt at Rome in 388, restitution was enforced, and the same would have happened at Callinicum (p. 167) if Ambrose had not insisted, unreasonably and to his lasting discredit, that it was sinful for a Christian emperor to help the Jews to triumph over the church. Probably incidents of synagogue burning were isolated and provoked by special local circumstances. It was never wise for Jews to circumcise their Christian slaves or to marry Christian wives and then convert them to Judaism. The powerful attraction exercised by missionary Judaism was long felt as a threat. The over-excited and distasteful anti-Jewish discourses of John Chrysostom were intended to dissuade Christians at Antioch from their propensity to observe Jewish customs and ceremonies. An unpleasant riot occurred in Alexandria in 414 and another at Minorca in 418. In both places events had occurred to move the populace to ungovernable excitement, and it would be unjustified to conclude that fanatical pogroms were a regular happening. At times of strain and economic crisis societies tend to seek a scapegoat in groups that have not been assimilated; but ordinarily the Jews could live and trade without fear. Towards the end of the sixth century there were occasions when Jews were subjected to forcible baptism, a compulsion deplored by Gregory the Great, though he had no objection to the generous use of incentives. The worst persecution suffered by the Jews occurred under the Visigoths in seventh-century Spain, where the Jewish population had long been numerous. Isidore of Seville remarked that the Visigothic kings, in the enthusiasm of recent conversion, had a zeal not according to knowledge. Under the legislation of Justinian certain high positions were barred to Jews. But a surprising number of laws ran in the direction of protection. In short, the situation of the Jews in the Christian Empire did not go steadily from bad to worse but tended to pursue a zig-zag course. There is evidence of relations between individual Jews and Christians becoming friendly to the point of intimacy; and, though nothing diminished the close particularism of Judaism, in the period here under review there was no such thing as a ghetto in cities.

Despite the Theodosian laws which ended pagan sacrifices and closed temples a long time passed before pagans were subjected to serious pressure. Theodosius I actually entrusted to the pagan orator Themistius the education of his son Arcadius, and made him city prefect of Constantinople. At Alexandria the atmosphere after the destruction of the Serapeum in 391 was less liberal. The *Palatine Anthology*[1] preserves several bitterly ironic epigrams by Palladas, an Alexandrian schoolmaster who found bishop Theophilus hard to bear and did not understand how his well organized bands of monks could claim the title of 'solitaries'. Hypatia's career at Alexandria a few years later illustrates both the freedom enjoyed by a pagan teacher and the risks of violence (below, p. 194). Her murder in 415 horrified Christian

1. The Greek Anthology of c. 980 A.D. in the manuscript from the Palatine library, Heidelberg, contains both pagan and Christian epigrams, and is an important source for this period.

opinion in Constantinople. The prosperity of Egypt depended on the annual flood of the Nile; in the summer after the dismantling of the Serapeum the flood was so great that the population of Egypt turned to Christianity in large numbers, and left the educated aristocracy isolated in its continued paganism. Panopolis (Akhmim) in upper Egypt remained a pagan stronghold, and at Alexandria the university circle remained Neoplatonic and critical of Christianity until 517 when the leadership fell to John Philoponus, commentator on Aristotle and Monophysite theologian (below, p. 207). At Athens the Neoplatonic school survived until 529 when Justinian closed it because of its tenacious adherence to paganism under pupils of the anti-Christian Proclus (whose works were to contribute much to the mystical theology of 'Dionysius the Areopagite', below, p. 207). But until Justinian's time pagans continued to occupy high government positions without molestation. A physician who attended the Byzantine emperor in 462 was remembered not so much for his paganism as for his bold bedside manner. In the fifth century many of the intelligentsia in the Greek East changed to Christianity, sometimes by unusual routes. In 441 the city prefect at Constantinople was a pagan poet from Panopolis in Egypt named Cyrus, who probably owed much to the friendly interest of the empress Eudokia (below, p. 196). Cyrus was exceedingly popular in the city and incurred the envy of the court eunuch Chrysaphius (below, p. 200) who engineered his downfall. Cyrus saved himself by becoming a Christian, whereupon Chrysaphius had him despatched to be bishop of a delinquent Phrygian town where the over-excitable and rowdy populace had lynched four successive incumbents of the see. Cyrus' sermons there were so brief (his first Christmas sermon consisted of one sentence) that he won the hearts of his turbulent flock. Strangely, the experience produced a genuine faith. In 451, after Chrysaphius' fall, Cyrus abandoned his orders and resumed secular rank at Constantinople, where he became famed for his generosity to the poor and for his intimate friendship with the nearby pillar saint, Daniel the Stylite (below, p. 180), who became his spiritual director.

Other unusual figures who passed from paganism to Christianity were Heliodorus, author of the novel about the loves of Theagenes and Charicles (*Aethiopica*), who became bishop of Tricca in Thessaly; and Nonnus, author of the *Dionysiaca*, who devoted his skill to putting St John's Gospel into Greek verse. But it is noteworthy that they were remembered by posterity for their literary achievements as writers within the pagan and classical tradition, not for their contributions to Christian literature. In general there was no prohibition on the expression of pagan thought and no restriction imposed on the diffusion of pagan literature, even if, like the *Saturnalia* of Macrobius written early in the fifth century, this literature was making direct claims for the old polytheistic tradition. Throughout the fifth century poetry and secular historical writing tended to remain in pagan hands. At the beginning of the sixth century Zosimus, probably a native of the pagan stronghold Gaza (above, p. 166), wrote an extant history of the empire from Constantine to the fall of Rome in 410 to show that disasters had followed on the abandonment of the old religion. But by 500 the most distinguished man of letters in Gaza was a Christian named Procopius (to be distinguished from Procopius of Caesarea, the historian, who may have been his pupil). He wrote both poems in the usual pagan tradition and theological commentaries, which were constructed out of citations from authoritative exegetes – the type of commentary that became known as a catena or chain and achieved considerable popularity. It is characteristic that the classical convention remained overwhelmingly powerful in poetry and history. Even in the time of Justinian the two principal historians of the age, Procopius of Caesarea and Agathias, still wrote as if Christianity were a phenomenon which they were almost embarrassed to mention and could only discuss in circumlocutions.

12

The Ascetic Movement

By the end of the fourth century the Church had virtually captured society. In worldly terms of status and social influence, the episcopate of even moderately important cities had become an established career to which a man might aspire for reasons not exclusively religious. Many local churches had become substantial landowners, supporting numerous poor folk. A bishop was expected by his people to be the advocate of their secular interests as well as their spiritual pastor. In ancient society success depended much on possessing a patron whose word to the right official could obtain for one a well paid post, or secure one's liberty when there was trouble with the police or the tax authorities, or even influence the courts if one was a litigant. The development, from the third century onwards, of the veneration of the saints as 'patrons' whose 'suffrage' would be influential in heaven, was a natural transfer to the celestial sphere of the social situation on earth. The intercessions that bishops were expected to make for accused persons sometimes passed into interference with justice if the magistrate was weak and the bishop strong. A substantial part of the surviving correspondence of Basil of Caesarea, Gregory of Nazianzus, and their pagan contemporary Libanius, consists of recommendations and requests to powerful officials on behalf of some individual in need. When in Libya in 410 the Neoplatonic poet and orator Synesius of Cyrene was elected metropolitan of Ptolemais, his election was in part the consequence of his success eleven years earlier in obtaining tax remissions for his province at a time of economic depression; and he hesitated for six months before accepting an office that meant the abandonment of learned reflection and gentlemanly pursuits because of the endless burden (of which Augustine constantly complained) of arbitrations and letters of intercession. Admittedly, Synesius' reluctance was reinforced by other reasons: he did not desire the separation from his wife which church custom by 400 had come to expect of bishops (though not, in the Greek East, of inferior clergy), and he had hesitations about the doctrine of the resurrection which to him was a valuable symbol but impossible as plain prose.

From the third century the question was being put with steadily increasing pressure whether the Church could occupy a position of influence in high society without losing something of its moral power and independence. Several circumstances contributed to the growing prominence of this issue.

The primitive Church had imposed high demands and strict discipline – so strict that in the second century it had to face painful controversy about the very possibility of repentance for sins committed after baptism. The debates about the holiness of the Church as an empirical society ended in the defeat of rigorism when Novatian was rejected at Rome in 251 (above, p. 119). But the old ideal was never lost, and could be reasserted without creating a schism.

Detachment from vanity fair was easier to those who expected the end of the world in the imminent future than to those who expected the historical process to roll on and who possessed some modest property to pass on to their children. St Paul had opposed at Corinth any rejection of marriage on the ground of a Gnostic dualism of spirit and matter, but had freely allowed that because the time was short those who had wives should be as though they had not. When it became apparent that the time would not be as short as the apostle supposed, the precariousness of life under the persecutions kept vividly alive the martyr's sense that true values did not consist in this world's goods.

During the second century there were individual Christians in local communities who renounced marriage and all but the minimum of possessions. They held before themselves and the local congregation the ideal of renunciation with devotion to prayer and to works of mercy. These ascetics were not organized in communities under rule with special clothing or a common purse – though there would have been good precedent for property-sharing in the communities on the edge of Judaism like the Essenes or the group at Qumran from which the Dead Sea Scrolls come, or the Therapeutae of Egypt described by Philo of Alexandria. The rapidity of church expansion in the third century greatly accelerated the acceptance of a double ethical standard: ordinary Christians living in the world might not keep the counsels of perfection, but would at least observe the precepts of Christ, and might hope to aspire to higher reward hereafter if they did more than the minimum that was actually commanded. Acute theological problems were raised by this doctrine of two types of Christian life and ethic. It long remained obscure[1] whether the distinction was merely a way of expressing the idea that there are at least two stages in a progress of moral and spiritual understanding and practice open to all, or whether the distinction meant that married people, living an active life in this world, constitute an inherently inferior type of Christian excluded as such from the highest reaches of prayer and from aspiring to the vision of God. In Origen, for example, passages suggesting the former interpretation are very common, but there are other places where the latter view seems to be dangerously implied. In one sermon he speaks of Christ's army as having a small *élite* of combatant troops and a multitude of camp-followers who assist the soldiers fighting against evil but do not actually fight themselves.

Once the camp-followers had become a flood, the combatants began to feel that they could not do their work effectively. It was a matter of time before the ascetics withdrew to live separately from the ordinary congregations, while still continuing to do works of mercy in caring for prisoners, sick, orphans, and widows. The ascetics badly needed order and discipline to concentrate on their objective without the pull of worldly distractions. But their withdrawal unquestionably weakened the ordinary congregations, and was regarded by many bishops with a misgiving that individual extrava-

1. Late in the fourth century it became controversial when Jovinian vehemently denied the superiority of the celibate life.

gances could do much to justify. Throughout the fourth century the monastic movement was straining to overcome the
deep distrust of many of the bishops. Its spirit seemed too
individualistic and separatist, critical of the town clergy.

Many of the ascetics may have been fairly simple folk,
but it was not long before the movement possessed a coherent
theological basis. In the writings of Clement of Alexandria
and especially of Origen all the essential elements of an
ascetical theology may already be found. It was a theology
dominated by the ideal of the martyr who hoped for nothing
in this world but sought for union with the Lord in his
passion. Just as the cross was God's triumph over the powers
of evil, so the martyr shared in this triumph in his own death.
The ascetics continued this spirit after the persecutions were
past. They strove to achieve the same self-sacrificing detachment from the world. The evangelical demand for sacrifice,
however, was fused with attitudes towards simplicity and
frugality inherited from the classical past. The monastic
movement had room not only for simple folk but also for
men educated in the tradition of Plato and his ideal martyr
Socrates, in the Cynic principle of self-sufficiency, and in the
Stoic doctrine that happiness consists in suppressing the
desire for anything one cannot both get and keep, and therefore demands the suppression of the passions for a life of right
reason.

The classical Greek influences increased the tendency for
the ascetic movement to be individualistic. In Origen's
commentary on the Song of Songs the bride of Christ is
primarily the church, as in St Paul; but there is a yet more
intimate interpretation according to which the bride is the
individual soul united to the divine Word in a sacred marriage. The imagery, which owed something to Plato's
Symposium, helped to foster the conception that the existence,
or at least the presence, of other persons is an embarrassing
distraction and hindrance to the soul's elevation to the bliss of
union with God. Neoplatonic ideals of the 'flight of the alone
to the alone' encouraged renunciation not merely of un-
necessary bodily indulgences but even of human society.

In popular estimation the hermit in his solitude was

accorded intense respect. The desert fathers in Egypt in the second half of the fourth century were constantly visited by individuals who used to ask according to the regular formula: 'Speak to me a word, father, that I may live.' The records of their answers were collected in writing to form the *Paradise* or *Apophthegms of the Fathers*. It was axiomatic that the words of one who lived so close to God would be inspired.

Early in the fourth century the models for future development were provided by two Egyptian ascetics, Antony and Pachomius. Antony, made famous by Athanasius' biography, renounced the property inherited from his parents and gradually moved farther from society until he finally retreated to inaccessible tombs to fight the devils out in the desert. Roughly contemporary with him, but far to the south in the Thebaid, Pachomius started a community of ascetics by the Nile at Tabennisi, where great numbers were set to strenuous manual labour under strict discipline; obedience in Pachomius' organization was military and complete. There was an ideological tension between the hermit-ideal and the belief that the monastic life required a community under rule with obedience to a superior as an essential principle. In practice, there long continued to be numerous ascetics who were neither solitaries nor incorporated in a community (*coenobium*), but wandered from place to place, and were regarded as an irresponsible, disturbing element.

The basic problem raised by the enthusiasm of the monks was the separatist and individualist character of the movement. Was the monk pursuing only his own salvation? Or had the movement a social purpose? Insistence on the primacy of the social purpose of the ascetic movement was the central feature of Basil of Caesarea's organization in Asia Minor, and made his achievement epoch-making. Whether Basil had heard anything of Pachomius is very doubtful. He rejected the hermit-ideal as a private and personal quest, divorced from the Gospel demand of love and service to one's neighbour. Basil was the first to give institutional form to the novitiate and the solemn profession, and to insist on obedience as a means of restraining the excess, the competitiveness, and the ostentation of histrionic individuals who were bringing the monastic movement into disrepute. Before Basil monks had understood poverty and chastity better than obedience. Severe penalties were prescribed by Basil for monks who set themselves austere fasts without leave. In his continual emphasis on restraint Basil anticipated the spirit of the Benedictine Rule.

A painful practical problem was to keep the ascetics from passing wholly outside the local church under its bishop. A prominent motive underlying Athanasius' *Life of Antony* was to show how devoted the saint was to orthodoxy. A synod at Gangra in Asia Minor about 340–41 expressed strong disapproval of monks who entirely abandoned church attendance. In some forms of the ascetic movement the sacraments were regarded as secondary or even indifferent. One pietistic mendicant sect, the Messalians or Euchites, who spread from Mesopotamia into Asia Minor in the middle of the fourth century, held that in each man there is an indwelling devil who can be ejected not by any sacramental grace but exclusively by intense prayer and ascetic contemplation sufficient to produce palpable inward feelings. It was easy for even the most orthodox monks to become indifferent not merely to the calls of secular society and civilization but also to the normal worshipping life of the Church. Basil of Caesarea sought to check this by instituting monastic communities with a Rule under which the authority of the local bishop was safeguarded. His principle of episcopal control worked admirably as long as the bishop was good. But within thirty years of Basil's death the bishop of Caesarea was using his monks to terrorize the city militia when it was protecting the exiled John Chrysostom. In Egypt the successors of Athanasius did not take long to discover that a force of peasant monks was an ideal instrument for destroying pagan temples and for conflicts with heresy. To the second and third generation of the monastic movement it was clear that the ascetic life had special problems of its own. It might easily provide a home for people wanting to contract out of responsibilities in civil society, for those bankrupted by oppressive taxation, sometimes for criminals on the run, sometimes for homosexuals, rather more often for people with compulsions to make some striking gesture and urges to be self-assertive in their mortifications. It was always likely, even at its best, to be a movement dependent upon striking leaders and personalities.

Sometimes monks were tempted to claim that they were entitled to do no work and to live on alms. Augustine in 401 had to write *On the Work of Monks* to explode this error.

In the fifth century the Judean desert became a favoured locality for a new type of organization, the 'Lavra', where a number of individual monks would have their cells in proximity to an outstanding leader, and would meet for common prayers and common meals, but would still preserve more solitariness than was common in a *coenobium*. In the sixth century under Justinian the lavras of Palestine became divided by doctrinal controversy about the orthodoxy of Origen.

In Syria and Mesopotamia asceticism occasionally took bizarre forms. The majority of the monks were very simple Syriac-speaking people, ignorant of Greek. Their recorded mortifications make alarming reading. A heavy iron chain as a belt was a frequent austerity. A few adopted the life of animals and fed on grass, living in the open air without shade from the sun and with the minimum of clothing, and justifying their method of defying society by claiming to be 'fools for Christ's sake'. At the monastery of Telanissos (Deir Sem'an) in Syria, Symeon the Stylite (*c.* 390–459) practised his idiosyncratic austerity of living on top of a column. Attacked at the time as mere vainglory, Symeon's austerity was real enough, and won the deep reverence of the country people. He attracted many disciples to the monastery and inspired later imitators like Daniel (409–93) who spent thirty-three years on a column near Constantinople (at the modern Rumeli-Hisar). Symeon's prestige was so great that the assent of the illiterate stylite was required by the government to the councils of Ephesus (431) and Chalcedon (451).

At the opposite end of the intellectual scale from Symeon stood the ascetics influenced by Origen, among whom Basil of Caesarea was distinguished, though he did not accept the speculative propositions that had made Origen's theology suspected of heresy. In Egypt, on the other hand, there were those who continued to think well even of the more speculative side of Origen's thought. It was expounded at Alexandria by Didymus the blind (at whose feet Jerome sat for a while) and at Constantinople by the archdeacon Evagrius, a close friend of Gregory of Nazianzus. A love affair led Evagrius to leave the capital for Jerusalem and finally the Egyptian desert where he became one of the most influential writers on the spiritual life. Evagrius introduced order and method not merely into the institutional organization but into the innermost processes of contemplation. He classified the principal or root sins as being eight in number, his list being gluttony, fornication, avarice, dejection (or 'lack of pleasure'), anger, weariness (accidie), vainglory, and pride.[1] He divided them among the different parts of the soul as distinguished by Plato. He differentiated types of contemplation arranged in a scale of advancing apprehension, from corporeal to incorporeal and so upward to the Holy Trinity. At the highest level, he taught, prayer was a wordless, mental act, and must be free of any physical pictures of God that the imagination, prompted by evil powers, might form. Evagrius loved sharp, pregnant, obscure maxims. Much in his language about the mystery of prayer entered permanently into the stream of Greek ascetical theology and, through John Cassian, passed to the West.

Cassian was a monk of Scythian origin who had undergone a long ascetic training in Palestine and Egypt before undertaking his pioneer work in the West. His sympathies were with Evagrius and his Origenist friends, so that he could not stay after 400 in the Egypt of Theophilus of Alexandria (below, p. 186). He moved to Constantinople where John Chrysostom made him deacon, then to Rome after John's fall in 404, and finally about 415 to Marseilles where he organized monastic communities of men and women after Eastern models. In his *Institutes* he described the external

1. Gregory the Great added envy to the list and amalgamated dejection and accidie.

order: the correct kind of habit, the proper liturgical offices, and the eight principal sins of Evagrius' catalogue. In his *Conferences* he expounded the inwardness of the desert tradition in the form of a series of discourses put into the mouths of famous Egyptian ascetics. Cassian's criticism of Augustine's doctrine of grace in the thirteenth *Conference* drew a counter-attack from the hyper-Augustinian Prosper of Aquitaine (below, p. 234), and the polemic threw lasting doubt on Cassian's orthodoxy. Nevertheless, it would be hard to exaggerate how much later Western monasticism owed to Cassian's moderation and insight. He arrived on the Western scene at a critical moment. Western Christians, moved by Latin translations of Athanasius' *Life of Antony* and Rufinus' account of the desert fathers in Egypt, wanted to have saints of their own. A zealous publicist from Aquitaine, Sulpicius Severus, writing about 403, achieved popular success with a largely fictitious biography of the ascetic bishop Martin of Tours, designed to show that Gaul could produce a saint superior even to the Egyptian ascetics. Martin was credited with extraordinary miracles and prodigies, and thanks to Sulpicius' historical novel became one of the most popular saints in the barbarian West, principally as a soldier-saint and patron of military virtues. But Cassian regarded this type of miracle-mongering with distaste, and repeatedly deplored the popular demand for it. It was not, he thought, the authentic ascetic tradition, of which the true end was simply prayer out of a pure heart.

By his moderation and restraint Cassian did for the West much that Basil had done for the Greek East, though without ever questioning the ultimate superiority of the solitary life to membership of a *coenobium*. Cassian's achievement is evident in the sixth century Rule of St Benedict and the closely related 'Rule of the Master', an anonymous abbot writing perhaps a few years before Benedict,[1] some of whose work was freely incorporated in the Benedictine Rule. Bene-

1. Perhaps the Master is Benedict himself. Before the founding of Cassino he founded twelve monastic houses near Subiaco, and it is possible that the two related Rules correspond to these two stages in Benedict's development.

dict directed that Cassian's *Conferences* (*collationes*) were to be read before compline. Later a light meal was taken during the reading; whence modern Italian derives its everyday word for luncheon (*colazione*) and English the term 'collation' for a light meal at an unusual hour.

By the accidents of history the name Benedictine has become associated with austerity and learning. Benedict himself had no special interest in either matter. His rule was one of simplicity and self-discipline, not of penitential austerity and self-inflicted mortification. There is not the least hint that he expected his monks to be recruited from those who had failed in the world or who, having soiled their conscience, came to make reparation. He did not think of founding monasteries to perform a special service to the Church or to Society. His monks were not clergy, but simple people, Italian peasants and rustic Goths. They needed to learn letters for their duty of devotional reading (nothing is said of learned study) and for the daily offices, 'the work of God' (*opus Dei*), which Benedict regarded as central to the life of the community. They were to be a family with the abbot as their father, to whom each was an equal care. Above all, they must stay in their monastery and not move from house to house. Although the Rule was intended for more than one monastery, it is clear that Benedict had no notion of founding a religious Order. When he prescribed that a substantial number of hours each day were to be devoted to work, he did not foresee the astonishing achievements of medieval and modern Benedictine scholars in the field of education and research. He wished rather to preserve his monks from the corrosion of character that results from idleness. He had no end in view other than that his monks should live in the presence of God and should get to heaven.

13

The Controversy about Origen and the Tragedy of John Chrysostom

THE respect in which Origen was held by Evagrius and his circle of Egyptian monks was not universally shared. About 375 a damaging and surprisingly influential attack on the orthodoxy of Origen was launched by Epiphanius (*c.* 315–403), bishop of Salamis (Famagusta) in Cyprus from 367, in his 'Medicine chest for the cure of all heresies'. Heresy troubled Epiphanius directly. In his own city of Salamis he impotently faced an active group of Marcionites. He made himself an authority on Christian deviations of all kinds, past and present. An ascetic himself, he interpreted his faith to require a rigorous hostility to every sort of intellectual pretension, including theological speculation. As all necessary dogmatic issues had been determined by authority, there could be no room for a man like Origen who claimed to regard such questions as open for inquiry and (in Epiphanius' view) had adulterated the purity of true faith with the poison of pagan culture. Epiphanius was a passionate puritan, and abhorred the incipient popular demand for installing images and pictures to decorate the walls of churches (below, p. 281).

Epiphanius condemned in Origen above all his tendency to reinterpret apparently literal statements as spiritual symbols, especially his spiritualizing doctrine of the resurrection. His onslaught was not merely exhuming the dead for trial, but specifically mentions the living influence of Origen in his own time on 'certain Egyptian monks'. In the 370s in the Nitrian desert on the edge of the Nile Delta[1] there was

1. The Nitrian desert was south-west of Damanhur. Ten miles further to the southwest was Cellia with many hermits. Scetis (Wadi 'n Natrun) was forty miles south, with many more hermits.

an Origenist group led by Ammonius and three brothers. On account of their stature the four were known as the Tall Brothers. They had suffered in the conflict against Arianism in Egypt after Athanasius' death (373) and were on excellent terms with bishop Timothy of Alexandria (381–5) and, until 400, with his successor Theophilus (385–412). When Evagrius went to Egypt (above p. 181) he placed himself under Ammonius' direction. Evagrius' writings became the principal medium for the diffusion of the group's theology. Despite obscurities they were clear in teaching that in prayer the imagination must not admit any pictures of God as having human form or any kind of spatial localization 'up there'. Indeed, any spatial shapes or forms in the mind at prayer had their origin in demonic deceit. It was the pained reaction of simple believers against this denial that in devotion God could legitimately be pictured as a paternal superman in the sky which precipitated controversy among the monks between the 'Origenists' and the 'Anthropomorphites' who thought God had human form.

Fostered by Epiphanius the dissension spread to Palestine in 393, where it bitterly divided the old friends Rufinus and Jerome living in ascetic hostels on the Mount of Olives and at Bethlehem respectively. Jerome who (as Rufinus imprudently liked to remind him) had once translated some of Origen's works and praised him as 'the greatest teacher of the church since the apostles', now became violently anti-Origenist. Jerome was a prickly, donnish figure of a familiar type: his immense scholarship could at times be put to the service of passionate resentments and petty jealousies. He could not endure criticism, and the nearer anyone stood to him the more likely it was that the relationship would turn sour. Yet he exuded malice in so brilliant a manner and wrote biblical commentaries of such scholarly distinction that everyone wanted to read him. So the quarrel among the western ascetics at the holy places came in time to implicate Rome. The principal battlefield, however, was in Egypt.

At first Theophilus of Alexandria supported the Tall Brothers, and even made one of them a bishop. In 399 his Paschal encyclical, announcing the date of Easter for the ensuing year according to custom, contained a long attack on the naïve 'Anthropomorphites'. The anti-Origenist monks answered by descending in force on Alexandria and creating such a storm that Theophilus executed a sudden volte-face. He expelled the Origenists from Egypt, and obtained the agreement of Pope Anastasius to a formal censure of the doctrines attributed to Origen, especially those propagated in the writings of Evagrius. Evagrius had died in January 399 just before the storm broke, but the Tall Brothers with Cassian and others had to leave Egypt. They made their way to Constantinople to complain at court and to put their case to the newly appointed bishop John (Chrysostom, the 'golden-mouthed' preacher, as he came to be called in the sixth century).

The Origenists' appeal to John Chrysostom led to tragedy. John was a man of outstanding qualities, but was in some respects ill fitted to be bishop of an affluent city filled with gossip and intrigue. Born the son of an army official at Antioch, he had in early youth renounced good prospects in the civil service to become a monk in the Syrian desert, but after injuring his stomach by mortifications had returned to Antioch in 386 to be a presbyter under bishop Flavian (above, p. 150). His education in rhetoric had been with the leading pagan orator, Libanius; in theology with Diodore bishop of Tarsus. He could now apply his brilliant oratorical gifts to the pulpit, and acquired a vast popular following by a series of sermons in 387 when the Antioch city mob had expressed indignation with excessively high taxation by smashing statues of the emperor, and all were in fear at the imperial vengeance. Most of John's surviving sermons were preached at Antioch and owe their preservation chiefly to the enterprise of private stenographers. Outspoken and direct, they remain today the most readable and edifying of all discourses among those of the Church Fathers, and are also a vivid source for the social history of the age.

When bishop Nectarius of Constantinople died in 397, the court, then dominated by the eunuch Eutropius, decided, after four months' hesitation, to kidnap John from Antioch and to make him bishop in the capital.

The star of Constantinople had been in the ascendant for many years past, and its secular and ecclesiastical dignity had been rapidly growing. The council of Constantinople (381) had declared that as 'New Rome' it should enjoy precedence after old Rome, a decision resented at both Rome and Alexandria. The Alexandrians consistently wanted weak and ineffective bishops at Constantinople. At the vacancy of 397 Theophilus of Alexandria had tried hard to put in his own candidate. Nevertheless he cooperated at first with John, e.g. in settling the long-standing schism at Antioch that had divided the church there since the fall of Eustace soon after the council of Nicaea. The appeal of the Origenist monks changed everything. It put John into the position of judging Theophilus' rectitude, and, since John had long enjoyed friendly relations with ascetics who venerated Origen, Theophilus had reason to suspect that John might not be impartial. Theophilus determined to overthrow John, and at Constantinople John played into his hands by making innumerable enemies.

When John first arrived in Constantinople in February 398, he forthwith initiated many measures of reform. His predecessor Nectarius had been kindly, lax in discipline, and easygoing with his clergy. Some of those whom he had ordained were highly unsuitable for holy orders, and John brusquely sacked them. As a deacon he had described his exalted ideals for the priesthood in a special book, and he now had the chance to put his ideals into practice. Nectarius, like Damasus of Rome (above, p. 161), had encouraged the clergy to minister to their flock by good food and drink as much as by pastoral instruction. John, having a chronically weak stomach since his desert austerities, ate alone and deeply offended those who had been wont to enjoy generous entertainment at the bishop's house. Unfavourable comparisons were made. In a sermon preached not long after his arrival John remarked that 'people praise a bishop's predecessor when they mean only to disparage the present occupant'. Malice suggested that John was keeping to himself the delights of the table and rich wine-cellar and was 'living like a Cyclops'. He offered very modest hospitality to the continuous stream of bishops who hung round the court hoping for favours and for financial support for their building programmes. One visiting Syrian bishop, Severian of Gabala, found that eloquent sermons in the capital were well paid, and was offended when after several months John suggested that his diocese needed him. John similarly annoyed a popular monk, Isaac, who found the bright lights of the city more exciting than his monastery. The devotion with which John's advice was sought by a rich widow, Olympias, and by other ladies provoked catty talk. Anxiety at John's reforms extended, moreover, beyond Constantinople. He discovered that in the province of Asia a number of bishops had been paying the metropolitan of Ephesus consecration fees, determined on a sliding scale proportionate to their annual emoluments. The bishop of Ephesus put himself beyond John's reach by dying, but all the bishops implicated in the simony were removed from office with the strictest rigour. In the eyes of John's critics these acts were outside his jurisdiction and manifestations of high-handed self-aggrandizement. In time, they feared, the bishops of Constantinople would be demanding consecration fees themselves and exercising jurisdiction throughout Asia Minor.

John was ascetic, aloof, energetic, and outspoken to the point of indiscretion, especially when he became excited in the pulpit. None of these qualities made him easy to live with in a sophisticated and affluent city. The rich resented as a personal affront his socialist sermons explaining that private property existed only as a result of Adam's fall, or pillorying those who cared nothing for the beggars at their door and wanted only to own ten fine houses with hundreds of servants and lavatories of gold. He offended the men by repeatedly proclaiming that a woman had as much right to demand fidelity of her husband as a man had of his wife. His unsparing sarcasms about feminine luxuries, delivered in the scathing tradition of Juvenal or Seneca, were not relished by ladies of high fashion.

To Theophilus of Alexandria all these difficulties were a godsend. He began his campaign by alerting Epiphanius, who sailed from Cyprus to Constantinople and made inflammatory attacks on the alleged cover that John was providing for the heresies of Origen. The Tall Brothers, however, reassured Epiphanius that they personally admired his writings, and extracted the admission that he had not read a line of theirs. In disillusion the good bishop left the capital, and died on the voyage home.

In June 403 Theophilus arrived on the Bosphorus. Nominally he had come to defend his treatment of the Tall Brothers, but in fact he intended to put John on trial. He gathered the malcontents to a council in Chalcedon (modern Kadiköy), near the Asiatic shore of the Bosphorus opposite Constantinople. The council met in the palace of the Oak, lately built by a fallen praetorian prefect, Rufinus, and there summoned John to answer their charges. John refused to appear before so partisan a court, and was deposed.

The decision of the Oak would have been utterly ineffective if only John had been able to keep on good terms with the emperor Arcadius and his impulsive German wife Eudoxia. Eudoxia had at first admired John. She had asked him to baptize her son, the future Theodosius II; and when the child fell ill she had eventually decided (after some doubts) that John's intercessions would be more likely to ensure the recovery of the child than those of his enemy Epiphanius who had offered his services. But by June 403 Eudoxia was irritated with John. She had taken over some property without due regard to the rights of the owners. When in a sermon on feminine frailty John cited the lurid example of Jezebel, his words were widely, perhaps rightly, understood to refer to the empress.

Accordingly the angry emperor ratified the decisions of the council at the Oak and decreed exile for John. John preached a wild, valedictory sermon to a packed church, explicitly comparing Eudoxia to Jezebel and Herodias, and then stepped down to accept his exile. The day after his departure, however, an earth tremor was taken to mark celestial disfavour; and the lesson was driven home at the palace by the angry hum of the enraged citizens for whom John was a hero. Arcadius and Eudoxia recalled him, and he was reinstated. But a few months later there were disturbing popular festivities at the erection of a silver statue of Eudoxia by Sancta Sophia.[1] John's disapproval was felt as an insult, and Eudoxia's hostility was fed by a violent pamphlet against John published by Theophilus of Alexandria denouncing him as Satan disguised as an angel of light. John lost control in the pulpit: 'Again Herodias raves,' he cried, 'again she dances, again she demands John's head on a charger.' The palace decided that this turbulent priest must go. The unanswerable charge was laid that John had reoccupied his throne before any synod of bishops had annulled the decision of the Oak, in defiance of a canon of the Dedication Council of Antioch of 341 (above, p. 137). Only John's popularity in the city kept him unmolested in his house. But sympathy for John's excited supporters began to fall away when they set fire to Sancta Sophia. John left for exile in the cold Armenian winter, but not before he had appealed to the bishops of Rome (Innocent I, 402–17), Milan, and Aquileia. In his exile the widow Olympias richly sustained him, and he maintained a voluminous correspondence with his supporters. The government decided that he must be moved to a remoter spot, and on the bitter journey he died at Comana (Tokat) on 14 September 407.

John's story was more than a private tragedy. He provided a spectacular illustration of the perennial ambiguity in the position of the bishop of Constantinople as both principal court chaplain and also a leading patriarch in a body with a long tradition of independence in relation to the state. The struggle did not die with him. Innocent I steadily refused to be in communion with John's enemies and demanded the vindication of his memory, so that the issue, instead of concerning the dignity of Constantinople, became the standing of Roman authority in the East. The firmness and ultimate victory of Innocent did much to enhance Roman prestige. But the vindication of John's cause came very slowly. At Constantinople, with Roman support, a large proportion of the people preferred to worship outside the

1. The inscribed base of the column, found in 1848, is in the Istanbul archaeological museum.

walls rather than accept John's successor Atticus (406–25); and it is to one of these 'Joannites', Palladius (a pupil of Evagrius), that we owe not only a dramatic and pardonably partial account of John's life, but also the principal document for the history of Egyptian monasticism, the *Lausiac History* (so called because he dedicated it to the high chamberlain Lausus). As long as Theophilus of Alexandria was alive, reconciliation was impossible. In 412 Theophilus was succeeded by his nephew Cyril, a man with similar opinions and much greater ability in defending them, who explained that he could not commemorate a Judas Iscariot among the saints with whom his church was in communion. After Innocent I's death (417) Atticus of Constantinople at last agreed to Roman demands that he should insert John's name in the diptychs (i.e. lists of the names of departed saints read at the eucharist), but Cyril remained loyal to his uncle's policy. Eventually in 428 a new bishop of Constantinople, Nestorius, chosen from Antioch like John, won Cyril's reluctant assent to the insertion of John's name in the Alexandrian diptychs, and established at Constantinople an annual festival in his honour. Thereafter John exercised a mounting literary influence by the legacy of his admirable sermons, which were taken as models of vigorous style and teaching.[1] In medieval Byzantium no figure seemed worthier to be given the credit for composing the traditional liturgy of the imperial capital, which therefore bears his name as the 'Liturgy of St Chrysostom'.

1. The nineteenth canon of the ecumenical council of Constantinople of 692 (called either 'Quinisext', because it supplemented the fifth and sixth ecumenical councils of 553 and 680, or the council 'in Trullo' because it met in the domed hall of the imperial palace) directed that preachers should model their discourses on those of 'the luminaries of the church' rather than compose their own. Anthologies of Chrysostom, with Basil, and Gregory of Nazianzus, came to have a great vogue.

14

The Problem of the Person of Christ

DIODORE, THEODORE, AND APOLLINARIS

JOHN CHRYSOSTOM had learnt his theology from Diodore, an ascetic presbyter of Antioch, appointed bishop of Tarsus in 378. Diodore was an unusual person, with a lively interest in cosmological questions, and wrote books not only on theology but on 'How hot the sun is' and on Aristotle's opinion on the ethereal matter of the heavens. His expositions of scripture laid more stress than was usual on the literal and historical meaning; while conceding the validity of typology (the interpretation of particular persons and events as specific prefigurations of Christ and the Church), he rejected the unrestrained use of allegory. He was critical of popular interpretations of the incarnation, as if it were a metamorphosis of a God or a mythological theophany. He abhorred the notion that Jesus was Son of God because he had no human father. Authentic theology, Diodore thought, carefully observed the distinction and spontaneity of the humanity of Christ, the pioneer and example of faith.

Here Diodore came into conflict with Apollinaris of Laodicea (above, p. 148), who suspected, with reason, that Diodore wanted to interpret the incarnation as no more than a supreme instance of inspiration and grace. In the eyes of Apollinaris this was to make the virgin birth less than necessary and to minimize the supernatural in a mistaken attempt to diminish pagan prejudices. To Apollinaris the virgin birth was of the first importance for dogma, and there was profound truth in the epithet 'Mother of God' (*Theotokos*) which individual devotion had been applying to Mary since the third century. In Diodore's view this epithet was only tolerable theology if one also added that Mary was 'mother of man'.

The condemnation of Apollinaris' thesis that in Christ the divine Word replaced the human mind seemed to give the seal of approval to the rival theology of Diodore. Diodore himself, however, did not succeed in formulating his doctrine coherently, and it was left to another Antiochene theologian to bring his embryonic ideas to a brilliant maturity.

Theodore (350–428) was a friend of John Chrysostom and a pupil of Libanius. He became bishop of Mopsuestia (=modern Misis, east of Adana) in the Cilician plain in 392. He attracted much attention by his writings on the incarnation and commentaries on Scripture. Developing Diodore's rejection of allegory, he upset traditionalists by denying that many so-called 'messianic' prophecies and psalms were predictions of Christ, and by describing the Song of Songs as a natural love poem which had no reference to the supernatural union betwixt Christ and his Church. Theodore's central thesis was that the redemption of humanity depends on the perfection and obedience of Christ as man. Jesus' identity with God consisted in the 'loving accord' between his will and the Father's.

Theodore was anxious to safeguard the reality of Christ's humanity which he rightly saw to be prejudiced by Apollinarianism. He expressed himself in technical language, insisting repeatedly that the union of God and man in Christ to form a single person (*prosopon*) in no sense destroys or qualifies the permanent duality of the two uniting 'natures'. The enthusiasm of devotion may say that 'God suffered and died'; but the theologian knows that God is impassible and immortal, and therefore that this transfer of human frailty to God, like the ascription of miraculous power to the humanity of Christ, does not strictly mean what it says.

Apollinaris had denounced such notions as implying 'two sons' of God, one being son by nature, the other son by grace, and had trenchantly demanded a definition of the union of God and man in Christ in terms of 'one nature and one hypostasis'. Some of the disagreement arose out of the terminology. By 'one nature' Apollinaris meant a single individual person; but his language was naturally understood by Theodore to mean the absorption of the humanity within the divine Being, in such a sense that the human temptations and conflicts described in the gospels became mere play-acting. Christ, according to St Luke, 'grew in wisdom'; according to St Mark, he knew not the hour of the eschatological triumph of God and cried 'My God, why hast thou forsaken me?' Theodore felt that to make the eternal Word of God the subject of these experiences was meaningless unless it led straight to Arianism.

CYRIL AND NESTORIUS

Theodore's theology of the incarnation was a profound theoretical challenge not merely to Apollinarianism but to the main Alexandrian tradition. From 412 until 444 the see of Alexandria was occupied by Cyril, nephew of his predecessor Theophilus, an acute theologian and a determined zealot in church politics. Cyril was deeply opposed to Theodore, and in a masterful commentary on St John's Gospel he attacked, without mentioning names, those who were regarding Christ as the supreme example of prophetic inspiration and grace and so spoke of two distinct natures 'after the union'. Nevertheless the controversy remained literary. Theodore was a man of eirenic spirit. He even dedicated to Cyril a commentary on Job.

Unhappily the debate became mixed up in church politics. Cyril of Alexandria was a distinguished and thoughtful theologian, but found it hard to keep his hands clean when questions of ecclesiastical politics were at stake. Brought up under his uncle's campaign for the suppression of heresy and paganism in Egypt, Cyril was deeply intolerant and had begun his episcopate with a series of violent incidents. His intolerance towards paganism and dissent led to painful riots between Christians and Jews in Alexandria, and in 415 to the fanatical murder of the Neoplatonist philosopher Hypatia, a virtuous and clever woman who had taught Synesius of Cyrene (above, p. 171).

In April 428 the court wanted a fine preacher as archbishop of Constantinople and brought in a monk of Antioch named Nestorius. Nestorius fully shared Cyril's views about the desirability of suppressing paganism and heresy, but had learnt from Theodore of Mopsuestia of the great dangers of Apollinarianism contained in the popular term 'mother of God'. At first Cyril of Alexandria cooperated with Nestorius, to the extent that he reluctantly inserted John Chrysostom's name in the Alexandrian diptychs (above, p. 191). But Cyril soon took offence when reports reached him of Nestorius' criticisms of 'mother of God'. About the end of 428 four Alexandrian citizens went to the emperor Theodosius II and complained of the rough way Cyril had treated them. Theodosius referred the complaint to Nestorius for examination. Cyril, like his uncle Theophilus, did not wish the bishop of the upstart see of Constantinople to be sitting in judgement upon the conduct of the bishop of Alexandria; and if, as Cyril suspected, Nestorius was unorthodox, his right to judge any matter could be called in question.

At the end of 428, in his annual letter to his suffragans announcing the date of Easter 429, Cyril openly attacked Nestorius' doctrines. Meanwhile Cyril's agents in Constantinople fostered the opposition there, putting it about that Nestorius disliked the title 'mother of God' because he did not believe that Jesus was God. In the spring of 429 an Alexandrian lawyer named Eusebius (later bishop of Dorylaeum in Phrygia) posted up in Constantinople a placard juxtaposing excerpts from Nestorius' sermons with utterances of the third-century heretic Paul of Samosata. This was directly to accuse Nestorius of denying the divinity of Christ. Slowly but surely Cyril built up an atmosphere of opposition and suspicion. But Nestorius was liked by Theodosius and the empress Eudokia, so that Cyril had to proceed cautiously.

In February 430 Cyril addressed to Nestorius a long letter (his 'second letter') expounding the Alexandrian doctrine of the person of Christ. He conceded that the difference between the divine and human natures in Christ is not abolished by the union; yet in union they constitute a single entity (*hypostasis*), so that one may ascribe the supernatural miracles of the Godhead to the manhood and the natural weaknesses of the manhood to the Godhead. Because of this union to form a single *hypostasis*, we may say as strict theology, not merely as devotional enthusiasm, that God was born at Bethlehem or that the impassible and eternal Word suffered and died. Nestorius' reply to all this, sent five months later, was a reassertion of Antiochene, 'two-nature' Christology.

As the year advanced the tension mounted. Cyril's chief problem was to undermine the court's support for Nestorius. Without mentioning Nestorius' name, he attacked his doctrines in treatises addressed not only to the emperor but also to the powerful ladies of the court. Theodosius' life was largely dominated by women. In youth he had been controlled by his elder sister Pulcheria (399–453). Learned, devout, ambitious and implacable, she chose for him in 421 his beautiful and literate wife Athenais who, on her marriage, changed her religion to Christianity and her name to Eudokia.[1] But Eudokia turned out to have a mind of her own and preferred to dominate Theodosius without Pulcheria's cooperation. Like a weather-cock the emperor's church policy tended to vacillate according to whether he was being controlled by his wife or by his sister. Nestorius was popular with Eudokia but hated by Pulcheria whom he had once snubbed. One reason why Cyril's anti-Nestorian campaign was unwelcome to the emperor was simply that the resulting quarrels between his wife and his sister were making his own life a misery.[2]

Cyril had much quicker success in enlisting the support of Rome. Nestorius made this easy for him by receiving at Constantinople some Pelagian heretics condemned by Rome, to the intense irritation of Pope Celestine. Cyril's agent in Rome zealously portrayed Nestorius as a rationalist who

1. Eudokia wrote (extant) poems about gospel narratives in the form of Homeric centos.

2. Eudokia succeeded in forcing Pulcheria's retirement from court in 439, but her own indiscretion with the Master of the Offices led her to withdraw to Jerusalem (442), till her death (460), in propitiation for her sin. Theodosius, however, preferred to be dominated by the eunuch Chrysaphius rather than by Pulcheria, who was not able to play a decisive role until 450. Pulcheria's finest hour was the council of Chalcedon.

denied the divinity of Christ and the need of man for grace. Rome commissioned John Cassian to write a refutation of this new version of Pelagianism, and in August 430 sent Cyril a formal letter, to be forwarded on to Nestorius, demanding recantation within ten days. It is a measure of the slow headway of Cyril's campaign that even this ultimatum was not delivered to Nestorius until 30 November, when Cyril accompanied it with a strong dogmatic letter (his 'third letter') tersely demanding Nestorius' assent to Twelve Anathemas. Cyril's Twelve Anathemas condemned the Antiochene Christology of the 'two-natures', above all, the division of the words and acts of Christ between his divine and human natures (i.e. the doctrine that the manhood, not the Godhead, wept and died, and that the Godhead, not the manhood, stilled the storm). They required Nestorius to admit that 'the Word of God suffered in the flesh'.

These formidable documents were handed to Nestorius eleven days after Theodosius had issued a summons for a council to be held at Ephesus at Pentecost (7 June) 431. Cyril's Twelve Anathemas seemed to Nestorius to provide complete proof of Apollinarian tendencies,[1] and he confidently awaited the coming council. He underestimated both the ability of Cyril to get his way and the extent of the distress caused by his own derogatory remarks about the title 'Mother of God'. Moreover, patriarchs of Constantinople could count on having enemies among the metropolitans of Asia Minor, who were jealous for their own liberties and powers. Memnon, bishop of Ephesus, became so zealous an adherent of Cyril that at Ephesus Nestorius had to be given military protection against the displeasure of Memnon's monks. Apart from the court, Nestorius could rely on support from bishop John of Antioch and his Syrian suffragans, but severe weather delayed the arrival of the Syrian bishops. Moreover, John of Antioch had his own problems. Juvenal of Jerusalem was ambitious to acquire for his see, as the mother church of Christendom, a worthy jurisdiction as 'patriarch' over

1. Cyril consistently disowned the accusation of Apollinarianism. He was, however, influenced by texts which he accepted as the work of Athanasius but were in fact Apollinarian forgeries.

several provinces. As this ambition could only be realized at the expense of the traditional rights of Antioch (safeguarded in the sixth canon of Nicaea), Juvenal was certain to be opposed to John of Antioch and a supporter of Cyril, though for reasons which caused Cyril some embarrassment.

The hard core of backing for Cyril, however, lay in the passionate instinct of popular devotion. Nestorius was utterly misrepresented when he was accused of teaching that Christ was merely an inspired man. But believers felt deeply that to question the full legitimacy of saying that the eternal Word died, or that Mary was mother of God, was distressing to pious ears. Was not the eucharist a re-enactment of the miracle of Bethlehem, at which the lifegiving Body and Blood of Christ were offered to be received by the faithful? Nestorius' distinctions between the humanity of Christ and the eternal Word appeared to prejudice the divine pledge of immortality in the sacrament. Cyril's language, on the other hand, allowed one to say without fear that at Bethlehem the Ancient of Days was an hour or two old. Nothing caused so much scandal as a remark of Nestorius that 'God is not a baby two or three months old'.

The action at Ephesus opened on 22 June 431 in St Mary's church where Cyril and his suffragans excommunicated Nestorius. Four days later the Syrians arrived under John of Antioch, forthwith met in synod, and deposed both Cyril and Memnon of Ephesus. Finally the Roman legates arrived and joined Cyril in accordance with Pope Celestine's instructions. Fortified by this Western ratification of his very dubious proceedings, Cyril assembled his party in synod to condemn Pelagianism (to gratify the West), to grant Cyprus ecclesiastical independence and Juvenal of Jerusalem his patriarchate (to annoy Antioch), and finally to pass a resolution prohibiting any 'addition' to the Nicene creed.

Two rival synods had cursed each other. In the resulting deadlock, decision rested with the reluctant emperor. Both sides sent delegations to court at Chalcedon, and the emperor ratified the rival depositions of Nestorius, Cyril and Memnon as if they had been acts of a united council. All three were kept

in custody. Meanwhile, Cyril expended vast sums on dou-
ceurs for influential people at the palace, and Nestorius
suddenly began to lose ground. Nestorius undermined his
own position by expressing a weary wish to return to his
monastery at Antioch. He had had enough. His offer was
accepted and a nonentity, acceptable to Cyril, was appointed
to succeed him. Cyril himself escaped from prison and rewarded his venal gaoler by promotion among the Alexandrian clergy.

Most unedifying of all was the complete breach between
John of Antioch and Cyril, which could only be healed in
433 by large concessions on both sides. John of Antioch and
the Syrians had to accept not merely the retirement but the
condemnation of Nestorius.[1] It was Cyril, however, who had
to make the doctrinal surrender. He had to abandon any
attempt to impose the Twelve Anathemas of his third letter
to Nestorius, and narrowly escaped being required to withdraw them altogether. He put his signature to a Formulary
of peace, originally drafted in 431 by the leading Syrian
theologian, Theodoret bishop of Cyrus. This Formulary of
reunion protected Antiochene theology in all essentials. It
declared that Christ was 'perfect God and perfect man consisting of rational soul and body, of one substance with the
Father in his Godhead, of one substance with us in his Manhood, so that there is a union of two natures; on which ground
we confess Christ to be one and Mary to be mother of God'.
A final sentence contradicted Cyril's anathema condemning
the dividing of Christ's words and acts between his human
and divine natures.

Cyril's assent to this formulary caused consternation
among his more advanced supporters. To reassure them he
glossed his acceptance of the phrase 'union of two natures'
by explaining that, although the analytical mind could in
the abstract distinguish two natures as being united in

---

1. In 435 Nestorius was exiled to the Egyptian desert where he suffered
much and, shortly before his death (450), wrote his tragic memoirs,
the 'Book of Heraclides', an interpolated version of which survives
through a Syriac manuscript (destroyed in the first World War in
Kurdistan).

Christ, yet the separation is abolished in the incarnate Lord so that there is only 'one nature after the union', analogous to the unity of body and soul to form a single person.

The reunion of 433 was a compromise achieved by ecclesiastical politicians under government pressure, and theologians on both sides were forced to swallow their principles, which they did unwillingly. At Edessa in 435 a newly elected bishop Ibas turned out to be a zealous disciple of Theodore of Mopsuestia, and the dogmatic controversy now began to concentrate on Theodore's writings. Disquiet in Roman Armenia had to be settled by the moderating influence of Proclus, second successor of Nestorius at Constantinople, who in a weighty 'Tome' interpreted the formulary of reunion of 433. Proclus taught that there is 'one hypostasis of the incarnate Word' and that 'one of the Trinity became incarnate'. A condemnation of Theodore of Mopsuestia in 438 was only averted by John of Antioch who successfully urged that it was wrong to pass posthumous sentence on one who had died in the peace of the church.

The incident showed that the truce of 433 was only being maintained under strain. It broke down as soon as new men replaced the old.

THE 'MONOPHYSITE' COUNCIL OF EPHESUS AND THE REACTION AT CHALCEDON

By 446 Cyril of Alexandria, John of Antioch, and Proclus of Constantinople were dead. At Antioch John was succeeded (442) by his weak nephew Domnus, a man only capable of sensible decisions when he had Theodoret of Cyrus at hand to advise him. At Alexandria Cyril was succeeded (444) by Dioscorus, leader of the extremist party that regretted Cyril's compromise of 433. At Constantinople the ambitious Proclus was succeeded (446) by Flavian, a diffident man unendowed with eloquence.

The policy of Theodosius II at this time was in the hands of the court eunuch Chrysaphius who had succeeded in ousting Pulcheria (above, p. 196). Flavian began his episcopate by offending Chrysaphius. The eunuch had frankly

indicated that a present would be a welcome sign of gratitude for the election. Flavian sent him some consecrated
bread, which Chrysaphius returned saying he would rather
have gold. With a man like Chrysaphius it was necessary
either to cooperate or to conquer, and Flavian was too honourable for the first and too weak for the second. Chrysaphius'
godfather was a distinguished archimandrite in Constantinople named Eutyches, a wily old man who shared all
Dioscorus of Alexandria's regrets and resentments at the
concessions made by Cyril in the peace of 433.

Chrysaphius, Eutyches and Dioscorus formed an intricate plan to overthrow the peace of 433, to impose the Twelve
Anathemas of Cyril as the standard of orthodoxy, and so to
crush the 'inspired man' Christology of the Antiochenes. The
plan would give Dioscorus the chance to show that Alexandria, not Constantinople, was the second see of Christendom. The Antiochene leader Theodoret at once saw the
threat, and published a long attack (entitled *Eranistes*)[1] on
the ultra-Cyrilline theology which was now emerging. In
the spring of 448 an imperial order confined him to his
diocese. In November 448 at Constantinople Eutyches,
evidently acting with all deliberation, challenged the orthodoxy of those who said that in Christ there are 'two natures
after the union', and was condemned by Flavian as an
Apollinarian. Eutyches appealed that the minutes of his
trial were incorrect and was upheld at an inquiry in April
449. At once Dioscorus of Alexandria accused Flavian of
requiring a test of orthodoxy other than the Nicene creed,
which the council of Ephesus in 431 had declared to be incapable of supplementation. The emperor decided to call a
council to meet at Ephesus in August 449.

Pope Leo was invited to attend the Council. He declined,
saying there was no precedent for such attendance, but sent
three legates and a doctrinal statement or 'Tome'[2] addressed

1. *Eranistes* means one who makes a garment from discarded rags.
Theodoret argued that Monophysite doctrine was a patchwork of
abandoned heresies.

2. The Tome was drafted by Leo's secretary Prosper (below, p. 234),
parts being plagiarized from one of Augustine's sermons and from a
letter of bishop Gaudentius of Brescia (c. 400).

to Flavian of Constantinople, intended to be accepted by the Council. At first Leo had been prejudiced against Flavian; throughout this period bishops of Rome tended to begin with the assumption that bishops of Constantinople were ambitious men who needed to be cut down to size. But when Flavian sent him a transcript of Eutyches' trial of November 448, Leo was appalled by what he read. Accordingly, his Tome directly attacked Eutyches' formula 'one nature after the union' (which Eutyches took from Cyril of Alexandria) and also the reluctance Eutyches had shown when asked to concede that Christ's lifegiving body was of one substance with ours. Leo asserted in the strongest language the permanent distinction of the two natures in the incarnate Lord. Nestorius, reading the Tome in his lonely exile, felt that the truth had been vindicated at last, and that he could die in peace.

But the council of Ephesus in 449 was controlled by Dioscorus of Alexandria, not by the legates or allies of Rome. The Roman legates could only protest in impotent Latin ejaculations as the proceedings moved majestically to their predictable climax, the condemnation of Flavian and rehabilitation of Eutyches. With the help of one of the Roman legates, the deacon Hilarus, Flavian wrote an appeal to Leo and was then carried away to prison, exile and (eventual) death. The council went on to depose the leading 'Nestorians' – Theodoret of Cyrus, Ibas of Edessa, and finally even Domnus of Antioch. Leo's Tome was never read to the synod. By November 449 Dioscorus' triumph seemed complete: he was able to exert influence so that his own presbyter Anatolius was appointed as Flavian's successor at Constantinople.

In the hour of his triumph Dioscorus utterly misjudged the realities of the situation. Three factors were fatal to the ultra-Cyrilline, Monophysite cause. First, there was Pope Leo in the West, militant in his enraged rejection of the 'den of robbers' (*latrocinium*) as he called the proceedings at Ephesus. Secondly, the ascendancy of Chrysaphius over the emperor was precarious, and in 450 he fell before the fury of Pulcheria whom he had scorned. An alliance between

Pulcheria and Leo was sufficient to make it certain that the decisions of Ephesus in 449 would not stand. But the third and final blow to Dioscorus came from his own creature, Anatolius, the successor of Flavian, who decided to reassert the full claims of Constantinople to be the second see of Christendom, and saw that the situation provided a golden chance of persuading Rome to accept these claims.

In July 450, when Theodosius II fell off his horse and died, the revisionist movement was already under way. Pulcheria at once took control, had Chrysaphius executed and Eutyches exiled, and took as her consort a veteran soldier Marcian, the favourite protégé of a powerful general, Aspar (an Arian barbarian). A vast council was summoned for October 451, and met at Chalcedon in the church of St Euphemia the martyr.

The great council of Chalcedon, the fourth ecumenical council, was under the firm control of Pulcheria and Anatolius of Constantinople. It systematically reversed almost all the decisions of Ephesus (449). Dioscorus was deposed (though not on doctrinal grounds), and went into exile to die in 454. Juvenal of Jerusalem dramatically crossed the floor of the house and was rewarded by being allowed to keep his patriarchate. Of the 'Nestorianizers' Theodoret and Ibas of Edessa were restored to office, while Nestorius himself was condemned as a heretic.[1] But the central question was doctrinal. Leo's Tome was received with courteous approval and pronounced to be in line with established orthodoxy. The bishops, however, were most reluctant to accept any new Greek formulary, and when it became clear that the Roman legates were demanding this, they tried to get one which (like the formulary of 433) left room for either 'one nature' or 'two natures'. The plea was rejected.

The final form of the Chalcedonian definition owed much to the Formulary of 433. It pronounced Christ to be (a)

1. Nestorianism soon found its centre in the Syrian school at Nisibis, whence it spread into Persia and thence across central Asia into China, and southwards to India. The Nestorian community had a continuous history in the mountains of Kurdistan until their calamitous sufferings in the First World War, since when many of the survivors have moved to San Francisco.

perfect God and perfect man, consubstantial with the Father in his Godhead, and with us in his manhood; (*b*) made known *in* two natures without confusion, change, division, or separation. The meaning of the preposition 'in' was explained by further clauses: (*c*) the difference between the natures is in no sense abolished by the union; (*d*) the properties of each nature are preserved intact, and both come together to form one person (*prosopon*) and one *hypostasis*.

The formula was a mosaic of phrases from different sources. Clause (*a*) came from the formulary of 433; (*c*) was quoted from Cyril's second letter to Nestorius, (*d*) from Leo's Tome. The 'in two natures' came also from Leo (who took it from Augustine), and it was this which caused much of the subsequent distress. The Roman legates and their Nestorianizing friends could not tolerate either Cyril of Alexandria's formula 'one nature after the union', or even the formula 'out of two natures' which obviously allowed a Monophysite interpretation. The council prefixed a lengthy preamble condemning both Nestorius and Eutyches and approving 'the letters of Cyril to Nestorius and to the Antiochenes'. Which letters of Cyril was left unclear. Before long the conclusion was to be drawn that Chalcedon had approved of not only the moderate second letter but also the extremist third letter to Nestorius with the Twelve Anathemas. This ambiguity (probably intentional) made it easy to argue that, despite its 'two natures' formula, Chalcedon implied no ultimate duality in Christ.

Before disbanding, the council passed twenty-seven canons, establishing Constantinople as a court of appeal from provincial synods, and, at a session from which the Roman legates were absent, enacted a resolution reasserting the privileges of Constantinople on the ground of its imperial status and the analogy to the dignity of old Rome. The Roman legates had been warned by Leo to expect this and protested that the resolution was contrary to the sixth canon of Nicaea. The sixth Nicene canon said nothing of Constantinople as that city did not exist in 325; it assured the traditional jurisdiction of the bishops of Alexandria in Libya as being analogous to the extra-provincial authority also exercised by Rome and Antioch (though it did not define the nature and scope of that authority). But the canon had come to be commonly interpreted as determining the hierarchical order of the great sees of Rome, Alexandria and Antioch. Once that assumption had been made, its wording was felt to be capable of improvement. The papal chancery added at the beginning 'The Roman church has always had the primacy'; and it was in this inauthentic form that the Roman legates cited the canon in their protest at Chalcedon.

The resolution on the dignity of Constantinople was so unacceptable to Rome that Leo took the enormous risk of delaying his 'ratification' of the dogmatic definition until 453. He did not see that the council of Chalcedon needed all the authority it could get if its decisions were to stand, and that his actions were widening the gulf between East and West. In Egypt and Palestine the 'two natures' formula provoked passionate violence and hostility. At Alexandria Dioscorus' successor Proterius found that by accepting Chalcedon he had lost his flock and could only hold his own by military support. The news of the death of the emperor Marcian in 457 was the signal for violent revolt at Alexandria: Proterius was torn to pieces by the frenzied mob, and the see was occupied by the ultra-Monophysite bishop, Timothy Aelurus.

THE SEARCH FOR RECONCILIATION

For the next century the Chalcedonians and the Monophysites fought and argued and intrigued. The Monophysites were ousted in 451, but they had not lost hope of recovery with the assistance of a sound emperor. Their hopes were almost realized.

In 482, under the emperor Zeno the Isaurian, a clever patriarch of Constantinople named Acacius devised an eirenic formula of union, called the Henoticon, to reconcile the Monophysite Egyptians and Syrians. The Henoticon condemned both Nestorius and Eutyches, explicitly approved Cyril's Twelve Anathemas, declared that 'one of the Trinity was incarnate', avoided any mention of either one nature or two, and concluded by condemning any heresy 'whether advanced at Chalcedon or at any synod whatever'. This was promulgated on the authority of the emperor without a council of bishops. It was signed by the pro-Monophysite patriarchs of Alexandria and Antioch, and the churches of the Greek East were once more in harmony and concord. The Henoticon failed to satisfy thoroughgoing Monophysites because it did not condemn Chalcedon outright. On the other side, the Roman see deeply objected not only to the unenthusiastic reference to Chalcedon but also to the fact that Acacius of Constantinople had coolly entered into communion with Monophysites without asking for approval from Rome. In 484, after infuriating and brilliant obstruction by Acacius, the Pope finally succeeded in excommunicating him and the Byzantine emperor. The breach was regretted at Constantinople, but it was more important for the emperor to retain the loyalty of Egypt and Syria than to keep in step with Rome and the now disintegrating barbarian West. The Pope for his part was able to maintain his condemnation largely because his own political independence was ensured by the Gothic, Arian power of Theodoric in Italy. The schism between Rome and the Greek East lasted until 518 when Justin I became emperor and pursued a church policy formed in accordance with the Chalcedonian views of his nephew (and successor as emperor) Justinian.

For thirty-six years the Henoticon remained the standard of orthodoxy in the East. During this period the best Monophysite theology appeared, especially under the tolerant reign of the great emperor Anastasius (491–518). Men like Severus of Antioch (465–538) and Philoxenus of Hierapolis in Syria (440–523) were theologians of high intellectual finesse. They urged with inexhaustible argument that Cyril of Alexandria's formula 'one nature after the union' was irreconcilable with Chalcedon and Leo, and they sharply disowned the extremist Monophysite doctrine (propagated by bishop Julian of Halicarnassus) that the physical body of Christ was incorruptible before the resurrection.[1] On the

1. In his senility the emperor Justinian came to adopt this opinion, labelled Aphthartodocetism. He died before he could enforce it.

Chalcedonian side equal energy and learning was devoted to showing the harmony of Cyril and Chalcedon. Both sides employed the rigorous tools of Aristotelian logic. The principal form of the argument from authority became the *florilegium* or anthology of carefully selected excerpts from orthodox fathers, designed to show that the unchanging orthodox tradition was in accordance with the compiler's convictions. The makers of these collections of excerpts were not always scrupulous about the integrity and authenticity of their texts, but the greatest of the Monophysite theologians, Severus of Antioch, undertook laborious researches to be sure of citing genuine texts. About 500–510 a moderate Monophysite, deeply influenced by the Neoplatonism of the pagan Proclus of Athens, put into circulation some writings on mystical theology under the name of St Paul's Athenian convert, Dionysius the Areopagite (Acts xvii, 34). The forger, whose identity baffles investigation, was soon successful, and before long Chalcedonian theologians had to write commentaries on the Areopagite to explain his text in a satisfactory way. Another prominent Monophysite was John Philoponus[1] (490–570), the first Christian head of the Platonic school at Alexandria, who wrote commentaries on Aristotle as well as acute expositions of Monophysite doctrine; he also conducted a running fight with a Nestorian merchant-traveller named Cosmas (later nicknamed 'Sailor to India', Indicopleustes) who supposed that the Bible provided literal scientific information about the natural world.

The intellectual ability was not entirely a Monophysite monopoly. For the Chalcedonian cause, one Leontius of Byzantium argued that, while Christ had two permanently distinct natures, yet his humanity had its concrete existence only within the one hypostasis of the divine Word, a position which he defended with the utmost finesse. This emergence of serious and sustained argument on both sides had the effect of making the Henoticon itself seem antiquated. The weakness of the Henoticon was its assumption that agreement

1. Philoponus held, against Aristotelian science, that the material universe (not merely its order) had a beginning. He in part anticipated Galileo.

could be determined by ecclesiastical politicians without much regard to theological principles. By 510–20 Chalcedonians and Monophysites were facing one another in strenuous disputations, each side being confident of its own logical skill and intellectual consistency.

The tolerant policy of the emperor Anastasius towards the Monophysites was resented by the strict Chalcedonians. Not all the controversy was conducted at the level of academic disputations about the technical terms. The difference also came to be expressed in the popularly comprehensible form of a liturgical difference.

Before 451 both the churches of Syria and of Constantinople had come to use as a liturgical acclamation the 'Trisagion', viz. 'Holy God, Holy Mighty, Holy Immortal, have mercy upon us'. As early as 431 Apollinarian sympathizers were adding 'crucified for us' after 'Immortal'. At Antioch under a Monophysite patriarch about 460 this strengthened version of the Trisagion passed into use. The Chalcedonians rejected the addition, as implying that God was crucified, and re-interpreted the Trisagion to refer not to Christ but to the Trinity. When in November 512 the emperor Anastasius was persuaded to allow the Monophysite form of the Trisagion to be used at Constantinople itself, a violent riot broke out which endangered Anastasius' life and throne and warned him of the passionate strength of Chalcedonian feeling in the capital. It was becoming clear that neither side was willing to rest content with the political compromise represented by the Henoticon.

The possibility of reconciliation with the Monophysites haunted the long reign of Justinian (527–65) and his wife Theodora. Justinian's reign was marked by a largely successful military effort to reconquer the barbarian West and Vandal Africa;[1] by a building programme of magnificent churches, some of which (like Sancta Sophia or SS. Sergius and Bacchus at Constantinople) remain today to evoke the

---

1. After Justinian's death (565) much was soon lost again: Spain to the Visigoths, N. Italy to the Lombards, 'Hungary' to the Avars, much of the Balkans to Slavs and Bulgars. These invasions created a major missionary problem.

beholder's admiration and amazement; by a systematic codification of the laws; and by continual dogmatic controversy in which the emperor himself played the unusual role of an expert theologian 'advising' the patriarchs how to act. The acceptance of Chalcedon was indispensable to Justinian's political ambitions for the recovery of the West, and he could not withdraw from this. But his wife Theodora (of whose colourful career the historian Procopius of Caesarea tells many malicious scandals) sympathized with the Monophysites. In 532 after a serious riot in Constantinople (the *Nika* riot), which destroyed the old Sancta Sophia, Justinian was given the courage to stand his ground against the mob only by the steely determination of Theodora, and her influence was thereafter very great.

Two controversies occupied much of the emperor's attention. In Palestine the mystical speculations of Origen as developed by Evagrius (above, p. 181) caused controversy which required imperial intervention. In 542/3 the emperor published a long refutation of Origenism, and the patriarchs agreed to the condemnation. The Monophysite problem was more intractable. One of the principal Monophysite objections to Chalcedon was that it had acquitted the Nestorianizing sympathisers, Theodoret of Cyrus and Ibas of Edessa. Might not the Monophysites be reassured if the assertion of the Chalcedonian definition, as interpreted in the light of Cyril of Alexandria, were to be combined with a condemnation of objectionable propositions ('chapters') cited from Theodore of Mopsuestia, Theodoret, and Ibas? It was a subtle plan, and the one serious difficulty was to bring Vigilius of Rome (Pope 537–55) to agree to it, since the West was convinced that it made no sense to affirm Chalcedon and simultaneously to condemn the 'Three Chapters'. Vigilius was brought to Constantinople where in 548 he signed a condemnation of Theodore personally as a heretic and of objectionable writings ascribed to Theodoret and Ibas. (This cautious wording was evidently deliberate.) But the signature was given by a man who knew that his action would be denounced in the West, especially in North Africa, and in 551 he withdrew it. Justinian, however, could hardly let him go. A council summoned to Constantinople in May 553, the fifth ecumenical council, agreed to the condemnation of both Origen and the Three Chapters; and to this decision Vigilius (after several further changes of mind) finally assented. He was lucky to die before reaching Rome and the storm awaiting him there.[1]

The painful affair of the Three Chapters did nothing to reconcile even moderate Monophysites, and actually had the reverse effect to that intended. From 553 onwards, a dedicated Monophysite bishop from Syria, Jacob Baradaeus, realized the full dimensions of the threat to the independence and survival of his party contained in Justinian's plan. He travelled round the East in disguise creating an underground Monophysite episcopate to coexist with the Chalcedonians. (To the present day the Syrian Jacobites, like the Armenians, Copts, and Ethiopians, reject Chalcedon.) On the Chalcedonians the immediate effect was to produce temporary schisms in the West; and the successive contradictory utterances of Vigilius did not enhance the authority of the Roman See.

THE DOCTRINE OF ONE WILL

In the seventh century the successive Persian and Arab attacks renewed the imperial government's determination to try and conciliate the Monophysite dissenters. A formula of conciliation was proposed, that while Christ had two natures, he had only a single 'activity' (a doctrine for which Dionysius the Aeropagite provided clear support) or, better, only a single, divine will. This 'Monothelete' doctrine, anticipated by Vigilius, was unwisely accepted by Honorius I (Pope 625–38), but strict Chalcedonians could not accept such a compromise for a moment. The Monothelete doctrine was condemned (in defiance of imperial policy) by Pope Martin I

1. Vigilius' successor, chosen by Justinian, was his deacon Pelagius, in youth a violent opponent of the condemnation of the Three Chapters, but rightly judged by the emperor to be capable of changing his mind. By autocratic authority and the minimum of explanation Pelagius succeeded in upholding the Fifth Council against its Western critics.

at the Lateran Council in Rome of 649, and then in the East at the sixth ecumenical council at Constantinople in 680–81.

The principal architect of the theological destruction of Monotheletism was Maximus the Confessor (*c.* 580–662), who was moved to give the Chalcedonian Christology the profoundest study that it received in antiquity. He saw that the Monophysite doctrine implied a pessimistic estimate of human nature. Chalcedon, he urged with arguments of the most subtle refinement, safeguarded the autonomy of manhood and granted an independent status and positive value to the order of creation. The Christ who is known in two natures is able to be the model for our freedom and individuality, and for a mystical union in which man's separateness as a creature is respected. At the same time Maximus could look beyond formulas and popular slogans. He had learnt from the Cyrilline interpretation of Chalcedon sanctioned by the fifth general council of 553, and recognized as fully orthodox in intention and fact both the Chalcedonian formula 'in two natures' and the Monophysite formula 'out of two natures' or even 'one nature of the incarnate Word' (provided that the difference 'after the union' is not abolished).

Despite the thoughtless slogans of the crowd and the over-subtle logomachies of the intellectuals, the Christological controversy was concerned with questions of basic and permanent importance for Christian theology: Did the Lord, to whom and through whom Christians pray, pray himself? Yet there were grave losses, terrible moments of fanaticism and intrigue, and far too much controversy for its own sake, conducted by men whose natural superiority to scruple was enhanced by the feeling that in the party they were defending, the cause of God was at stake. The alienation of Egypt and much of Syria from the Chalcedonian government was a serious political matter, and gravely weakened those key provinces before the Moslem invasions (though the Monophysites were never so disaffected as actually to welcome the Arabs as deliverers). The Arabs took Jerusalem in 637, then Antioch (638), Egypt and Alexandria (641), and before many years passed were threatening Constantinople itself where they were only repelled by the use of 'Greek fire'. They had conquered North Africa by 707, and Spain four years later. By this rapid Islamic conquest many principal provinces were lost to the Christian empire. The shape of Christendom was transformed, and the process was initiated which would in time transfer its centre of gravity to Western Europe.

The Moslem presence did not bring the Christological controversy to an end, but it imposed new demands on theology and on apologetic argument. The Moslem disapproval of pictures and images had close affinity with the great iconoclastic explosion of the eighth century. It was a Christian monk living in Moslem Palestine, John of Damascus (*c.* 675–*c.* 749), who summed up the achievement of Greek patristic theology in his work 'On the orthodox faith', and classified the basic doctrinal statements of the past concerning the Trinity and the Incarnation in a vast anthology of authoritative citations. He was one of the first Christian schoolmen.

15

The Development of Latin Christian Thought

JEROME AND THE BEGINNINGS OF MATURITY

LATIN Christianity before the last quarter of the fourth century was far behind the mature development of the Greek churches. The best guide on advanced theological questions remained Tertullian, who had become a Montanist. Cyprian still continued to enjoy immense prestige. In the Roman eucharist he was specially commemorated. That he was being read is proved by a surviving list of his writings made at Rome in 359, which includes particulars of their length to warn buyers against bookshops overcharging. Evidently the Donatist appeal to his sacramental theology, so unacceptable at Rome, had not clouded his reputation. But Cyprian's interest in theology, apart from the church and sacraments, was negligible. The West had nothing to parallel the achievement of Origen either in biblical scholarship or in speculative reflection. The earliest Latin exegete, bishop Victorinus of Pettau, martyred in the persecution of Diocletian, wrote simple commentaries dependent on Greek models. At the same period the crisis of pagan attack elicited two essays in defence, one by Arnobius of Sicca in Numidia, and the other an altogether better work entitled *The Divine Institutes* by Lactantius, professor of Latin at Nicomedia, who was also responsible for a gruesome tract on the terrible deaths suffered by persecutors. None of this writing could be called weighty and powerful as theology. The impact of the Arian controversy stimulated a deeper seriousness in Western thought on fundamental questions. In the fifties of the fourth century Hilary of Poitiers was exiled by Constantius to Asia Minor and learnt how to explain a complicated controversy to the uninformed Latin world. At the same moment in Rome Marius Victorinus, a Neoplatonic philosopher whose conversion in 355 caused a sensation, turned the full subtlety of his mind to the intricate logical questions raised by the Arians and argued decisively for the Nicene formula. Gradually Western theologians began to acquire more self-confidence.

At first they borrowed from the Greek East. In Ambrose there is close, often verbal dependence on Philo, Origen, and Plotinus. Rufinus of Aquileia (*c.*345–410) found a ready public for translations of Greek theological classics, especially Basil, Gregory of Nazianzus, and Eusebius of Caesarea's *Church History* which he extended with a supplement down to the death of Theodosius I (395). Rufinus' friend Jerome (Eusebius Hieronymus) similarly published translations of Origen's sermons and of Eusebius of Caesarea's *Chronicle* likewise brought up to date; Jerome also wrote pungent Biblical commentaries, principally modelled on Origen.

Although Jerome was born (347) not far from Aquileia and studied in youth at Rome, he spent a large part of his life in a Greek milieu at Bethlehem, from 386 until his death in 419. Nevertheless his attitude to the Eastern tradition was critical and his relations with the Greeks in Jerusalem were often strained. He was not sure whether the Jerusalem liturgy was a model to be followed as many Western pilgrims thought. One sermon to his Latin monks at Bethlehem consists of a criticism of the Greek custom of celebrating Christ's birth on 6 January instead of on 25 December. The Western communities at the Holy Places lived in enclaves that had curiously little contact with the indigenous Christians of the land.

Jerome's mental world was Latin. The dissenters who provoked his crushing polemical onslaughts, often expressed in a hyperbole embarrassing to his friends, belonged to the West: Helvidius who held that the Lord's 'brethren' were sons of Mary and Joseph; Vigilantius who deprecated manifestations of popular devotion, such as vigils and the cultus of the saints, as pagan infiltrations into the church; Jovinian who denied the spiritual superiority of celibacy to marriage; Pelagius who seemed to question human need for grace;

above all, Rufinus who dared to translate Origen. Jerome
was competent in Greek (as also in Hebrew), but had no
first-hand intimacy with the classics of Greek literature. On
the other hand, Cicero, Sallust, Lucretius, Virgil, Terence,
Horace, and Juvenal he knew and loved so well that he
could not help filling his writings with reminiscences of
them. Whether this was fitting in a monk he was not sure.
About 374 when he was a beginner in the ascetic life, he fell
ill during Lent and in a nightmare was caught up to the
Judgement Seat to hear the terrible condemnation, 'You
are a Ciceronian, not a Christian.' But his ascetic promise
of renunciation was ineffective. Perhaps he need not have
been so embarrassed, for the high literary quality of his
writing may be reckoned among the factors which helped
to give Western Christians a stronger sense of poise and
security. It was a reassurance that the most learned and
cultivated man of the age was one of them, not a Greek.

The West's sense of natural pride in its own traditions was
enhanced by Pope Damasus and by the stimulus which he
gave to the liturgical commemoration of saints and martyrs.
Damasus decorated the shrines of Rome with hexameter
epigrams. His contemporary Ambrose at Milan wrote hymns
for liturgical use at the annual festivals of the great saints.
The Western church acquired also at this time a lyric poet of
high artistry and genuine feeling – the Spaniard Prudentius
(*c.* 348–*c.* 405). Prudentius' chief interest lay in the growing
popular devotion to the saints and martyrs of Spain and
Italy. The same interest dominated Sulpicius Severus who
wrote to show the world that in the fearless simplicity of
Martin of Tours the West had a saint whose miracles were
quite the equal of Antony's in Egypt. Sulpicius' friend Paulinus, a rich Aquitanian landowner, renounced his wealth to
settle in 395 in Campania by the shrine of the popular saint
Felix of Nola, in whose honour he used to write a long poem
for each annual festival. Two saints, however, above all others
drew pilgrims to their shrines in Rome: St Peter and St
Paul. Each year Paulinus of Nola made a pilgrimage to
Rome for the solemn procession round the city on 29 June;
and both Ambrose and Prudentius wrote poems in honour

of this Roman patronal festival. The possession of such pre-eminent apostles and martyrs provided the West with its most important ground of confidence as it faced the older churches of the Greek East.

The time was ripe for the emergence of an independent Latin theology. Jerome was producing the biblical scholarship, but he was no thinker. This task fell to the lot of a young African named Augustine, who by the range and profundity of his mind came to tower not only over all his immediate contemporaries but over the subsequent development of Western Christendom.

THE CONVERSION OF AUGUSTINE

Augustine was born on 13 November 354 at Thagaste, a small Numidian town (now Souk-Arrhas in Algeria), the son of lower middle class parents, Patrick and Monica. Patrick was pagan, becoming a Christian only shortly before his death (370). Monica was a devout believer, probably of Berber stock, and had high hopes for her brilliant son. The boy's education, partly financed by a wealthy benefactor, was completed at Carthage. He acquired an easy mastery of Latin literature, and like Jerome was always able to sharpen his style with allusions to Cicero and Virgil. His instinct for fine prose was irrepressible. Education in the art of self-expression in public speech was the normal ancient route to success at the law or civil service. But his father's early death meant that he had to support his family. He took up teaching at Thagaste, but soon moved through successive professorships of rhetoric at Carthage (374), Rome (383), and Milan (384) where he hoped that his influential friends could find him a provincial governorship. His conversion to Christianity in the summer of 386 radically altered the direction of his life.

In his *Confessions*, written some eleven years later, he described his personal quest in one of the most moving works of Christian prose. At his birth Monica had had him signed with the cross and entered as a catechumen. (At this period it was still rather unusual for infants to be baptized.) But in adolescence his childhood faith became submerged by adventures in sensuality which in the retrospect of the *Confessions* he judged with severity. At the age of seventeen he took a concubine of low social standing, in accordance with the accepted custom of the time,[1] and was faithful to her until Monica's (unrealized) ambitions for a successful marriage for her son abruptly brought the relationship to an end. In 372 she bore his son Adeodatus (Given by God). In the same year Augustine's mind began to turn back towards Christianity, moved at first by a desire for truth inspired by the reading of one of Cicero's philosophical dialogues (*Hortensius*, now lost but then part of the regular school curriculum). But the style of scripture seemed to him distressingly inferior to the Latin classics. He despised the Old Testament as old wives' fables and the church as a body lacking in cultural distinction. It was a mood that made him easy game for the propaganda of the Manichees (above, p. 169), who rejected the Old Testament and claimed to offer reason where the church childishly appealed to authority. For ten years Augustine was an adherent of the Manichees, converting several of his friends to the sect as well. But doubt and disillusionment eventually produced withdrawal into a state of suspense and scepticism, which coincided with the time of his move to Milan in 384.

At Milan, for the first time in his life, Augustine met a Christian intellectual who commanded his respect. Ambrose's sermons in the cathedral charmed him at first by their eloquence, but soon moved his mind by their argument, by their combination of Christian devotion with the language of Neoplatonic mysticism, and by their convincing interpretations of problematic passages in the Old Testament which answered the mocking objections of the Manichees. Augustine

1. How conventional and respectable this then was is illustrated by a canon of a Spanish synod of 400 decreeing that, so long as a man was faithful to his concubine as if she was a wife, their relationship constituted no bar to communion. Pope Leo I thought monogamy preserved if a man left his concubine to contract a legal marriage.

At Rome early in the third century Pope Callistus, a freedman, had recognized unions between emancipated ladies of high birth and men of low social rank, to whom legal marriage was impossible (above, p. 88).

became fascinated by Neoplatonism and ardently read
Plotinus and Porphyry. The axioms of Platonism became to
him almost like the air that he breathed. Plotinus' philosophy
had stimulated an intense interest in the inward mind of man
as a correlate of God; and Augustine possessed powers of
analytical introspection to the highest degree. His conversions to Neoplatonism and to Christianity were so nearly
simultaneous that it was many years before he began to be
seriously critical of Platonism as a religious metaphysic.

Emotionally the focal point of the crisis came in a Milanese
garden in the summer of 386. The next months he spent in
quasi-Platonic retreat (like Cicero at Tusculum) with a group
of his closest friends at Cassiciacum, a country estate a few
miles from Milan. Their long discussions he made the basis of
four Platonizing dialogues (*Against the Academics, On Happiness,
On Order,* and *Soliloquies*) which together amount to a claim
to present the basic Christian answers to the questions put
by the dominant philosophy of the time. The strong Platonic
element in his conversion was also an influence in making it a
decision for a celibate life, though at this stage Augustine had
no intention of following a specifically monastic, far less a
priestly, vocation. On Easter Eve 387 he and his son were
baptized by Ambrose. In the autumn his mother Monica
died at Ostia, and twelve months later Augustine returned
to Africa which he was never again to leave. He established
a little ascetic community at Thagaste, the interest being still
partly philosophical. But in 391 on a passing visit to Hippo
(Bône) he was coerced by popular pressure, and in spite of
his tears, into accepting ordination as presbyter. Thenceforth
his ascetic society had to move to Hippo and took on a more
ecclesiastical character.[1] In 395 the old Greek bishop of
Hippo, Valerius, had Augustine consecrated as coadjutor
bishop to prevent any other church from carrying him off.
No one in Africa knew that the eighth canon of Nicaea
directed that there should not be more than one bishop in a
city.

Ordination marked a change in the movement of Augus-

1. Many of Augustine's monks became bishops elsewhere and so
diffused his ideals in Africa.

tine's mind almost as profound as that of his conversion. Hitherto his writings had concerned either questions of Christian philosophy or polemic against the Manichees which turned on such intellectual problems as the nature of evil and the relation of authority to reason. When Augustine became a bishop, it marked the watershed in his life. He began seriously to grapple with the exegesis of the Bible, especially the letters of St Paul. At the time of his preparation for baptism in 386–7 Ambrose had advised him to read Isaiah, but Augustine had soon abandoned the attempt as being too difficult. Now, however, his concerns were different. Biblical exegesis became a central preoccupation, and his grasp of theology greatly deepened. This had a direct effect on his evaluation of human nature in general and of his own capacities in particular. In 397 the *Confessions* appeared, an original masterpiece of introspective autobiography, expressed in the singularly difficult form of a long prayer to God, frequently modelled on the Psalms. Yet the autobiography is characteristically set in a larger framework so as to become an almost accidental example of the perennial truth of the soul's restlessness until it returns home to its Maker. The personal story is exquisitely told, but mainly as an illustration of a theological thesis. It is a mistake to read the *Confessions* as if it were a simple autobiography with alien theological digressions intruding upon the narrative.

THE DONATIST SCHISM
AND THE PROBLEM OF COERCION

At Hippo Augustine directly faced, in a way that was new to him, the pain of Christian division; and the agony was the greater for him because of his acutely conscientious sense of responsibility. The city was split between the two rival communities of North Africa, Donatist and Catholic, and each body treasured the memory of every single insult. Every injury over nearly a century past was remembered as if it had happened the previous day. Under the hot Numidian sun nothing was forgiven or forgotten. Yet the Donatists and the Catholics affirmed the same creeds and read the same

Latin Bible. Donatist churches could only be distinguished from Catholic ones by the Donatist custom of whitewashing the walls (for which their motive may have been puritan disapproval of the incipient practice of painting figures in churches). Perhaps also a Donatist celebration of a popular feast day could be distinguished by a little extra gusto; for they were particularly attached to the honour of their martyrs, and believed that the Catholic community failed to take the matter with full seriousness. The Donatists, however, seem to have had as large a share of the educated upper classes as the Catholics, and the tension between the two communities was all the sharper because class and economic factors had not been prime causes of the division. Naturally enough some non-theological factors entered into the tensions. It was an embarrassment to respectable and honest Donatists when their cause was supported with brutal violence by wandering Berber bands called Circumcellions,[1] whose seasonal work at the olive harvest gave them plenty of leisure for terrorist attacks on Catholic churches. It was no less embarrassing for Catholics to try and explain away the tough methods used against the Donatists about 347 by a military commander named Macarius, sent to Africa by Constans on a campaign of repression. The Donatists had their own special commemorations lest they should forget their brothers who had died under Macarius.

Each community made the exclusive claim to be the one mystical body of Christ and the sole ark of salvation, the Mother without whom one cannot have God as one's Father. The Donatists consistently followed their hero Cyprian in entirely rejecting the validity of all sacraments other than their own, so that Catholics changing their allegiance to Donatism were 'rebaptized' (in Donatist eyes, baptized for the first time). The Donatists held that the Catholics were compromised and tainted as a community by Caecilian of Carthage who had been consecrated bishop (they affirmed) by men responsible for surrendering copies of the sacred scriptures and church vessels during the great persecution.

1. Augustine explains that they wandered *circum cellas*, round the martyrs' shrines. Their suicides brought odium on Catholics.

The African Catholics commemorated this Caecilian at their eucharist as a departed saint with whom they were in communion. In Donatist eyes this was to declare themselves to be involved in a pollution of the moral and ritual purity of the church which St Paul declared to be without spot or blemish or any such thing.

The Catholics' answer to the Donatists depended not merely on their denial of the factual truth of the charges brought against Caecilian's consecrators. They also rejected in principle the puritan view of the church as a holy and exclusive community in its empirical reality, and affirmed that the church was like Noah's ark with clean and unclean beasts, or like the field of the parable in which wheat and tares remained side by side until the harvest of the Last Judgement. Secondly, they observed that since the Donatists were not in communion with Jerusalem, Rome, and the churches outside Africa, they could not claim to be the catholic, i.e. universal, church. Thirdly, the Catholics developed a different understanding of the sacraments. According to the Donatist (and Cyprianic) view, the validity of the sacrament depends on the proper standing of the minister; it is valid if received within the church, invalid outside it. But if Caecilian's consecrators had been in a state of mortal sin, they had put themselves outside the church of the martyrs who had died rather than surrender Bibles and sacred vessels to the police. The African Catholics at the Council of Arles (314) had come to accept the doctrine which Pope Stephen upheld against Cyprian in 256, viz. that the sacraments belong not to the ministry but to Christ; therefore validity depends on whether the Lord's command to baptize in water in the name of the Trinity has been fulfilled. (The medieval schoolmen neatly summarized the difference between the two doctrines as the distinction between Cyprian's view that the sacrament is valid *ex opere operantis*, on the ground of the personal quality or standing of the minister, and Stephen's view that it is valid *ex opere operato*, on the ground of the action done.) Augustine followed the Roman tradition of Pope Stephen and accordingly accepted the validity of Donatist baptism; but he conceded to the Cyprianic view that baptism bestowed in a schismatic community was an ineffective means of grace until the recipient was reconciled with the Catholic church. In the sacraments, he urged, the priest's actions belong to God who at the moment of ordination has imprinted upon the priest an indelible mark (*character*); therefore, ordination is independent of the moral and spiritual condition of the person ordained, and the efficacity of the sacraments does not depend on the devout state of mind of the baptizing or celebrating priest. All that is required of the priest is awareness that in the sacramental action which he is administering it is the whole church which is acting.

When Augustine became bishop of Hippo, the schism in Africa was eighty-five years old, and the two opposed communities had become resigned to living side by side, with a mutual dislike maintained by occasional outrages, but in the main without intolerable discomfort. Augustine felt that it was impossible passively to accept such a situation of deadlock. He inspired a series of church councils under the metropolitan at Carthage so that the Catholic bishops could reach a common mind on questions of church discipline, and could present the Donatists with a united front. At that moment the climate of opinion in government circles was favourable to a renewed attempt to suppress dissenters. The closing decade of the fourth century was the heyday of imperial edicts against paganism and heresy. The West had enjoyed toleration for a time under Valentinian I, but this policy was exceptional. The political world of the empire was not a liberal democracy where people wanted to think they were doing just as they liked, but a state where personal freedom counted for little, where repeated laws and edicts tried to prevent all social mobility by tying sons to their father's occupation and status, where the secret police (*agentes in rebus*) seemed ubiquitous, and where the screams of those under judicial torture and the gibbets of arbitrary executions were common sounds and sights. If such stern measures were everyday matters in the political sphere, it did not seem so very obviously wrong to apply some minor inducements, and perhaps even a few financial and civil disabilities, to those who were felt to endanger the unity of society by religious dissent.

Augustine was at first strongly opposed to the use of any coercion against the Donatists, not because he thought that the emperor had no right in principle to use force in the interests of peace and order, but mainly because he thought that government pressure would produce a resentful mass of feigned conversions with which the Catholics simply could not cope. Gradually, step by step, Augustine was brought round to another opinion. From 405 onwards the government put a mounting pressure on the Donatist community, and the policy met with surprising success, until Augustine felt unable any longer to resist the practical arguments of his fellow-bishops. The problem of sincerity and honesty he left to God. Augustine knew that the motives which bring men to the truth are often complex, and may include elements of fear or self-interest that have to be regarded as a temporary stage towards a full, glad, and willing assent. Moreover, the highest function of penal action is remedial: what looks like a deterrent penalty of harsh severity may do good as the offender learns to recognize its justice and beneficent social intention. And had not the Lord in the parable said 'Compel them to come in'? It was by such reasoning that Augustine's mind was reluctantly and painfully moved to accept a policy of coercion, understood, however, as paternal correction. It was a fateful theoretical justification of the imperial policy. The protests against the condemnation of Priscillian (above, p. 170) had been forgotten. But at least the nature of the disabilities imposed by the government on the Donatists was not of so stringent a nature as to pass beyond Augustine's limiting doctrine that it must be 'rebuke', not crude physical force.

It was characteristic of Augustine that his mind had to find an intellectual justification for what was being done. The controversy, however, was seldom conducted at a profound level of thinking. Much of the debate between Donatist and Catholic consisted of unending repetition of two rival accounts of the origins of the schism. The Donatists had their last chance publicly to state their case at a great conference at Carthage in May–June 411, presided over by an imperial commissioner. The surviving minutes of the conference provide a vivid picture of exasperated men in the summer heat and dust, made more trying by the Donatists' refusal to sit down with the 'ungodly', arguing *ad nauseam* about incompatible versions of what had or had not occurred in the time of their great-grandfathers. It is hard to read the record of the proceedings, which had comic moments, without being oppressed by the futility and tragedy of it all. In any event, the government's purpose in calling the conference was predetermined: its function was to justify the replacement of fruitless, jangling argument and counter-argument by a policy of strong state pressure. In January 412 the emperor Honorius formally proscribed Donatism by an edict which laid down a sliding scale of fines graded according to social status, exiled Donatist clergy, and confiscated Donatist property. The intransigent Circumcellions were driven to a last fling of infuriated atrocities, but Augustine came to feel that the problem of insincere conversions was not as serious as he had once feared.

Before many years passed, however, the schism which had for so long split the African churches was temporarily pushed to one side by the ravages of invasion. In 429 the Arian Vandals, who had poured into Gaul in 407 and on into Spain in 409, crossed the straits of Gibraltar and spared neither Catholic nor Donatist. Augustine's last letters dealt with the problem of conscience whether clergy might join with the refugees. In Gaul and Spain the bishops of many cities, such as Toulouse, had been the principal organizers of the resistance to the invaders; but some bishops had gone with those who fled before the murdering, plundering hordes. What were the African clergy to do? Augustine did not want all the best priests to be lost in the coming massacre. Yet there was a clear duty to be there to minister to those who would be clamouring for baptism or for the last rites before the cruel invaders cut their throats. Augustine recommended that some should go and some stay, and that to avoid invidious decisions the clergy should cast lots. He himself stayed in Hippo for the Vandal siege, but died on 28 August 430 before the barbarians broke through the defences.

The Donatist community, though reduced by government

pressure and Vandal attack, survived both, and even Justinian's reconquest of North Africa in the sixth century. In Numidia its continued strength was enough to cause distress to Pope Gregory the Great in 590, and the Pope found it particularly galling that the local government authorities in Africa were reluctant to implement the anti-Donatist laws. But a century later both Catholic and Donatist succumbed to the flood of Islam. There were Catholic Christians in the Maghreb until as late as the twelfth century, but the Donatists disappear from history.

'THE CITY OF GOD' AND THE PELAGIAN CONTROVERSY

The virtual ending of the Donatist controversy at the Carthaginian conference of 411 released Augustine's energies for other interests. He longed to finish an extended work on the doctrine of the Trinity which had occupied his few leisure moments since 399. But even this had to be deferred for a while because of other urgent pressures. In 410 the Western world, still reeling under the barbarian blows in Gaul and Spain, suffered the numbing shock of the sack of Rome by Alaric and the Goths. Refugees poured into Africa and the safer Greek East. Large questions of divine providence in history were urgently raised in a mood of frantic emotion. Why had the patronage of St Peter and St Paul been ineffective to save their city? Pagans believed that the inconceivable, unimaginable catastrophe was the result of the empire's abandonment of the now angry gods to whose celestial favour Rome had owed her greatness.

At Augustine's suggestion Orosius, a priest from Spain who perhaps at the time of the Vandal invasion had moved to Africa, answered the pagans with a short history of the world designed to show that pre-Christian history was a long record of misery and disaster far worse than anything happening under the barbarian attacks, which were God's just judgement on the surviving pagans. Meanwhile, from 413 to 427 Augustine himself was engaged on an immense apologia for Christianity, *The City of God*, in which he saw the Church as existing for the kingdom of God, the true 'eternal city', beyond the rise and fall of all empires and civilizations. Even 'Christian' Rome could claim no exemption from the chaos and destruction brought by the barbarians. Augustine never supposed that the interests of the Roman empire and the kingdom of God were more or less identical. In relation to the church, he thought, the government had a positive function to preserve peace and liberty. But the barbarians who attacked the empire were not necessarily enemies to the city of God. It would be the western church's task to convert its new barbarian masters.

The City of God moves from a criticism of pagan religion and philosophy to an evaluation of government and society. Its title implies a contrast to Plato's political dialogue, the *Republic*. Man's true end, Augustine argued, lies beyond this life. No earthly state can ensure security from external attack or internal disruption. History is a catalogue of almost incessant war. Man without God is victim of fear and self-love, driven by vain ambitions for imperialistic domination. 'Without justice governments are merely large-scale gangsterism.' Yet the organization of society apart from God is not wholly evil. The Roman conquerors possessed energy and courage. Their empire conferred benefits that Christians have received as God's gifts. Although government, like private property and slavery, exists only in consequence of man's fallen nature, yet it restrains dishonesty and anti-social behaviour. A ruler, whether Christian or pagan, rightly demands obedience unless his command is to do wrong. Christians rightly pay taxes and accept their share of responsibility in government, magistracies, and defence in 'just' wars. Moreover, just as the state is not simply the 'earthly city' of self-love, so also the Church militant here in earth is not identifiable with God's city. There are wolves within and sheep without. (Here Augustine owed much to a Donatist theologian Tyconius, who expounded a doctrine of the 'mixed' nature of the Church in a *Commentary on the Apocalypse* and in a book of *Rules* for interpreting scripture.) The Church exists for the kingdom of heaven, and God alone knows the elect. So the meaning of history lies not in the flux of outward events, but in the hidden drama of sin and redemption.

The City of God became a treatise on human nature and destiny, a theme of another debate. About 411, while Augustine was away from Hippo perhaps on Donatist affairs, a notable refugee from Rome landed at the harbour and called to pay his respects on his way through to Jerusalem. The disappointed visitor was a British monk named Pelagius who had lived in Rome for several years and there acquired a considerable reputation as a moralist and spiritual director. Pelagius went on his way without meeting Augustine, but left behind him in Africa a friend and travelling companion named Celestius, a lawyer whose too eloquent advocacy of Pelagius' opinions soon created a buzz of anxiety at Carthage.

During his years at Rome Pelagius had been disturbed by the easygoing moral tone of affluent Roman society which sat lightly to the precepts and counsels of the gospel. He had been especially alarmed when a bishop had quoted in his hearing a prayer from Augustine's *Confessions*: 'Thou commandest continence; grant what thou commandest and command what thou wilt.' The use made of these words seemed to Pelagius to undermine moral responsibility and to preach cheap grace. Pelagius was equally anxious at the apparent infiltration of Manichaean pessimism into the Church. In the time of Damasus a notable commentary on the Pauline epistles had appeared in Rome by an author whose name is not certainly known but whose mind was strikingly original.[1] The unknown commentator had explained St Paul's words in Rom. v, 12, to mean that 'in Adam all sinned as in a lump', and had remarked that this transmission of sin to Adam's posterity might presuppose that human souls are derived from the parents, like human bodies. Such doctrines were deeply disturbing to Pelagius. He wrote his own commentary on the Pauline epistles to make it clear that there is no hereditary transmission of sin passed down since the fall of Adam through the reproductive process. According to Pelagius, we sin by a voluntary imitation of Adam's

1. The commentary became transmitted under Ambrose's name. Hence the author is called 'Ambrosiaster'.

transgression, corrupted indeed by external environment and by successive wrong choices that weaken the will's resolution, but never by a fault inherent in the 'nature' with which we are born into the world.

Pelagius regarded it as a disastrous concession to the Manichees to admit that the nature of man can be corrupt to the point that his will is powerless to obey God's commands. To him it seemed essential to the very notion of morality to affirm that in all sin there is personal assent, and vice versa – without assent there is no sin. Therefore Pelagius was driven to deny any element of evil within the newborn child. The consequence of Adam's sin was, he thought, to set a fatally bad example of disobedience, but it transmitted neither sin nor death to his posterity. Adam did not become, he was created mortal (a proposition that Pelagius seems to have learnt from a Syrian disciple of Theodore of Mopsuestia who came to Rome about 399–400). This denial of sin in infants does not imply (Pelagius explained) that the newly born do not need baptism and redemption in Christ. From John iii it is certain that the unbaptized are not admitted to the kingdom of heaven. But it is monstrous to suppose that unbaptized babies without sin are consigned by a just, not to say merciful, God to the pains of hell. They must be received into some third place, or limbo, of natural felicity.

Pelagius was accused of denying man's need for grace. He was much misrepresented in the course of the controversy. In fact he affirmed that in the forgiveness of sins there is an unmerited gift of grace. But otherwise he spoke of grace as divine aid conveyed through moral exhortation and the supreme example of Christ. Advance in the moral and spiritual life depends on free choices of the will confronted by possibilities of either right or wrong.

The controversial aspects of these propositions were so provocatively urged in Africa by Pelagius' friend Celestius that Celestius was formally censured in 412 at a synod in Carthage, and took himself off to Ephesus. The departure of both Pelagius and Celestius to the East did not, however, bring the controversy in the West to an end. At Syracuse Pelagian opinions were sedulously canvassed. A fellow-countryman of Pelagius from Britain, living in Sicily, published tracts which gave a socialistic interpretation to the central Pelagian thesis that if God has given commands (e.g. 'Sell that thou hast . . .') it is our responsibility to obey them. Horror of exploitation follows naturally from saying that only freely chosen acts are moral.

In 412–13 Augustine began to publish tracts criticizing his critics, though still treating Pelagius with great respect and even as late as 413 sending him a courteous letter. But gradually the temperature of the controversy began to rise. At Carthage in 414 Demetrias, the young daughter of one of the richest families of Rome, the Probi, took the veil as a consecrated virgin. Her mother and grandmother wanted the praises of this great event to be suitably sung, and elicited lengthy essays of spiritual counsel for Demetrias from several distinguished ecclesiastics, including Jerome and Pelagius. Pelagius' letter to Demetrias contained matter which Augustine regarded as so dangerous that he wrote to warn Demetrias' mother against it.

Venom began to be injected into the controversy by the behaviour of Jerome. Many of the western pilgrims who found their way to the Holy Places became the target of pungent criticism in Jerome's correspondence. Pelagius was no exception, and he was unwise enough to criticize Jerome's very Origenist commentary on Ephesians. Jerome retorted that Pelagius was 'a corpulent dog', 'weighed down with Scottish (i.e. Irish) porridge'. In 415 Augustine sent to Jerome his young friend Orosius from Spain. Advised by Jerome, Orosius created a storm at Jerusalem by declaring that the doctrines of Pelagius and Celestius had been formally condemned as heretical by an African synod: they denied original sin and human need for grace. The last thing Pelagius wanted was bitter public controversy. After a preliminary decision at Jerusalem in Pelagius' favour the matter came before a synod of Palestinian bishops at Diospolis (Lydda) in December 415. Pelagius, whose accusers did not even appear, easily satisfied the bishops that the propositions of Celestius condemned at Carthage in 412 were either opinions which he disowned or notions for which he accepted no responsibility.

He certainly did not teach (he said) that man could avoid sin
without God's help.

Pelagius' statements at Lydda show a man unwilling to
go beyond the simple proposition with which he had started,
namely that, while God's grace was necessary for a good
work, there must also be a free, independent act of will
which is man's unqualified responsibility. But as Augustine
read over the minutes of the council it seemed to him that
Pelagius had been guilty not of simplicity but of deep dishonesty and craftiness: Pelagius had not made it clear what
he meant by grace, viz. external teaching and example,
rather than that love of God poured into our hearts by the
Holy Spirit according to the doctrine of St Paul. The Africans held separate councils in the provinces of Numidia and
Proconsular Africa, which hysterically denounced Pelagianism as denying both prayer and infant baptism, and then re-
mitted the matter to the urgent attention of Pope Innocent I.
Innocent replied that on the evidence sent by the Africans the
Pelagians must be held excommunicate unless they repudia-
ted such views. In his pulpit Augustine exulted that the
matter was now finally settled: two councils had sent their
findings to the Apostolic See and back had come concurring
answers. *Causa finita est.*

It was an excessively confident utterance. Three months
later Innocent I died and was succeeded by Pope Zosimus
(417–19). Celestius decided to put his case personally to the
new Pope. He travelled from Ephesus to Rome where he
assured Zosimus that he entirely submitted to the judgement
of the Apostolic See, and that he certainly believed in infants'
need for baptism. Pelagius stayed in Jerusalem but sent
Zosimus a new book explaining what he thought about free
will. The Pope was much impressed both by the high morality
of the Pelagians and by their exalted opinions of papal
authority. He told the Africans rather curtly that they had
been listening to prejudiced accounts of Pelagius who on
fundamentals must be accounted orthodox. The horrified
Africans reacted to this so explosively that for six months
Zosimus hesitated, assuring them that no final decision had
yet been reached. Suddenly the Pope found that his hand was

forced, not by the anger of the African bishops but by the emperor. Augustine and his friends had been taking advantage of Zosimus' hesitations and had sent urgent representations directly to the court at Ravenna. On 30 April 418 an imperial edict banished the Pelagians from Rome as a threat to peace. The lobbying that led up to this edict is shrouded in obscurity. Perhaps Augustine's enlistment of government intervention was made easier by his use of the socialistic tract by the Pelagian Briton in Sicily where the strongest language is used to pillory the irresponsibility of the rich towards the poor and the maintaining of power by torture and cruelty. Here at least was plausible evidence that Pelagianism could mean social revolution. Perhaps reports had reached Ravenna that in Rome the church was being split in two by factions for and against Celestius and the Pelagians. For at the next papal election in 419 two rival bishops were consecrated by different parties whose *raison d'être* is not perfectly clear. The effect of the edict on Zosimus was crushing. He bowed to the inevitable, issued a formal condemnation of Pelagius and Celestius, and looked about for other ways of expressing his resentment at the way in which the Africans had acted.[1] Celestius and his friends appealed to Alexandria and then to Constantinople, where in 428 Nestorius compromised himself by listening to them (above, p. 196). But the Pelagians never recovered their ecclesiastical position.

The theological discussion, however, was far from being concluded, and it was only at this stage that Augustine began to give a really full exposition of his theology of grace.

According to the doctrine that Augustine opposed to the

1. An African priest of Sicca Veneria (El Kef) named Apiarius was excommunicated by his bishop, one of Augustine's best pupils, and appealed to Zosimus. The Pope curtly demanded Apiarius' reinstatement, justifying his right to judge the appeal by invoking the Serdican canon (above, p. 139), which he cited as 'Nicene' (below p. 238). The Africans, who had never heard of the council of Serdica, obtained from the East authentic texts of the Nicene canons to demonstrate that Rome had no such jurisdiction. Augustine, whose expressions of regard for Roman authority were ordinarily warm, was much distressed by this papal overriding of African independence, especially since Apiarius was a very tiresome person. Zosimus' support for him was a blunder.

Pelagians, the entire race fell in Adam (the Latin version of Rom. v, 12 said so). The transmission of hereditary sinfulness is bound up with the reproductive process. The general belief that virginity is a higher state than marriage proved for Augustine that the sexual impulse can never be free of some element of concupiscence. In any event the practice of infant baptism for the remission of sins presupposes that infants arrive polluted by sin; since they have committed no actual sin, remission must be for the guilt attaching to a fault in their nature. Therefore if babies die unbaptized they are damned, even though it will be a 'very mild' form of damnation. Mankind is a lump of perdition, incapable, without redeeming grace, of any act of pure good will, and all the virtues of the good pagan are vitiated by sin ('splendid vices', as a zealous adherent of Augustine soon put it). If all humanity were consigned to hell, that would be nothing but strict justice. Nevertheless God's mercy is such that, inscrutably, he has chosen a fairly substantial minority of souls for salvation by a decree of predestination which is antecedent to all differences of merit. To complain that this election is unjust is to fail to consider the gravity of the guilt attaching to original sin, and yet more to actual sin.

A necessary corollary of this doctrine of predestination is that grace is irresistible. If we are so corrupt that we no longer have free will to do good, grace must do all; and that this power is irresistible is a plain deduction from the divine decree of predestination which otherwise would be frustrated. It is the purpose of God to bring his elect, infallibly, to a certain end. Accordingly, the empirical test of the operation of grace lies in a man's consistent goodness of character right through to the end of his life, a 'final perseverance' which is a foreordained gift of God, independent of merit.

Augustine's propositions provoked a quick reaction in several quarters. A frontal attack came from Julian, bishop of Eclanum (near Benevento), an avowed Pelagian. Julian's fundamental thesis was that grace brings nature to its divinely intended perfection, but is not radically discontinuous with it since nature also is the good gift of the Creator. Nothing 'natural' can be evil. The sex instinct is only wrong when used in a way outside the limits laid down by God, and it is quite wrong to confuse original sin with concupiscence. The trouble arose, Julian thought, because Augustine had brought his Manichee ways of thinking into the church, was defaming the good handiwork of the Creator under the influence of a hagridden attitude to sex resulting from the adolescent follies described in the *Confessions*, and was denying St Paul's clear teaching that God wills all to be saved.

Julian of Eclanum was a competent thinker and uninhibited controversialist, but he fell with the Pelagians and took refuge in the East with Theodore of Mopsuestia. Meanwhile Augustine's doctrines, which became harder with each successive reiteration and restatement, drew pained protests from many to whom Pelagianism was abhorrent. The lazy conclusion was being freely drawn from Augustine's tracts that salvation was predetermined and that one need make no efforts after goodness. Among the monastic communities founded by John Cassian in southern Gaul there was consternation when they received a copy of Augustine's work *On Rebuke and Grace* (427). To Vincent of Lérins the Augustinian doctrine was a most disturbing innovation, quite out of line with 'orthodoxy' which Vincent defined as that body of belief which is held undeviatingly by the universal church – *quod ubique, quod semper, quod ab omnibus*. In his *Conferences* John Cassian went so far as to provide an alternative positive doctrine. Augustine, he agreed, was right in teaching that at every point divine grace is needed. The human heart is like a flint which God strikes; but when God sees the first sparks of response, he pours in his grace. The capacity for making the first turn of the will towards God is the gift of grace. But the actual turning is a cooperation of the natural will with God's gracious help. Cassian entirely rejected the idea that grace is a power than can be neither resisted nor lost.

The controversy now centred on the psychology of faith, and especially on the mysterious question, How does it first come into being? Cassian's doctrine did not succeed in meeting the objection that if God pours in his grace when he sees human will responding, the response of the will is in

some sense prior to the gift which is therefore not uncondi-
tional. It was an ingenious compromise, and was attacked
by a hyper-Augustinian enthusiast, the layman Prosper of
Aquitaine (above, p. 182). In time, however, Prosper himself modified the stern rigour of his doctrine. He became
Pope Leo I's secretary, and perhaps under his moderating
influence withdrew from the full-blooded predestinarianism
of Augustine's last years. By 450 Prosper appeared as an
advocate of the doctrine that when St Paul said 'God wills
all to be saved' he meant what he said.

The religious strength of the full Augustinian doctrine lay
in its overwhelming consciousness of human dependence,
awe, and reverence before the majesty and sovereignty of
our Maker. The acknowledgement that we are dependent on
God for our creation requires the further acknowledgement
that we depend on grace for our redemption. 'What have
you which you have not received?' Augustine gave this
doctrine a special character and depth by his own consuming
interest in the subjective and psychological aspect of faith.
In his own experience he had known the meaning of moral
impotence. It seemed to him quite unreal to speak with the
Pelagians of a free will and an uncorrupted nature with the
capacity to delight in that which is good. In the first place,
Augustine could not think in terms of a neat antithesis
between nature and will; for him all acts of the will are expressions of a person's nature. In the second place, it was
precisely the delight in righteousness which he found himself
unable to achieve by any act of will. He could acknowledge
the rightness of the divine commands laid down in the Ten
Commandments. But his will and effort could only be directed towards the good life if the Holy Spirit poured the love
of God into his heart. In the third place, Augustine's psychological realism made it impossible for him to think of free
will as if it were a simple choice between open alternatives,
unaffected by the pressures imposed by motives and desires
that we bring with us into situations of moral decision. For
him 'freedom' means the power to choose the good and to do
it, which is just what fallen human nature is incapable of
achieving.

The theologians in the monasteries of southern Gaul liked everything about Augustine except the hard extremism of his doctrine of predestination and grace. But at least they came to agree with him that divine grace is prior to any human response; it was so decreed at a council held at Orange in the Rhône valley in 529. Both Prosper of Aquitaine and Vincent of Lérins produced short summaries of Augustine's teaching concerning the basic essentials of the creed; and Prosper went so far as to publish a guide to Augustinian theology in verse.

It was a theologian living in Southern Gaul, or perhaps in Spain, in the second half of the fifth century who produced the catechetical compendium beginning 'Whoever will be saved . . .', *Quicunque Vult*, which soon (if not from the start) passed under the august title of the Creed of St Athanasius. The influence of Augustine's Trinitarian doctrine upon this document is marked, especially in one important respect.

THE HOLY TRINITY

In his great work *On the Trinity* Augustine expounded a view of the doctrine of God which, while it was nearer than he realized to that of the Cappadocian Fathers, was deliberately formulated in language that differed from the Greek tradition. Augustine did not think the Cappadocian language (inherited from Origen) about 'three *hypostases*' was really satisfactory since it suggested too strong an emphasis on the separateness and plurality of the divine 'Persons'. Further, the Greek Fathers had spoken of the Father's individuality as consisting in being the source or fount of the Godhead of the Son and Holy Spirit; the Son is 'begotten', while the Spirit 'proceeds' from the Father. Augustine was anxious to eliminate every possibility of Arianism and subordinationism from his doctrine of the Trinity. Therefore the unity of the Trinity needed to be safeguarded by the affirmation that the Spirit proceeds from the Father and the Son. He illustrated his meaning by the analogy of the psychological process of thinking. Because we are made in the image of God, he argued, we may expect to find some 'footprints' of the Trinity in the soul of man. Augustine diffidently suggests that there is a triad within the personality of man consisting of the 'memory' (by which Augustine means the profound centre of the personality, including the subconscious mind), intelligence, and will. The intelligence is a reflection, in some measure, of the divine Reason who is the Son; the conative, appetitive will mirrors that Love which is the Holy Spirit.

Augustine's doctrine of the 'double procession' became for his successors much more than an illustration or analogy. It appears as formal theology in the 'Athanasian' Creed, and in Spain during the sixth century came to be affirmed as an indispensable anti-Arian proposition. Gradually the word 'And the Son' (*Filioque*) came to be added to Western creeds, including Latin translations of the creed of Constantinople (381), until in the seventh and eighth centuries the addition to the ecumenical creed began to be the subject of mutual criticism and even recrimination between the Greek East and the Latin West. How, the Greeks asked, could the West justify the interpolation in the text of the ecumenical council's creed? Perhaps because of a sensitivity to the force of this question the last church in the West to make the addition in the creed was Rome. It was a step that contributed a little to the widening gulf between East and West.

16

The Papacy

THE rapid emergence of the Roman see as a pre-eminent centre of both leadership and juridical authority is a striking feature of the life of the Western churches from the second half of the fourth century onwards. The role of the Roman community as a natural leader goes back to an early stage in the history of the church. It can be clearly seen in their brotherly intervention in the dispute at Corinth before the end of the first century. Perhaps the first seeds of the future development can be discerned already in the remarkably independent attitude of St Paul towards the authority of the church of Jerusalem and in his creation of a Gentile Christendom focused upon the capital of the Gentile world. The standing of the Roman church was enhanced by its important part in the second century conflicts with heresy, and by its consciousness, expressed as early as 160 in the monuments erected to the memory of St Peter and St Paul, of being the guardian of the apostolic tradition. By the end of the second century Pope Victor insisted, in a manner which other churches thought autocratic, that all churches, including those of the Greek East, should observe Easter on the same day as that determined by the church of Rome. But before the third century there was no call for a sustained, theoretical justification of this leadership. All were brethren, but the church in Rome was accepted as first among equals. The 'Petrine text' of Matt. xvi, 18, 'Thou art Peter and upon this rock I will build my church', cannot be seen to have played any part in the story of Roman leadership and authority before the middle of the third century when the passionate disagreement between Cyprian of Carthage and Stephen of Rome about baptism apparently led Stephen to invoke the text as part of his defence against Cyprian. But it was not until Damasus in 382 that this Petrine text seriously began to become important as providing a theological and scriptural foundation on which claims to primacy were based.

From Damasus onwards there is a marked crescendo in the expression of the claims made by the bishops of Rome. It seemed to be a clear lesson of the Arian controversy that the whole church needed a much stricter discipline and more centralized control. The traditional method of ensuring good order was by regular meetings of provincial synods enacting canons, and the Council of Nicaea in 325 had done much to elevate the authority of provincial metropolitans in relation to their fellow bishops. In both East and West in the second half of the fourth century the systematic collection of the canons passed by various synods at different times was felt to be a pressing need. Basil of Caesarea in Cappadocia took a special interest in gathering together past rulings and trying to form them into a coherent system of ecclesiastical legislation that would bring order and discipline where much anarchy had prevailed. In the Roman chancery a collection also began to be made; the canons of the Western synod at Serdica, which established the appellate jurisdiction of the Roman see, were joined to those of Nicaea, though without any note to indicate the source of the Serdican canons, with the consequence that in the fifth century more than one pope tried to quote the Serdican canon about appeals to Rome as if it enjoyed Nicene authority (cf. above, p. 231).

The conflicts of the Arian controversy weakened the respect in which episcopal synods were held. They still enjoyed high reverence and authority, but not as much as they had before the controversy began since there had been too many instances of rival synods producing incompatible manifestos. Eusebius of Caesarea early in the fourth century remarked that councils are indispensable to the good order of the Church. Towards the end of the century Gregory of Nazianzus felt that no good ever came of such meetings (admittedly his sad disillusion was an expression of his personal disappointment at Constantinople in 381; above, p. 150). In the West scepticism about the authority of episcopal synods was stronger than in the East. During the fourth century the 'Arians' met in a succession of synods, and Athanasius unkindly contrasted their frequent meetings and successive creeds with the unchanging mind of orthodoxy formulated right from the start in the creed of Nicaea. Nicaea alone, Athanasius argued, enjoyed proper authority and inspiration with the right to demand assent of all true Christians. The same attitude appears in Western writers of the fourth century. Pope Damasus boldly claimed that the unique authority of Nicaea rested on the fact that its decisions had been approved by his predecessor, Pope Silvester. In the dispute about John Chrysostom with Theophilus of Alexandria, Pope Innocent I objected to Theophilus' invocation of a canon passed by an Arian council of Antioch, on the ground that the canons of Nicaea were the sole conciliar canons recognized by the Roman church.

Councils were less important as a locus of decision to the Western churches because the see of Rome, as the West's only apostolic 'foundation', enjoyed a pre-eminence unparalleled by any single bishopric of the Greek world. For although Jerusalem had a greater aura of holiness than Rome, the bishops of Jerusalem were not a force in church politics before the fifth century. Moreover, the metropolitan system was much more developed and recognized in the East than in the West. An individual bishop in Gaul or Spain might naturally write directly to Rome for guidance and help rather than to his metropolitan.

Damasus and his successors began to treat requests for guidance as analogous to the questions sent to the emperors by provincial governors, and composed answers in a formal, chancery style modelled on imperial rescripts. Damasus' underlying assumption was that he was the historical successor of St Peter as no other bishop was (though he recognized that by tradition St Peter had presided over the church in Antioch before coming to Rome). Moreover, this fact of *historical* succession could be interpreted as conferring a *juridical* inheritance of the power to bind and loose entrusted to the apostle by Matt. xvi, 19. On the basis of this juridical theory papal letters began to take the form of decretals. From Damasus and his successors there appeared a series of rulings with the end of obtaining a greater uniformity in Western church discipline. The principal subjects of concern were the age and qualifications of candidates for holy orders, the degrees of kindred and affinity that constitute a bar to Christian marriage, and the need for requiring celibacy in bishops, priests, and deacons (sub-deacons were added by Leo I).

The influence of local Roman usages in liturgical custom also began to grow in this period. The forms of worship in use at important churches were always liable to be taken as models to be followed by smaller communities in the provinces. During the fourth century the increase in pilgrimage to the Holy Land, stimulated by the example of Constantine and his mother Helena with their splendid foundations at Jerusalem and Bethlehem, led to widespread imitation of the rites of the church of Jerusalem, even in the West. About 384 an aristocratic lady from Spain named Egeria wrote a travel diary of her journey by Sinai to the Holy Places and described, in a fascinating colloquial Latin, the characteristic ceremonies and special shrines of Palestine. Naturally the influence of Rome was even more immediate and direct upon liturgical developments in the West. In 416 Pope Innocent I claimed that the gospel had spread to other Western provinces exclusively from Rome[1] and that therefore all Latin churches should follow Roman rites. It is fair to note here that Innocent was not on this occasion writing to an African or Gallic bishop but to a nearby Italian suffragan at Gubbio. In practice the endeavour to bring the Western churches generally into conformity with Roman liturgical usage was not effectively pursued before Charlemagne's time. Pope Gregory the Great expressly disapproved of the policy of imposing the Roman liturgy on all other churches. In the time of Damasus the policy of encouraging

1. In actual fact Greek missionaries probably played a part in the evangelization of North Africa, perhaps also Marseilles and the Rhône valley, and even Northern Italy, not to mention Rome itself.

conformity with Rome's customs was fostered, up to a point, by Ambrose at Milan. He was glad to note Milan's harmony with Rome, but did not think that uniformity should be carried so far as to obliterate distinctive usages of the Milanese tradition. In his catechetical lectures *On the Sacraments*, which have been preserved probably through an unofficial private transcript made by one of his hearers, Ambrose cites some of the principal eucharistic prayers from the liturgy of Milan. The formulas are akin to those which later documents attest for the Roman church in the eighth century, but there are noteworthy local variations. When Monica was troubled about differences between churches in liturgical observance, Ambrose advised her to adhere to the local tradition, whatever it was: in Milan she should follow Milanese ways, and when in Rome should do as Rome did. Augustine also, whose African liturgy belonged to the same general family as those in use in Italy, regretted the confusion caused when clergy came back to Africa and introduced liturgical practices which they had seen abroad.

In Italy it was natural that the authority of Rome was particularly strong in relation to the numerous Italian episcopate. But more distant provinces were harder to control, especially the Greek-speaking regions of Greece and Macedonia. Until 379 they belonged to the Western half of the empire. Damasus found that in his negotiations with Constantinople and the East he had an invaluable ally in the then bishop of Thessalonica. When in 379 the government transferred the administration of Greece and Macedonia to the Eastern half of the empire, this ecclesiastical alliance between Rome and Thessalonica became important in a new way. In 381 the Greek council at Constantinople proposed that ecclesiastical jurisdiction should simply follow civil boundaries. This would entail the transfer of Greece and Macedonia to the sphere of influence of Constantinople, and was an additional reason for Damasus to resist the decisions of a council that he much regretted anyway (above, p. 151). To enforce Rome's continued influence in this area, Damasus and his successors adopted the practice of appointing the bishops of Thessalonica to be their vicars apostolic. From time to time, from the fifth century on, patriarchs of Constantinople attempted to alter the situation, with full support from the emperor; but the papacy was able to maintain its vicariate until the eighth century.

In the Latin-speaking provinces Rome's authority did not need such active personal representation as at Thessalonica. But in 417, by a mistake of judgement on the part of the erratic Pope Zosimus (above, p. 231), an ambitious bishop of Arles was entrusted with a comparable vicariate, analogous to that of Thessalonica, with a right of jurisdiction over the other Gallic metropolitans. The reason for this advancement of Arles was a recent change in the city's secular status. By 401 the prefecture at Trier looked vulnerable to attack, and the seat of the civil and military administration passed from Trier to Arles. The decision of Zosimus caused such a storm among the other Gallic metropolitans that it was quietly dropped by the succeeding popes. But later bishops of Arles reasserted their dignity. In 445 bishop Hilary of Arles felt sufficiently free, in the chaotic state of the West at that time, to act in independence of Rome. Hilary was brought to submission by Pope Leo I but only with the help of a thunderous rescript from the Western emperor Valentinian III, which decreed that all bishops in the Western provinces must submit to papal authority on the pain of secular penalties. Arles had become so important a city in this period that the ambitions of its bishops could not be kept down for long. It reached its peak of ecclesiastical authority early in the sixth century under Caesarius, bishop 502–42, whose admirable sermons do much to illuminate the pastoral problems of the time.[1] But under Frankish rule in Gaul the importance of Arles became much diminished, and by the time of

1. The sermons particularly attack the survival of many peasant superstitions (some Arlesians did no work on Thursdays out of respect for Jupiter), and express disapproval of clergy who made concessions to popular religion by giving amulets inscribed with Biblical texts. Caesarius had to admonish his flock not to leave the church after the psalms and lessons but to stay for mass, and tried to encourage private Bible-reading at home. To raise the standard of preaching, he recommended that clergy should follow the Greek custom (cf. p. 191) of reading sermons by acknowledged masters instead of producing their own poor efforts.

Pope Gregory the Great at the end of the sixth century the papal vicariate was quite unimportant.

The greatest of the fifth-century popes was Leo I (440–61). He inherited all Damasus' romanticism about the past and his sense that the grandeur of Rome's imperial greatness was continuous with its high Christian dignity. St Peter and St Paul, he explained in a sermon on 29 June, had replaced Romulus and Remus as the city's protecting patrons. There is nothing whatever in Leo of Augustine's detached pessimism towards the empire as a political institution, and *The City of God* does not appear to have influenced him deeply. His letters and decretals, composed in an incisive prose without trace of irony or literary allusions, reflect the mind of a man who admired the style of the imperial chancery. But Leo was not a man in whom imperial dignity and legal form were more prominent than pastoral simplicity and charitable zeal. In direct sermons to his congregation he exhorted them to vigilance in giving alms for the poor and in the observing of four short annual fasts, probably instituted under Damasus, during Lent, after Pentecost, in September, and during Advent – the times which later came to be specially associated with ordinations as 'Ember' seasons. He discouraged his flock from mixing their Christianity with sun worship on the steps of St Peter's. As a result of a scandal he unearthed an alarming Manichee infiltration into his congregation, which he checked by a careful watch on the reception of the chalice at mass (the crypto-Manichees only wished to receive communion in one kind, as they disapproved of drinking wine). Leo also served his city with distinction as an ambassador, successfully pleading the cause of the city in 452 before the terrible Attila and his Huns. When the Vandals arrived from Africa in 455, Rome was defenceless; but Leo at least dissuaded the invaders from senseless massacre and destruction even if he could not stop them stripping Rome of its treasures and deporting many into slavery.

In his decretals and letters Leo consolidated the essentially juridical doctrine of Petrine authority as that had been developed since Damasus sixty years earlier. The personality of Leo as a man, despite the large number of surviving documents from his pen, is curiously elusive just because he could only write in the name of the great institution with which he had merged his identity. Leo believed himself to be successor of St Peter in more than any merely historical sense. When he preached or wrote a letter, he believed that St Peter himself was speaking and writing; or at least that his hearers and readers should receive his words as such. Because the pope is legal heir of all that St Peter was, there is no diminution of the power of the keys, but a *plenitudo potestatis*. It is symbolic that Leo should have been the first Pope to be buried at St Peter's.

When Leo sent to the Greek East the Tome which was to be received at Chalcedon in 451 (above, p. 203), he forbade the bishops in council to subject it to the scrutiny of discussion. Now that the matter had been defined there was nothing to discuss, and they were humbly to receive the Tome as an utterance of blessed Peter himself. Although in practice and for tactical reasons Leo might occasionally appeal to the decisions of church councils, his theory of authority allowed them little weight. The Greek bishops could hardly have looked at the matter in the same way. At Chalcedon the Tome was approved as a truly worthy and Petrine utterance, but on the clear ground that examination had shown it to be in conformity with received standards of orthodoxy. The Council retained their independence of judgement. Leo, however, held that the doctrinal definition of Chalcedon was valid and irreformable because it received papal ratification. In practice Leo sensibly realized that the maintenance of the authority of the Chalcedonian definition in the East depended much less on Rome than on the policy of the emperor at Constantinople. The Monophysites regarded Chalcedon as a temporary set-back that they would soon reverse. When the emperor Marcian died in 457, the Monophysite party made the most strenuous efforts to win over his successor to an anti-Chalcedonian standpoint. Pope Leo took firm counter-measures. He provided the new emperor with an arsenal of argument in favour of his Tome and the Chalcedonian definition, flatterously adding that 'by the Holy Spirit's inspiration the emperor needs no human instruction and is incapable of doctrinal error'. After such language it was not quite so easy for Leo's successors at Rome consistently to complain when the Henoticon was issued in 482 on the sole authority of the Byzantine emperor.

The long thirty-four years of schism between Rome and the Eastern patriarchates which resulted from the Henoticon (above, p. 205) led the popes of this period to use a sustained fortissimo about their supremacy in the endeavour to subdue the independence of Constantinople and Alexandria. Pope Gelasius I (492–6) claimed that 'the see of blessed Peter has the right to loose what has been bound by the decisions of any bishops whatever'. The support which the Eastern patriarchs were receiving from the emperor Anastasius I led Gelasius to expound a bold doctrine of the relation between ecclesiastical authority and kingly power: Just as in mundane matters (he wrote) the clergy are bound to obey the emperor, so in ecclesiastical affairs the emperor ought to submit his neck to the prelates, and above all to the pope as chief prelate, who must give account to God for the manner in which the emperor discharges his responsibilities.

In less than five years Gelasius I accomplished much for the Roman see. He put a stop to an abuse in the churches of Calabria where communion was being given in only one kind. He tried to suppress the festival of the Lupercalia in Rome, an event directly echoed in the traditional collect for the third Sunday after Easter of which Gelasius was the author. Several of his prayers passed into the Latin liturgical tradition; and in modern times scholarly conjecture, now recognized to be mistaken, has commonly ascribed to him responsibility for the Latin sacramentary contained in an eighth-century manuscript presented to the Vatican Library by Queen Christina of Sweden. But the admission that the 'Gelasian Sacramentary' is not his does not take away from the reality of his liturgical achievements.

In the memory of Dionysius Exiguus, the Roman canonist of the first half of the sixth century responsible for introducing the Christian Era as a system of dating, Gelasius appeared the ideal pastor. Gelasius' successors were generally less impressive men. From 498 until 506 two rival popes,

Symmachus and Laurentius, fought one another for the office, partly with physical violence, partly (on Symmachus' side) with skilfully forged documents which made on Symmachus' behalf the claim that 'the apostolic see can be judged by no one'. The proposition passed into the theory of medieval canonists. The unedifying wrangle was ended only by Laurentius' withdrawal into private life. The schism was the more painful for the fact that the government of Italy at this time was in the hands of the Arian Ostrogoth, Theodoric, at Ravenna; his tolerant detachment did little to shorten the agony.

Still greater humiliations were to come upon the papacy after the ending of the breach with Constantinople in 518–19. The restoration of Chalcedonian orthodoxy in the East in place of the Henoticon was the prelude to Justinian's reconquest of Italy, which had the uncomfortable consequence of depriving the sixth-century popes of the liberty they had enjoyed during the long schism. The miserable career of Pope Vigilius (p. 209) is merely one illustration of this subservience to Byzantine imperial policies. In 568, however, three years after Justinian's death, the Byzantine control of Italy, exercised through the imperial exarchate at Ravenna, was checked by the advent of the Lombard invaders. The Lombard occupation of northern Italy created a political situation which made it possible for Pope Gregory the Great to restore to the papacy a measure of independence of action and to direct his gaze away from the Byzantine world, which he cordially disliked, towards the missionary problems of the new barbarian kingdoms now dominating the West.

To the evangelization and civilization of northern Europe, the papacy gave crucial support. Simultaneously the tendency to centralization sowed the seeds of future problems at the same time as appearing to offer solutions. From Leo and Gregory the popes inherited a responsibility for guarding the apostolic faith and claimed jurisdiction over all churches. The eastern Churches, conscious of their ancient traditions, were normally glad to include Peter's see among those with which they were in communion, but did not think universal jurisdiction desirable or possible.

17

The Church and the Barbarians

FROM the time of Constantine onwards the Roman emperors found that to obtain the best soldiers for the army they had to look to the Germanic tribesmen north of the long Rhine–Danube frontier, whose attacks had almost brought the empire to its knees during the middle years of the third century. Gradually the Goths became indispensable for the defence of the empire, and many of them reached high office; they began to take wives from Roman families. One of the emperor Julian's many complaints against Constantine was that he had promoted barbarians to important offices; but it was noticed by pagan observers that before long Julian himself was appointing a barbarian to the envied honour of the consulship. The appointments were resented by those who thought that the great Roman families should continue to hold a monopoly of such dignities. But at least the immigration was gradual and controlled. The situation changed quickly from 375 onwards. The pressure of the Huns from what is now south Russia precipitated an urgent move into the empire on the part of the Goths, and the movement became at once one of huge masses producing political and social disturbance. The Eastern half of the empire used barbarian generals almost as much as the West, but had a northern frontier that was relatively easy to control compared with the long indefensible Western frontier along the length of the Rhine and Danube. On 31 December 406 the Rhine froze, and the Vandals, Alans, and Suevi poured across into Gaul regardless of losses (the Vandals alone are said to have lost twenty thousand men at the river crossing). Two years later they were again on the move in search of food and pasture, and crossed the Pyrenees into Spain. In 429 the

Vandals crossed the Straits of Gibraltar and swept into
Africa, capturing Carthage in 439 where they established a
pirate kingdom (a little larger than modern Tunisia) which
lasted until Justinian's time.

The Germanic invasions produced chaos in the West. The
collapse of Roman political control and administration was
rapid, and the task of organizing local resistance often fell in
the main to the bishops. One Hun attack on a town in
Thrace was resisted only by the energy of the local bishop who
placed a huge ballista under the patronage of St Thomas and
then fired it himself to such purpose that he scored a direct
hit on the barbarian chief. At Toulouse heroic tales were told
of the leadership of the bishop during the siege. At first the
barbarians were regarded as a merely temporary scourge
that would be removed soon if people were truly penitent.
To Salvian, the socialistic presbyter of Marseilles, they had
been sent as a judgement on the vices of the empire in which
the rich had wickedly oppressed the poor. But probably even
Salvian did not suppose that the judgement was to be of
long duration and that the invaders had come to stay.

It was only slowly that the church took up the task of
missionary work among the tribesmen; but, as the political
threat grew, the hope of turning them into men of peace imparted high urgency to the project. With those who came into
the empire during the fourth century some progress was
made. In 381 the Council of Constantinople directed that
'the churches of God among the barbarian races must be
governed according to custom', a reticent canon which at
least informs us of the existence of groups of orthodox Germanic Christians within the empire. John Chrysostom
preached in the Goths' church in Constantinople, where they
used their own language for Bible and liturgy, and he also
sent missionaries to the Goths in the Crimea and north of
the Black Sea. Missionaries soon penetrated the Caucasus
and established churches among the Hunnish tribes. By the
seventh century we hear of missions among the Bulgars, and
even in central Asia among the Turkmen where the Nestorians were active.

Many of the Goths, however, were converted in the

fourth century not to orthodoxy but to Arianism by Ulfila (*c.* 311–83). His mother's parents had been Cappadocian Christians carried off in a Gothic raid of the third century. In 341 he appeared in the empire as a member of a Gothic embassy to Constantius, was consecrated bishop by Eusebius of Constantinople, and returned to undertake a mission among the Visigoths for whom he invented the Gothic alphabet and translated the Bible. The Goths became the principal missionaries to the other Germanic tribes, each of which tended to become Christians a few years after settling within the empire. Such was the pattern of events with the Visigoths, Vandals, Suevi, Burgundians, Heruls, and Ostrogoths. Immigration into the civilized Roman world was felt to entail an acceptance of Christianity. One inscription from southern Gaul commemorates two barbarians in such a way as to imply that their racial origin was part of the stain washed away in baptism. But the fact that the barbarians' form of Christianity was mainly Arian was crucial. It meant that their attacks on the empire strongly reinforced the identification of the Catholics with the Roman imperial ideal. It also meant that as immigrants within the empire their racial distinctiveness was preserved by their religious dissent. The Franks alone among the invading German tribesmen were initially converted to Catholic orthodoxy with their king Clovis, 'the new Constantine', probably about 506; it was not until later in the sixth century that the Burgundians, Suevi, and Visigoths successively changed over from Arianism to Catholicism. For a period after the middle of the fifth century the Catholic communities in Gaul, Spain and especially North Africa suffered sporadic persecution from their Visigothic, Suevic, and Vandal rulers respectively. But most of the barbarians had a regard for Roman law and institutions, and for much of the time made it easy for Roman patriots to collaborate with them or at least not to feel impelled to interfere. Moreover, the Germanic tribes had a strong common interest with the empire in their efforts to resist the terrifying Huns under Attila (d. 453). The correspondence of Sidonius Apollinaris, a cultivated Gallic gentleman who became bishop of Clermont about 469, illustrates how the old Gallo-Roman aristocrats met the situation. They could either retire to their estates and libraries, or accept bishoprics and use the episcopal office as a vantage point for social and political cooperation with the barbarian government and at the same time as a guarantee of their own independence. The great bishops of southern Gaul in the sixth century, Caesarius of Arles and Avitus of Vienne, found it possible to work with their Visigothic and Burgundian rulers without compromising with Arianism in religion.

In Italy it was the same. The policy of collaboration with the barbarians kept at least a ghostly line of figurehead emperors in office until 476 (or 480), though power was now in the hands of barbarian army commanders. It ended in 476 because the barbarian general Odoacer decided to pension off the cipher emperor Romulus Augustulus at Ravenna and to make himself 'king' of Italy. Since the Renaissance the year 476 has come to be invested with deep symbolic importance as the moment of final collapse for the Western empire. At the time it was not seen in this light. Not much had changed. A Byzantine chronicler of some forty years later admittedly looked back on the year as marking a significant break in the continuity of an institution that had begun with Augustus. But the psychological impact at the time seems to have been negligible compared with the emotional effect of Alaric's sack of Rome in 410. At Constantinople there was still a powerful Roman emperor, claiming sovereignty over the West, and at his instigation Odoacer was attacked and killed by Theodoric the Ostrogoth. Theodoric in turn settled at Ravenna and took the title 'king', but at least he nominally acknowledged the ultimate sovereignty of the emperor at Constantinople, so long as his own independence of action was not restricted.

Under Theodoric's rule (493–526) the old Roman senatorial landowners, now committed to Christianity, continued to live much as they had in the past. Little changed. They valued their church, but treasured no less the glories of Rome and the poetry of Virgil. The Ostrogothic court did not discourage civilized pursuits. The high level of culture achieved by the Arian court at Ravenna may be seen today from the style of Theodoric's palace church (now S. Apollinare Nuovo) with its rich mosaics and noble decoration. The University Library at Uppsala in Sweden possesses an exquisite codex of the Gospels in Ulfila's Gothic, inscribed on purple parchment in silver ink, which was probably written for Theodoric at Ravenna. The separateness of being Arian helped Theodoric to preserve his independence as he faced the orthodox Greek empire. It was an interest that many of the most influential Christians of the West also shared, and cooperation between them and the Gothic king was not difficult.

But the ending of the church schism between Rome and Constantinople in 518–19 (above, p. 206) made Theodoric suspicious, with some reason, that the Byzantine emperor wanted to exploit the reunion for political purposes. The chief casualty of these suspicions was Boethius (*c.* 480–*c.* 524), an aristocratic scholar and rich senator. Boethius wrote not only about the doctrines of the Trinity and the Incarnation, but also works about Platonic and Aristotelian philosophy, including a translation of and commentary on Porphyry's 'Introduction' (*Isagoge*) which became very influential in medieval philosophy. In 523 he fell under suspicion of treasonable dealings with Constantinople, and during his imprisonment before execution wrote his *Consolation of Philosophy*, remarkable for its strictly classical and pagan character almost untouched by Christian motifs. He reconciles providence both morally with innocent suffering and logically with free will.

Boethius probably regretted the existence of the Goths and thought about them as little as he could. It was different for his contemporary Cassiodorus (*c.* 485–582). Cassiodorus not only held high office with success under Theodoric and his successors, but also compiled a long history of the Goths (of which an epitome by the Goth Jordanes survives). He realized the pressing need, created by the new situation of the barbarian settlements, for educational institutions, and even planned an institute of higher studies at Rome modelled on the schools of Alexandria and Nisibis. But Justinian's decision to drive the Goths out of Italy ended all Cassiodorus' hopes of Romanizing and civilizing the barbarians in a common Christian and classical culture. He retired to his picturesque estate at Squillace in Calabria to establish a monastic community called 'Vivarium' (fishpond), designed to be a centre of religious studies. The foundation was differentiated from others by the fact that Cassiodorus tried to give his community a specially learned character.

A few years earlier, about 529, Benedict of Nursia had founded his monastery at Monte Cassino in central Italy (above, p. 182). The Benedictine monks were enjoined to spend on manual labour such time as was not devoted to worship, divine reading, or meditation. No doubt some of this manual labour was devoted to producing copies of the Bible, or Cassian, or Basil, which were recommended reading in the Benedictine Rule. In the time of Cassian early in the fifth century, manual labour, which might well take the form of writing a biblical manuscript, was prescribed as a remedy against idleness which made the monk peculiarly vulnerable to diabolical attack.

In Cassiodorus' institution at Vivarium, however, this manual labour of copying manuscripts was to serve intellectual ends that were not narrowly religious. Vivarium was a lovely place with excellent fishing, conducive to pleasant recollection in tranquillity; and Cassiodorus' books were finely bound. He wanted his monks not merely to learn scripture by heart, as Benedict's might, but to understand it and expound it. Accordingly he laid down a course of secular studies according to a programme outlined by Augustine in his tract 'On Christian Doctrine'. The idea that a monastery could be an intellectual and educational centre was not quite new. In the Greek East it had long been usual for boys to be sent to monasteries for education. Shortly before Cassiodorus, a fervent admirer of Augustine named Eugippius, who had been associated with Severinus in establishing Christianity among the barbarian invaders in what is now Austria, had been abbot of a monastery at Lucullanum near Naples. Dionysius Exiguus (p. 245) translated for him some Gregory of Nyssa. But Cassiodorus critically remarked of Eugippius that 'he was not learned in secular literature'. It was a new thing that at Vivarium monks were directed to read Cicero, Quintilian, and Latin translations of Aristotle, Porphyry, and Galen.

In the Benedictine ideal the exclusive quest for God required detachment from all worldly studies and secular literature. The liberal humanism of Cassiodorus was eventually to be absorbed within the Benedictine tradition, in a confluence to which the Irish monks were to make some contribution, but it did not happen easily or quickly. When Pope Gregory the Great (540–604) renounced a distinguished secular career as prefect of Rome to become a monk, his model saint was Benedict of Nursia, whose biography he wrote in his *Dialogues* of 593. Gregory characteristically felt that conversion entailed turning his back on the world in all its forms, including literature. In the finely cut prose of his letters and sermons he seldom allowed himself a classical allusion, and his great achievements as pope (from 590) did not include the creation of a learned Roman clergy. Gregory's *Pastoral Rule* for clergy was other-worldly and monastic. It was only a late medieval legend which attributed to Gregory the destruction of the Palatine Library in Rome; but perhaps when he passed it he looked the other way.

It is at first astonishing to turn from Gregory the Great's letters, full of the common sense and wisdom of an experienced administrator, to his *Dialogues* with their portentous accounts of bizarre prodigies and visions of Italian saints. The extravagance (and the regional patriotism) of Sulpicius Severus' portrait of Martin of Tours had evidently come to outweigh the restraint and sobriety of John Cassian. Yet the *Dialogues*, so distasteful to a modern reader, also bring out one of the reasons why Gregory was the man for the times. As pope he contributed more than anyone to bridging the gulf between the sophisticated past of the Roman empire and the now barbarian society of the West. Uncompromising in his insistence on the otherworldly and supernatural, he also took it for granted that Christianity was in complete accord with the simple aspirations of very ordinary mortals without pretensions to high culture. He liked to send wonder-working relics, such as filings from St Peter's chains, to barbarian princes. Against puritan iconoclasts he vigorously defended pictures and images in churches which were 'the poor man's Bible'. He urged that the Church should take over old pagan temples and festivals and give them a Christian meaning. There is a deep consistency apparent in Gregory's unself-conscious identification of the church with the barbarian culture within which it now had to do its work in the West.

With the highly civilized society of the Byzantines Gregory's relations were never easy or relaxed. For six years (579–85) he had lived in Constantinople as resident representative of the Roman church. Yet in all that time he did not trouble to learn Greek, and never trusted the Greek Christians of whom he inherited the conventional Latin opinion that they were 'too clever to be honest'. Towards the patriarch of Constantinople he continued the traditional Roman attitude of cool suspicion; and when as pope he discovered that the patriarch was awarding himself the epithet 'ecumenical', a title which had admittedly been in regular use at Constantinople for nearly a century, Gregory violently protested that church dignitaries ought not to use honorific titles. His Chancery called him 'servant of the servants of God' (a phrase first used by Augustine in referring to his mother).

Italy in Gregory the Great's time was largely occupied by Lombard invaders, and the territory controlled by the Byzantine emperor's Exarch at Ravenna was relatively small. Rome, however, was a Byzantine city, and remained so through the seventh century. The pope was a subject of the emperor at Constantinople. But Gregory's personal prejudices were anti-Greek. He had also learnt from Augustine to think with a certain detachment about the connexion between the church and the empire. Above all, he recognized that the barbarian kingdoms of the West were not just transitory armies of occupation which would soon move on to other pastures, but a permanent social and political fact with which the church needed to come to terms. The Visigoths in Spain were now Catholic. In northern Gaul the Franks had been converted directly to Catholicism early in the sixth century, and in the view of bishop Gregory of Tours (c. 540–94), the historian of the Franks, their coming was a divine deliverance sent to rescue a decadent imperial society and to safeguard it from the corrupting Arianism of Theodoric and the Ostrogoths. It seemed natural for Gregory the Great to adopt an equally positive attitude to the Franks and Visigoths. Moreover, beyond them the pope could see the need for a mission to the pagan Anglo-Saxons in England.

Communications between Britain and the continent had been temporarily endangered by the great sweep of the barbarian tribes into Gaul and Spain during 407–9. Britain ceased to be a province within the empire and was left to fend for itself against the invading Picts and Scots, for which purpose the fateful decision was made to invoke the help of some Saxons. But it was some considerable time before the Saxon invaders swelled to such numbers that the British were driven entirely into the western parts of the island. In the first half of the fifth century at least, the British churches remained intact, causing anxiety to their Gallic brethren chiefly by their strong sympathies with Pelagius. The desire to correct this propensity to Pelagianism may have been among the motives which led Pope Celestine to send Palladius to be bishop among the Irish in 431, and it was certainly the need to crush Pelagianism which took bishop Germanus of Auxerre to England in 429 and again about twelve years later. Soon after Palladius' time Patrick was at work as a missionary bishop in Ireland, founding monastic communities. In his autobiographical Confession, written in awkward colloquial Latin, Patrick complained that in certain quarters he was unkindly criticized for his mediocre education; perhaps Ireland already possessed Christians with a superior Latin culture. At any rate by the sixth century the Irish monasteries were becoming notable centres of study, including not only theology but also grammar and a lively interest in the right methods of calculating the date of Easter, a matter in which the conservative and isolated Celts had come to differ from the churches of the mainland. In 563 the Irish monk Columba founded a monastery on Iona which extended the Christian mission to the wild tribes in Scotland. His Pictish mission was not the first such undertaking, since more than a century earlier Ninian seems to have established a mission church at Whithorn (Candida Casa) in Galloway. But the new monastery at Iona became an energetic centre for the diffusion of Christianity and the Celtic monastic ideals through Scotland and northern England.

In England and Wales the Saxon invaders gradually won the upper hand. The British Christians became divided by dissension, and about 540 a sombre picture of moral decline and administrative chaos was drawn by a deacon named Gildas. By the end of the sixth century the pagan kingdom of Kent, with its capital at Canterbury, dominated most of England south of the Humber. The Kentish king Ethelbert, however, married a Christian Frank. Pope Gregory saw in this the opportunity for a mission, and therefore sent the monk Augustine from Rome. On his way through Gaul Augustine appears to have been consecrated bishop; he landed at Thanet with a supporting body of monks, and proceeded to baptize Ethelbert and many of his people. It was a tribal conversion. Gregory's intention was that Augustine should establish the principal English bishoprics at the old Roman cities of London and York; but in practice the Kentish capital at Canterbury became and remained Augustine's see and chief missionary centre. Gradually, despite many obstacles and discouragements, the mission was extended to other parts of the country.

Tension was felt, however, between the new mission in Kent and the old communities of British Christians in the north and west. The Celts were deeply conservative about their method of calculating Easter and about the form of the tonsure, and disliked the different ways of Augustine and his clergy. Their relationship with the Kentish mission was soon complicated by the Northumbrian mission led by Aidan, a monk of Iona who founded his monastery at Lindisfarne in 635. In 657 Aidan's pupil, the abbess Hilda, established a double monastery, for men and for women, at Whitby. But at a synod in Whitby in 664 the Church in the north of England was persuaded to agree with the continental date for Easter, and was brought into line with Canterbury: 'Those who serve one God should observe a single rule of life and not be at variance in the celebration of the heavenly sacra-

ments.' Pope Gregory the Great, with his generously Augustinian views about the needlessness of liturgical uniformity,
might have found some of the statements made at Whitby
rather extreme; but it was an evident practical necessity that
the Celtic and Saxon churches inhabiting the same island
should be in harmony with one another and with the continent on so important a matter as Easter.

Harmony between the British and the mainly dominant
English had not been entirely achieved by 731, when the
learned and saintly monk Bede at Jarrow completed his
Church History of the English People. Accordingly, his great
work had a thesis: that the Church alone can provide the
cement capable of bonding the fractious tribes in different
parts of the British Isles, and indeed can remain united in
itself only with leadership from St Peter's successor in
Rome, to whose authority it has owed the founding of the
see of Canterbury. To persuade the Celtic Christians of this
truth required time. Axioms similar to Bede's operated in
the life of Bede's heroic contemporary Boniface of Crediton,
who took the gospel to Germany and whose apostolic
labours ended with his martyrdom in Frisia in 754.

18

Worship and Art

LITURGY

THE early Christians shared with the Jews the conviction
that 'religion' included an interpretation of the whole of
life, and was very far from being limited to a matter of cultic
acts and ceremonies. But they also shared with the Jews the
idea that God had given certain covenant signs of his grace.
The Christians regarded circumcision as a particular form
limited to Judaism and not intended to be binding on Gentile
Christians; but they kept the washing of baptism which had
been an important constituent in the ceremonies of the
admission of a Gentile proselyte to the Jewish synagogue.
The bread and wine of the Jewish passover and other sacred
meals were invested for the Church with an intense significance by their association with the Last Supper and the
Crucifixion when, as St Paul put it, 'Christ our passover was
sacrificed for us' (1 Cor. v, 7). One stream of language in
early Christian literature used to contrast Judaism as a
religion of externals with Christianity as a worship of God
'in spirit and in truth'. But the Christians were well aware
that if they were to be a society with a coherent community life they could not live on a purely individualistic
inwardness. They needed form and order, and they knew
that the visible signs of baptism and eucharist were *dona
data*, God's gifts to his church, *verba visibilia*, a visible actual-
ization of the very substance of the gospel.

As early as St Paul's time it was customary for the Christians to meet for worship on Sunday in commemoration of
the Lord's resurrection; and this weekly association of 'the
Lord's day' with the resurrection led in time to the transfer
of the annual celebration of Easter from the date of the Jewish
passover (Pascha) on the fourteenth day of the month Nisan

to the Sunday following it. (For the tensions this change produced, see above, p. 84.) Soon other observances of Jewish origin were general in the Church, such as Pentecost. By the fourth century the calendar included Ascension Day, and the nativity of Christ which the Greek East celebrated on 6 January, the West on 25 December (above, pp. 126, 214).

Like the Jews, the early Christians kept certain days for fasting. Jewish custom kept Mondays and Thursdays as fast days (cf. Luke xviii, 12 'I fast twice in the week'). By the end of the first century at least, the Christian fast days were Wednesdays and Fridays. A fast day was soon called a 'station', or day of military duty on the watch. In the 'Shepherd of Hermas' Christians were warned that on station days the fasting God required was abstinence from evil acts and desires. From the text of Mark ii, 20 it appeared that Christians should specially fast on the day 'when the bridegroom was taken away', i.e. in commemoration of the Passion. The fast immediately preceding the Easter festival became increasingly important, and included an all night vigil, soon with special Paschal candles. The pre-Paschal fast tended to lengthen. By the beginning of the fourth century the fast before Easter lasted seven days in the Greek East but forty days in the West. The forty-day Lent was first introduced to the Greek churches in 337 by Athanasius after his exile to the West (above, p. 135) in which he felt put to shame by the seriousness of Western austerity. As Easter was especially associated with baptism the period of Lent was used as a period of instruction during which the bishop would give lectures for catechumens. From the fourth century onwards the ceremonial structure of Holy Week evolved, first with the special observance of Maundy Thursday, then (by the sixth century) Palm Sunday, though a form of blessing of palms is not found before the ninth century. The custom of holding no celebration of the eucharist on Good Friday is found as early as 416 in Pope Innocent I's letter to the bishop of Gubbio (above, p. 240).[1]

1. In the sixth century the Byzantines had a special rite for Wednesdays and Fridays in Lent when they used elements consecrated on the preceding Sunday, hence called the Liturgy of the Presanctified.

The form and pattern of the actual rites used in the period before Constantine and the Nicene council can be known only very imperfectly from scraps and fragments of evidence often contained in casual passing allusions or in illustrations of an argument about other matters. The practice of baptism in North Africa in 200 is described by Tertullian. After a preparatory fast the ceremony began with an act of renunciation of the devil and his works and with a declaration of faith. It appears from other third-century evidence (Hippolytus, Cyprian) that this declaration took the form not of a declaratory creed but of a repeated answer 'I believe' to three interrogations concerning belief in Father, Son, and Holy Spirit respectively. At each answer the candidate was dipped in the water. After coming up from the font the candidate was anointed with oil and hands were laid on him with prayer for the gift of the Holy Spirit. He received milk and honey as tokens of his entry into the promised land. (There is evidence that a similar ceremony with milk and honey occurred in some pagan mystery rites, but the biblical typology dominated the Christian understanding of its meaning.) The sacrament was normally administered by a bishop or, with his leave, by a presbyter, or deacon, or exceptionally by a layman. At Rome, as in Africa, at this time the anointing was given after baptism in water. But this order was not universal. In third-century Syria, according to a church order entitled *Didascalia Apostolorum,* the anointing came before the baptismal washing. Or there might be two anointings, both before and after; or even three as in Hippolytus. The variation is no doubt evidence of hesitation about the status of the rite. But the oil as a sign of the gift of the Spirit was quite natural within a semitic framework, and therefore the ceremony is probably very early. Some Gnostic sects disparaged water baptism, and laid all the stress on 'the baptism of the Spirit' conferred by the holy anointing. In time the biblical meaning became obscured: Ambrose explained it to his catechumens as like the anointing of an athlete before running a race.

Although it was regarded, e.g. by the author of the *Didache,* as in principle desirable for baptism to take place at a river or lake, in practice well before the end of the first century it had become customary to baptize simply by pouring water on the candidate's head three times. The symbolism of partial immersion in running water, however, was preserved by constructing special baptisteries in the house churches or, after the fourth century, adjacent to the main church building. The candidates would descend a few steps and stand in water. The ceremony was one of the most intense solemnity, made more formidable by exorcisms. When baptism was given to the sick or to infants, care was necessary not to risk health, and accordingly water was poured on in very small quantities. Third-century evidence in the letters of Cyprian and elsewhere shows that some over-anxious believers were not quite sure of the true validity of sick-bed baptism, but Cyprian regarded such scruples as mistaken and superstitious. Baptism meant dying to sin and rising again to newness of life with Christ; therefore it was specially associated with Easter and Pentecost. For the same reason baptisteries were often octagonal, symbolizing the Lord's resurrection on the 'eighth day'. (For this number symbolism cf. 1 Peter iii, 20.)

The earliest second-century texts (*Didache*, Ignatius of Antioch, Justin Martyr) agree that the regular Sunday worship of the Christians was first and foremost 'thanksgiving', *eucharistia*, a term which gradually replaced the more primitive term 'breaking of bread'. The Greek word *eucharistia* became so technical a word for the service that it passed into Christian Latin in transliteration, though the Latin Christians also spoke of it as a giving of thanks, *gratiarum actio*, and *agere* came to mean 'celebrate'. Hence the Western title for the great eucharistic prayer, *canon actionis* or 'rule of celebrating'.

Except among the Gnostic sects who were notoriously casual about such matters, only the baptized were admitted to the sacred meal. The Roman eucharist of 150 is described by Justin Martyr in a passage intended to reassure pagan readers that Christian rites are not black magic. After readings from 'the memoirs of the apostles' and from the Old Testament prophets, the president (evidently the bishop) preached a sermon, at the end of which everyone stood for a solemn prayer ending in the kiss of peace. Then bread and 'a cup of water and of wine mixed with water' were brought to the president who 'to the best of his ability' offered a prayer of thanks to the Father through the Son and Holy Spirit, concluding with the people signifying their ratification by the word *Amen*. Justin parenthetically explains for his uninitiated readers that the Christians are accustomed to use this Hebrew word meaning *So be it*. The communion followed at which each person partook of the bread and wine distributed to them by deacons, and received it not as common food for satisfying hunger and thirst, but as the flesh and blood of Christ. Finally pieces of the sacred bread were taken round to the sick and those in prison. It is clear that, although attending the service meant risking one's life or liberty, all Christians regarded it as an absolute obligation to be present each Sunday if it was in their power. Justin saw in the universal Christian custom of a weekly eucharist a direct fulfilment of the prophecy of Malachi i, 10 that in every place a pure sacrifice would be offered to the Lord from the rising of the sun to its setting.

Justin's presiding bishop was entirely free in the wording he chose for the great prayer of thanksgiving. There was no prescribed form of words. Nevertheless there was evidently an expected pattern of themes which were going to crystallize out into prepared forms. As early as the *Didache* such forms, no doubt intended to serve as models, were being provided. After the *Didache* the earliest extant forms of prayer, other than the briefest fragments, are preserved in the *Apostolic Tradition* of Hippolytus, a church order specifically mentioned on the statue erected in his honour (above p. 89). The text of this work does not survive exactly as Hippolytus wrote it, and has to be painfully reconstructed from later compilations which drew upon it, in particular from a Latin version of about 400 preserved in a manuscript at Verona written *c.* 494, from Coptic, Arabic, and Ethiopic adaptations which used an early (lost) Coptic translation, and from later church orders, written in the name of the Lord or the apostles, which borrowed material from it (notably the late fourth-century *Apostolic Constitutions* and the fifth-century *Testament of the Lord*).

Hippolytus begins the *Apostolic Tradition* by explaining that because of certain grave irregularities on the part of an irresponsible authority (probably Callistus is in mind) he has felt it urgently necessary to lay down norms of usage for church practice. Even so, Hippolytus does not expect a celebrant at the eucharist to adhere rigidly to his form of words:

It is not at all necessary for the bishop in giving thanks to recite the same words as we have given as if they were to be learnt by heart. But let each pray according to his capacity. If he can pray in a long and solemn prayer, it is good. But if in his prayer he prays at modest length, no one may prevent him, provided only that his prayer is orthodox.

Certain fixed forms were a necessity if the congregation was to join in, as in the prefatory dialogue between celebrant and people immediately preceding the great prayer of thanksgiving. As Hippolytus' prayer is so early an example, it deserves to be quoted in full:

BISHOP: The Lord be with you.
PEOPLE: And with your spirit.
BISHOP: Lift up your hearts.
PEOPLE: We lift them to the Lord.
BISHOP: Let us give thanks to the Lord.
PEOPLE: It is meet and right.
BISHOP: We give you thanks, O God, through your beloved Son
  Jesus Christ, whom in the last times you sent to us as saviour
  and redeemer and as angel [i.e. messenger] of your will, who
  is your inseparable Word, through whom you made all things,
  and whom by your good pleasure you sent from heaven to a
  Virgin's womb, who was conceived and was made flesh and
  was manifested as your Son, born of the Holy Spirit and the
  Virgin;
    Who, fulfilling your will and procuring for you a holy people,
  stretched out his hands when he suffered that he might free
  from suffering those who have believed in you;
    Who, when he was betrayed to a voluntary passion to des-
  troy death and break the devil's chains, to tread down hell and

lead the just to light, to fix hell's limit and to manifest the resurrection, took bread and gave thanks to you and said: Take, eat, this is my body which is broken for you. Likewise also the cup, saying: This is my blood which is shed for you. When you do this, do it in remembrance of me.

Remembering therefore his death and resurrection, we offer you this bread and cup, giving you thanks that you have counted us worthy to stand before you and minister to you as priests.

And we beseech you to send your Holy Spirit on the offering of the Holy Church. Gather them together and grant that all who partake of the holy things may be filled with the Holy Spirit for the confirmation of their faith in the truth, that we may laud and glorify you through your Son Jesus Christ, through whom be glory and honour to you, Father and Son with the Holy Spirit, in your holy church, both now and for ever, Amen.

The invocation of the Spirit in the final paragraph has been much debated, and this is one of the points where it has been argued that Hippolytus could not have written this and that the wording of the invocation reflects fourth-century developments. For in the Greek churches of the fourth century the invocation of the Spirit (or *epiclesis*) became very prominent, and any eucharistic prayer that lacked such an invocation would be likely to have one inserted. There are, however, weighty arguments to counter these sceptical doubts. First, the Latin and Ethiopic versions are unanimous witnesses to the text; and while the crucial sentence, 'we beseech you to send your Holy Spirit on the offering', is absent from the fifth century *Testament of the Lord* which in all other respects incorporates Hippolytus' prayer, the author of the *Testament* may have had special motives for omitting the clause. Secondly, the words are more an invocation of the Spirit on the action of the church in making the offering than an invocation on the bread and wine in themselves, and contain nothing that a theologian of 200–220 could not have said. Twenty years before, Irenaeus had written of the invocation of the divine Word by which the bread and wine ceased to be ordinary food and drink. Thirdly, when the late fourth-century author of the *Apostolic Constitutions* drew on Hippolytus, he took over much of the prayer but felt it necessary to modernize it at precisely this place, adding the supplement: 'And we beseech you to look kindly on the gifts placed before you, O God in need of nothing . . . and send down your Holy Spirit on the sacrifice, the witness of the sufferings of the Lord Jesus, that he [i.e. the Spirit] may make this bread the body of your Christ and this cup the blood of your Christ'. The fact that he had to abandon the original formula of Hippolytus at the critical moment is significant; it brings out the point that no fourth-century reviser or interpolator would have composed an *epiclesis* in a form that to his age would have seemed very inadequate and old-fashioned theology.

The importance of the invocation of the Spirit in the great eucharistic prayer or *anaphora* is mentioned by several Greek writers of the latter half of the fourth century as being the principal moment in the action of the service (e.g. Cyril of Jerusalem, Basil of Caesarea, and Theophilus of Alexandria). An unusual instance occurs in an anaphora ascribed by the manuscript tradition (viz. an eleventh-century codex on Mount Athos) to Serapion bishop of Thmuis, friend and correspondent of Athanasius of Alexandria, and certainly belonging to some church in fourth-century Egypt, where neither Arianism nor Nicene theology had influenced the language of worship. Here the prayer is, first, that the divine Word may come upon the elements 'that the bread may become the body of the Word' and 'that the cup may become the blood of the Truth', and, secondly, that all the communicants may receive the medicine of life to their benefit and not to their condemnation.

Besides the invocation of the Spirit there are several other points worthy of notice in Hippolytus' eucharistic prayer. There is the direct link with the Last Supper made by the recital of the words of institution, which occur in a relative clause, a formal feature which recurs in both Eastern and Western liturgies and was a mark of deep solemnity. Hippolytus has no *Sanctus*.[1] The three-fold angelic hymn is quoted

1. It has been conjectured that the original text had a *Sanctus* where the Epiclesis now stands, but there is no solid basis for this guess in the ancient texts.

from Isaiah in the letter of Clement of Rome to the Corinthians to illustrate the harmony of the heavenly host which the Corinthians are enjoined to imitate, but there is no evidence that for either Clement or Hippolytus the *Sanctus* was a necessary constituent of the Roman liturgy. As late as 400 the use of the *Sanctus* was much less widespread in the West than in the East, and the later Roman tradition marked the canon of the mass as beginning *after* the *Sanctus*, which might be taken to suggest that it was an addition to a previously composed structure. Hippolytus also makes repeated statements that the sacred bread and wine are 'antitypes' or figures of the body and blood of the Lord – language also found in Tertullian. Hippolytus accordingly enjoins on the faithful intense reverence for the eucharist. It should be received early before any other food, and the greatest care should be taken to see that nothing was dropped or spilt. At this period it was common for pieces of the eucharistic bread to be taken home and received privately, after daily prayers, during the week. Hippolytus had to warn communicants against leaving the sacred bread about the house where an unbaptized person, or even a mouse, might accidentally eat it.

As the congregations swelled in size during the fourth century, so the liturgy tended to be extended. Sometimes these enlargements could go to enormous lengths, as in the eucharistic formulas provided in the eighth book of the *Apostolic Constitutions*. Often older prayers were expanded by inserting biblical quotations – so that it is a paradoxical law of early liturgical study that the greater the biblical element in any given prayer the less primitive it is likely to be. In the Greek East in the second half of the fourth century ceremonial began to become quite elaborate. Greek clergy began to wear ornate clothes, and the ritual acquired a high dramatic splendour. At the same time the pressure of the multitude joining the church, and perhaps also the struggle against Arianism, led to a marked insistence on holy awe and on the transcendent wonder of the eucharistic action. The catechetical lectures of Cyril of Jerusalem, about 350, show both the beginnings of elaboration in ceremonial and also the emphasis on the intense awe appropriate for the rite. Cyril provides the earliest evidence for the introduction of the symbolic washing of the celebrant's hands (*lavabo*), and for the use of the Lord's Prayer at the conclusion of the great eucharistic prayer (a use which in Augustine's time was almost universal). Cyril gives elaborate instructions to prevent any irreverent dropping at the communion: the communicants are directed to receive the bread in hollowed palms, the left hand supporting the right. Above all, Cyril repeatedly mentions the solemn invocation of the Spirit by which, to faith, the bread and wine become Christ's body and blood, and speaks several times of the 'fearful' presence upon the holy Table.

This attitude of fear and trembling is even more prominent in Basil of Caesarea and especially in John Chrysostom who speaks of the Lord's Table as a place of 'terror and shuddering'. The eucharistic rite described in the recently discovered catechetical lectures of Theodore of Mopsuestia was marked by the most advanced ritual splendour. Important consequences followed from these developments. Before the end of the fourth century in the East it began to be thought necessary to screen off the holy Table by curtains. When Justinian's great church of Sancta Sophia was built in the sixth century, there was not only a gorgeous curtain before the canopied altar, embroidered in gold with a figure of Christ Pantokrator blessing his people and holding the gospel book in his left hand, but also a screen with three doors on which were figures of angels and prophets and the monograms of Justinian and Theodora over the central door. This was the first iconostasis, so copied elsewhere[1] that it became a necessary feature of all Greek churches. The doors in the screen were used for ceremonial 'Entrances' at the reading of the Gospel and the Offertory.

The later fourth century also saw great enrichment in the ornaments and vessels. At Antioch in John Chrysostom's time the church possessed finely wrought chalices, candelabra,

1. Compare the influence in the West of the 'barley-sugar' columns supporting the altar canopy in Constantine's church of St Peter's, Rome.

silk veils, white vestments, and sometimes silver-work decorating the altar itself. At Thessalonica early in the fifth century a church was built, dedicated to St Demetrius, with a fine silver canopy over the altar.

In the West liturgical elaboration proceeded considerably more slowly. Moreover, it was not until the latter part of the fourth century that the Western liturgy began to develop a life of its own; for until the time of Damasus the eucharist at the city of Rome had continued to be celebrated in Greek, so great was the influence of conservatism from the days when the Roman community had been wholly Greek-speaking. The earliest evidence for the order and formulae of the early Latin mass, apart from a few allusions in Tertullian and Cyprian, is found in Ambrose of Milan, whose lectures to catechumens 'On the Sacraments' were preserved by the private enterprise of an anonymous stenographer (above, p. 241). In this work Ambrose quotes the principal eucharistic prayer in customary use at Milan in his time. It is noteworthy that, in contrast to Cyril of Jerusalem with his emphasis on the invocation of the Holy Spirit as the decisive moment of consecration when the elements of bread and wine were transformed, Ambrose places all his stress upon the effect of the recitation of the dominical words of institution. As Ambrose's formulae are akin to those which later became a fixed part of the canon of the Latin mass,[1] they deserve quotation. After praises to God[2] and 'intercessions for the people, for kings, and the rest', the celebrant continues:

Grant to us that this offering be approved, spiritual, and acceptable, as the figure of the body and blood of Our Lord Jesus Christ; who the day before he suffered took bread in his holy hands, looked up to heaven, to you, holy Father, Almighty, everlasting God; giving thanks he blessed, broke, and gave the broken bread to his apostles and disciples saying, All of you take and eat this; for this is my body which is broken for many. Likewise also after supper the day before he suffered he took the cup, looked up

1. *Missa* = (a) dismissal (of soldiers); (b) by 400, any act of public worship; (c) by 800, 'mass', because of its dismissal formula, *Ite missa est.*

2. These may have included the *Sanctus*, but Ambrose does not mention this.

to heaven, to you holy Father, Almighty, everlasting God; giving thanks he blessed and gave it to his apostles and disciples saying, All of you take and drink of this, for this is my blood. As often as you do this, so often will you make my memorial until I come again.

Therefore remembering his most glorious passion and resurrection from the dead and ascension into heaven, we offer to you this unspotted victim, a spiritual victim, an unbloody victim, this holy bread and the cup of eternal life.

And we pray and beseech you to accept this oblation by the hand of your angels, as you deigned to accept the gifts of your servant, righteous Abel, and the offering made to you by the high priest Melchizedek.

Ambrose's prayer corresponds in plan and partly even in actual wording to the central core of the later Roman mass as it appears in the eighth century, which contains an expanded and modified version of the same basic formulae in the *Quam oblationem, Qui pridie, Unde et memores, Supra quae,* and *Supplices.* But his prayer that the offering be approved was expanded into a longer form in the *Te igitur* with which the Roman canon begins, a restatement of the offertory in which the priest asks that God will accept and bless the gifts offered and will grant peace and unity to the church.

Although Ambrose goes on to expound the Lord's Prayer in what follows, he does not make it explicit whether this had its place at the conclusion of the great eucharistic prayer. But since Augustine records that this practice was almost universal in his time, and since Augustine was very familiar with Milanese use, it is as good as certain that Ambrose was familiar with this custom. Two allusions in Jerome and Augustine strongly suggest that the Lord's Prayer was commonly introduced by the words '... we are bold to say' (*audemus dicere*).

Accordingly the basic elements and structure of the Roman liturgy were fixed in the period from Damasus to Leo the Great. But the earlier part of the service was still fluid. Two notable modifications to this introductory part, before the dismissal of the catechumens, were made under Eastern influence. By 500 the *Kyrie Eleison,* which formed a regular part of Greek litanies in the time of Egeria's pilgrimage to the Holy Places about 384, had been incorporated in the first part of the Latin mass, and, curiously, kept as a Greek formula, untranslated. The *Gloria in excelsis* was a Greek hymn, first attested in the *Apostolic Constitutions,* which had long been in use in the East without forming part of the eucharistic liturgy (like the *Te Deum* in the West);[1] it began to find its way into the text of the mass on special occasions by 500, though it did not achieve universal use in the West for another six hundred years.

The Creed properly belonged to baptism and made a late appearance in the eucharistic liturgy. In any event the Western baptismal creed was the so-called 'Apostles' Creed', while the Greek East used for baptism the Nicene creed of 325. Local baptismal creeds in the Greek East long continued to be used after 325, but orthodox bishops inserted the principal Nicene terms. So it was that at Constantinople in 381 there lay before the council called by Theodosius (above, p. 150) a formula which was called Nicene, because it contained the assertion that the Son is identical in substance with the Father, but had in fact derived its basic structure from a local baptismal creed perhaps already in use. This Nicene-Constantinopolitan creed first entered the eucharistic liturgy in unusual circumstances. The fifth-century Monophysites inserted it as a dramatic public protest against the 'innovations' of the council of Chalcedon. The Chalcedonians simply answered this exclusive claim to a monopoly of orthodoxy by making the same insertion. Gradually the custom of including the Nicene-Constantinopolitan creed in the eucharist spread to the West, but it only began to become important under Charlemagne who was anxious to lay great emphasis on the Western *Filioque* (above, p. 236). At this time the creed found its central position after the reading of the Gospel.

Two other late additions to the Latin mass were the appending of the *Benedictus* to the *Sanctus* during the sixth century,

1. The first use of the *Te Deum* is found at Arles under Caesarius (d. 542), but it is certainly older, probably a remaking of a third-century hymn cited by Cyprian. The authorship of the *Te Deum* is unknown.

and the *Agnus Dei* which appeared by the end of the seventh century.

The early Western liturgy owed something to Greek models, which was natural enough. For example, the *Supra quae* and *Supplices* of the Roman canon and the closely related formula of Ambrose (above, p. 269) asking that God would accept the sacrifice brought by his holy angel, as he had once accepted the gifts of Abel and Abraham, are very closely paralleled in the Alexandrian Liturgy of St Mark (which also places the formula immediately before the commemoration of the faithful departed). But it was likewise very natural that there should be wide varieties of regional usage. There is no reason to suppose that such varieties had not always existed from the beginning – the quest for an original, universally observed 'apostolic liturgy' is a mirage. Yet in both East and West diversity of custom in such sacred matters was felt by some to be a difficulty. By the seventh century it had become usual to employ unleavened bread for the Western eucharist, while the Greek East (except for the Armenians, whose history on this point is lost in obscurity) used ordinary leavened bread. In time this diversity was to become a matter of controversy. Another difference of practice was that in the East it was usual to have only one celebration of the eucharist under the bishop on a Sunday; in the West there gradually spread from the city of Rome the practice of holding celebrations taken by presbyters in suburban parish churches, which in fourth-century Rome were called 'title-churches' because they bore the names of the original donors of the title to the property and provided for the maintenance of the clergy by their endowments.

Beside the main Sunday eucharist it was customary by 400, at least in important cities, for the eucharist to be celebrated daily. From the third century the anniversary of a martyr's death, called his 'birthday', was commemorated at his grave by a celebration. At first the veneration of the majority of the martyrs was a matter of private devotion which was then taken over by central authority as it became popular. Special prayers began to be composed for these lesser feasts, and were collected. An early seventh-century manuscript in the Verona Cathedral library contains the earliest extant collection of Latin prayers, the compiler of which seems to have had at least two earlier collections before him originating in the city of Rome. The modern ascription of this sacramentary to Leo the Great is unsupported by the Verona manuscript and is impossible; but some of the liturgical material it contains certainly goes back to the time of Leo, since one of his Embertide sermons (no. 78) contains numerous allusions to formulas of prayer found in the later sacramentary. Leo may have written some of these prayers.

DAILY OFFICES

In addition to the Sunday eucharist, participation in which was an indispensable sign of church membership, and the special celebrations on the days of saints and martyrs usually supported by smaller groups, there were also daily private prayers. Hippolytus in the *Apostolic Tradition* directed that Christians should pray seven times a day – on rising, at the lighting of the evening lamp, at bedtime, at midnight, and also, if at home, at the third, sixth and ninth hours of the day, being hours associated with Christ's Passion. Prayers at the third, sixth, and ninth hours are similarly mentioned by Tertullian, Cyprian, Clement of Alexandria and Origen, and must have been very widely practised. These prayers were commonly associated with private Bible reading in the family. Of these times of private prayer two gradually became more corporate in character, so that by 400 it became common, at least on certain days in the week, for the morning and evening prayers to be taken by the clergy in the church building. Egeria (above, p. 240) vividly describes the solemnity and large attendance at daily morning and evening prayers in Jerusalem.

In ascetic communities the cycle of offices was fuller. The hours of prayer were shaped into an obligatory and institutional system in the rules for ascetic communities. In Basil the Great's Rule there were eight offices; but John Cassian had only seven at Marseilles – in accordance with the Psalmist's practice, 'Seven times a day will I praise thee'.

At Rome about 500 the daily offices numbered six. The basic material for the monastic office was provided by the Psalter, and the clergy in Rome developed a system whereby the Psalter was recited in full once a week, with Psalm 119 (118) providing for Terce, Sext, and None. They also had an ordered cycle of lections. This Roman system was taken over in the Benedictine Rule, but Benedict added the dawn office of Prime and the final office at the completion of the day (Compline, *Completorium*). It was usual to begin the night office with 'O God make speed to save me, O Lord make haste to help me', with the *Gloria Patri*, and with 'O Lord open thou my lips, and my mouth shall show forth thy praise'. Benedict also added the hymns of Ambrose as insertions in the offices, and prescribed the *Te Deum* for the vigil of the Lord's Day and the *Benedictus* and *Benedicite* for Lauds. The widespread use of the *Benedicite* in the devotions of the Greek East is attested in John Chrysostom. The Greek use of the *Nunc Dimittis* for evening prayers is mentioned in the fourth-century *Apostolic Constitutions*, but it did not form a part of Benedict's Compline and only later found its way into the Roman office. At Arles in the time of bishop Caesarius early in the sixth century the *Magnificat* was being used at mattins, and appears there also in seventh-century Ireland in the Book of Mulling, an Irish gospel book now in the library of Trinity College, Dublin. It is probable that Benedict's monks used the *Magnificat* at Vespers for which his Rule prescribes a 'Gospel Canticle'.

EARLY CHURCH MUSIC

Twice in the letters of St Paul (Col. iii, 16, Eph. v, 19) we find allusions to the use of singing in worship. As singing and chanting were already the custom of the synagogue there can be no surprise here. Philo of Alexandria describes the developed musical life of the ascetic community, the Therapeutae, near Alexandria. He says that they wrote hymns in all manner of metres and tunes, with notation to indicate that the rhythm was to be of a solemn character fitting for sacred music. They had choirs of both men and women, chanting sometimes in harmony, sometimes antiphonally. It is likely enough that the first Christian chants were simply taken over from synagogue usage. This helps to explain, for example, the continued use of the untranslated Hebrew word 'Alleluia' for a chant of praise. A passing hostile comment in the second-century pagan critic Celsus shows that the chants used in Christian worship (which he seems to have heard) were not only unusual to his pagan ears but so beautiful that he actually resented their emotive effect as an instrument for dulling the critical faculty.

A few Greek hymns survive from the period before Constantine (besides a special hymn by Clement of Alexandria, which may not have been intended for liturgical use). One is a rollicking second-century hymn of joy, which may well have been sung at the Paschal vigil since it takes the form of a wedding hymn of exultation that the lost bridegroom has been found. It runs:

V. Praise the Father, you holy ones. Sing to the Mother, you virgins.
R. We praise. We the holy ones extol them.
V. Be exalted, brides and bridegrooms; for you have found your bridegroom, Christ. Drink your wine, brides and bridegrooms.

Secondly, there is a mutilated strip of third-century papyrus from Egypt on which is preserved an anapaestic hymn where all the creation joins the church in praising the Trinity: 'While we hymn Father, Son and Holy Spirit, let all creation sing Amen, Amen. Praise, power to the sole giver of all good things. Amen, Amen.' This papyrus is of quite exceptional interest since the scribe noted down the music of the chant and provided dynamic signs which can be deciphered with the help of analogies in later Byzantine texts.

A third early example is the evening hymn, established in general use in the time of Basil the Great and still forming a part of Greek Vespers, sung at the lighting of the evening lamp. John Keble's translation is remarkably literal and accurate:

> Hail, gladdening Light, of his pure glory poured
> Who is the immortal Father, heavenly, blest,
> Holiest of Holies, Jesus Christ our Lord.

Now we are come to the sun's hour of rest,
The lights of evening round us shine,
We hymn the Father, Son and Holy Spirit divine.
Worthiest art thou at all times to be sung
With undefiled tongue,
Son of our God, giver of life, alone:
Therefore in all the world thy glories, Lord, they own.

Clement of Alexandria is the earliest Christian writer to discuss what kind of music is appropriate for Christian use. He directs that it should not be the kind associated with erotic dance music; the melodies should avoid chromatic intervals and should be austere. Perhaps he had in mind some of the Gnostic sects among whom there would probably have been much less sense of inhibition and restraint. The second-century *Acts of John* preserve a Gnostic hymn intended to be chanted during a ritual dance (familiar to modern English choirs as providing the words for Gustav Holst's *Hymn of Jesus*); but in orthodox eyes dancing did not succeed in becoming a natural and approved vehicle of religious expression, except in Ethiopia.[1]

As choirs grew in size, it became possible to have two groups of singers chanting alternately. This practice of antiphonal singing came in during the second half of the fourth century. It spread across from Mesopotamia and Syria, and may perhaps have owed something to synagogue precedents. One of Basil the Great's letters is devoted to a defence of his boldness in introducing the practice at Cappadocian Caesarea in face of outraged conservatism. It is very possible that Ambrose's hymns at Milan were sung antiphonally.

The use of music in worship was not quite universally approved. In the fourth century a few strong-minded puritans wanted to exclude it altogether, and found a measure of

1. Sacred dances were acceptable both in the Jewish tradition (as many Old Testament passages illustrate) and in, for example, the pagan mysteries of Dionysus. But among the Christians they appear either in fringe sects, such as the Melitians in Egypt, or in the exciting popular carnivals on the feasts of martyrs, concerning which Basil the Great, Ambrose, and Augustine express anxious disapproval. As for ballet as an art form, in antiquity this was vulgar, aggressively erotic, and the object of censure to pagan intellectuals like Libanius, Julian, and Macrobius, as well as to moralists like John Chrysostom.

support from those who felt that the chanting obscured the meaning of the words. Athanasius of Alexandria tried to meet the difficulty by demanding speech rhythm in chanting the psalms. On the other hand, the musicians had their chance with the singing of the Alleluia, the performance of which became quite long and elaborate. In his *Confessions* Augustine records how moving he found the psalm chants in use at Milan, observing that, while he felt guilty of a grave fault if he found the music more important to him than the words, he knew that the words were invested with a far greater power to come home to the mind when they were associated with music of haunting beauty. Augustine observes that there is no emotion of the human spirit which music is incapable of expressing, and that it is excessive austerity to exclude it from church services.

What music the early Christians sang can hardly be told. Only a solitary specimen, the third-century Egyptian papyrus already mentioned, has been preserved. The surviving Greek and Latin manuscripts containing musical notation belong to the medieval period. It is highly probable that the singing in the great centres like Jerusalem, Alexandria, Antioch, Constantinople, and Rome, provided a model for the imitation of smaller towns. By the end of the sixth century the chanting practised at the city of Rome had become a model for other Western churches; and by the ninth century responsibility for the invention of the Roman system came to be ascribed to Pope Gregory the Great, so that the local Roman chants were known as 'Gregorian'.

By a comparable process many of the hymns used in the Western churches quietly became ascribed to Ambrose. There were also other poets whose hymns achieved wide recognition. Venantius Fortunatus (540–600), bishop of Poitiers, wrote hymns of genuine sensitivity and pathos – *Vexilla Regis*, *Pangue Lingua*, and *Salve Festa Dies* remain in use today. Rather earlier in the sixth century at Constantinople there lived the greatest hymn-writer of the Eastern churches, Romanos, who died soon after 555. A converted Jew, he came to Constantinople from Syria and wrote hymns for Justinian's splendid foundations in the capital. He created the Kontakion,[1] an acrostic verse sermon of many stanzas, each stanza being sung from the pulpit by a soloist with an answering refrain from the choir. Romanos partly inspired the author of the most famous of Greek Lenten hymns, the so-called *Akathistos* (i.e. to be sung standing) in honour of the Blessed Virgin.

CHRISTIAN ART[2]

The second of the Ten Commandments forbade the making of any graven image. Both Tertullian and Clement of Alexandria regarded this prohibition as absolute and binding on Christians. Images and cultic statues belonged to the demonic world of paganism. In fact, the only second-century Christians known to have had images of Christ were radical Gnostics, the followers of the licentious Carpocrates. If the emperor Alexander Severus actually had a private chapel with statues of Orpheus, Abraham, Apollonius and Christ, as he is uncertainly reported to have done (above, p. 110), it must have given a bitter-sweet gratification to his Christian subjects. Yet before the end of the second century Christians were freely expressing their faith in artistic terms. Tertullian mentions cups on which there were representations of the Good Shepherd carrying his sheep. Clement of Alexandria gives instruction about the picture appropriate for a Christian's signet ring. In antiquity signet rings were not a luxury, but indispensable for correspondence. Clement recommends that Christians should use seals with representations that, without being specifically Christian, are readily capable of a Christian interpretation, such as a dove, a fish, a ship, a lyre, or an anchor. They should avoid seals with symbols suggesting idolatry or drink or erotic passion. It is noteworthy that Clement's suggestions for appropriate seals are all types that a pagan might use; that is, they are neutral from a

1. The Kontakion got its name in the ninth century from the rod (*kontos*) round which the text was rolled.
2. The scope of this brief history does not include illustrations. Much can be found in e.g. W. F. Volbach, *Early Christian Art*; D. Talbot Rice, *The Art of Byzantium*, etc.

religious or moral point of view, and either pagans or
Christians could happily use them. Likewise the Good Shepherd carrying his sheep was a conventional pagan symbol of
humanitarian concern, *philanthropia*. The Christians were
taking a common type and investing it with a new meaning
possibly with reference to Christ the good shepherd of his
sheep (John x). Another conventional type which the Christians soon began to use was the 'Orans', the figure with
hands uplifted in prayer.

It was the same story with church buildings. The first
Christian churches were ordinary private houses, and remained so until the time of Constantine. When the time came
for the church building to acquire a 'public' character, the
architects used existing forms, such as the rectangular basilica
with an apse. The conventional form was so filled with new
content that an optical illusion was created that the basilica,
or the Good Shepherd, or the Orans type was distinctively
Christian. But this was not at first the case at all.

Early Christian paintings first appear not in churches but
as funerary decoration in the Roman catacombs. The style
of painting is not dissimilar to that found on many ordinary
pagan houses at Pompeii. Human beings are in nothing so
conservative as in funeral customs, and in the decoration of
tombs and sarcophagi many of the conventions of the pagan
workshop were simply continued. It would be extremely surprising if anything else had happened. Catacomb art is full
of old motifs and, since the technique and style are popular,
no large aesthetic claims can be made for it. The content,
however, is of much greater interest than the form. The motifs
of pagan convention which the Christians used were symbols
which were capable of Christian reinterpretation. The four
seasons might suggest life from death. The peacock symbolized immortality, the dove peace hereafter; above all the
fish, the Greek word for which (*IXΘYC*) formed an acrostic
'Jesus Christ Son of God Saviour', was a favourite Christian
emblem, especially of the eucharist. About 182 the Phrygian
bishop Abercius (or Avircius) of Hieropolis wrote his own
epitaph containing his autobiography. 'A disciple of the
pure Shepherd', he explains, he had visited the Roman

church, 'a golden-robed and golden-sandalled queen', and had also travelled through Syria to Nisibis; everywhere he had found brethren – 'with Paul before me I followed, and faith everywhere led the way and served food everywhere, the Fish from the spring, immense, pure, which the pure Virgin caught and gave to her friends to eat for ever, with good wine, giving the cup with the loaf'. It was part of the same group of angling or nautical symbols when the Christians used anchors in paintings or in the design of sarcophagi. The epistle to the Hebrews had spoken of hope as the anchor of the soul. Or the journey through life could naturally be compared to a storm-tossed voyage ending in the heavenly harbour.

But besides these themes and symbols which a Christian would understand but which a pagan would not read with the same meaning, there were certainly paintings with biblical scenes: Adam and Eve, Noah's ark, the sacrifice of Isaac, Moses striking water from the rock, Jonah and the great fish, Daniel in the lion's den, the three young men in the burning fiery furnace, and others. The favourite New Testament themes were the baptism of the Lord, the Paralytic carrying his bed or being let down through the roof of the house to Jesus, the Samaritan woman at the well, the raising of Lazarus, and Peter walking on the water. The earliest known example of a church with such pictures on the walls is the third-century house church at Dura on the Euphrates, where a private house built in the first century A.D. was adapted for Christian use in the year 232. This little house church was rather overshadowed at Dura by a large and opulent Jewish synagogue nearby, the walls of which were splendidly decorated with Old Testament scenes and figures. The Dura synagogue proves conclusively that the Jews could have elaborate decoration in their synagogues if they wished, and probably early Christian representations of biblical scenes owed much to Jewish models. It is probably significant that in the choice of biblical scenes favoured by the early Christian artists Old Testament subjects outnumber New Testament scenes in the period before Constantine. One particular example of Jewish precedent may be

given. The Phrygian town of Apamea had a Jewish population which disregarded the claims of Ararat to be the site
where Noah's ark ran aground and affirmed that on a hill
near their city they had the very remains of the ark itself.
(The place was among the sites visited by that curious trav-
eller and antiquarian, Julius Africanus – above, p. 103).
Late in the second century and early in the third, the town
mint of Apamea issued a series of coins portraying Noah and
his ark. The type so very closely resembles the manner in
which Noah is portrayed in Christian catacomb art that it is
very difficult to deny a connexion. Probably, therefore,
other Old Testament scenes in early Christian art were taken
from Jewish models.

With the conversion of Constantine the Church no longer
had to be reticent in expressing its faith. Churches became
public buildings. In architecture, sculpture, mosaic decoration, and in paintings the symbols of Christianity and the
themes of the gospel provided a rich material for artistic
expression, and some of the greatest achievements in the
civilization of late antiquity lie in the realm of art. But the
process had already begun within the church even before
Constantine appeared. The Spanish council of Elvira recorded its shocked disapproval of some churches with paintings on the walls, but the fact that such places existed was
not suppressed, and the tide became a flood in the course of
the fourth century.

Nevertheless, the older puritanism was not stifled or killed.
About 327 the learned historian Eusebius of Caesarea received a letter from the emperor's sister Constantia asking
him for a picture of Christ. She evidently supposed that an
authentic likeness was more likely to be obtainable in Palestine than elsewhere. Eusebius wrote her a very stern reply.
He was well aware that one could find pictures of Christ
and of the apostles. They were for sale in the bazaars of
Palestine, and he had himself seen them. But Eusebius did
not think the painters and shopkeepers selling these memen-
toes to pilgrims were Christians at all. Similarly at Caesarea
Philippi he had seen a group of bronze statuary in which a
woman bending on one knee stretched out her hand as a

suppliant to a standing man whose hand reached towards her. From Eusebius' description the group was evidently a type familiar on Hadrian's coins, showing the emperor restoring rights to his provinces. By 300, however, Hadrian was forgotten. The citizens of Caesarea Philippi were now interpreting the bronze pair to represent Jesus healing the woman with the issue of blood, and could even show visitors the house where she lived. (This interpretation of the Hadrianic statues, which adorned a fountain in a public square, was so widely accepted that under Julian they were damaged by pagan vandals.) The story told by Eusebius has an incidental interest in marking the first step towards the creation of the medieval legend of Veronica.[1] His own attitude to the statues is one of sympathetic interest, but takes it for granted that only pagan artists would dream of making such representations.

A similarly iconoclastic view was taken by Epiphanius of Salamis (p. 184) who was horrified to find in Palestine a curtain in a church porch with a picture of Christ or some saint. He tore it down and lodged a vehement protest with the bishop of Jerusalem. Though Epiphanius did all he could to prevent the introduction of pictures in churches, he was fighting a losing battle. By 403, when he died, portrayals of Christ and the saints were widespread. It was a move of popular devotion roughly contemporaneous with the rise in the veneration of the Blessed Virgin who, by 400, was occupying a mounting place in private devotion that was soon to pass into the official liturgy. The first known church dedicated to her is that at Ephesus where the council of 431 was held (p. 198). In the next decade Pope Sixtus III

1. The Veronica legend arose from a remarkable fusion of several legends. By the fourth century the woman with the issue of blood was named Berenice. According to one form of the Abgar legend (above, p. 61), current by 400, Christ sent his portrait to a princess of Edessa named Berenice. The two ladies were identified, and in the Latin West the name became Veronica. In later legend she acquired her picture of Christ on a towel which she offered him on the *via dolorosa*. The towel, preserved at St Peter's, Rome, has in modern times attracted less attention than the Shroud of Turin, the work of a fourteenth-century artist for which no claims can be made on historical grounds.

(432–40) built the great church of St Mary Major in Rome with its superb mosaics on the walls and the triumphal arch. The mosaics on the side walls portray Old Testament scenes. Those on the triumphal arch show the Annunciation, the Presentation of Christ in the Temple, the Magi offering gifts and visiting Herod, Herod ordering the massacre of the Innocents, and an apocryphal story of Christ in Egypt. At one time the walls also showed mosaics with a line of martyrs offering their crowns to the Virgin and Child, as in the extant Arian mosaics at S. Apollinare Nuovo, Ravenna; but these have entirely perished. The mosaics of St Mary Major mark a watershed in the development of Mariology. They remain largely within the older tradition in which the Virgin appears in the context of representations of Christ's birth at Bethlehem and is subordinate to Christ. But at the same time the mosaics are the earliest evidence in art for the tendency to accord her an independent position. This independence was accelerated by the popular Monophysite Christology of the fifth century which transferred to St Mary the redemptive value that had been attributed to the humanity of Christ. In a Monophysite devotion Christ as man ceased to be very important; his resurrection was that of a God. Because of this loss of a sense of solidarity between Christ and the rest of the human race, the faithful increasingly looked towards Mary as the perfect representative of redeemed humanity. This theme was powerfully portrayed in Christian art from the sixth century onwards, and was much enhanced by the growing popular belief that the Virgin either had not died or had already been granted resurrection and admission to heaven.

A considerable body of Christian art of the fifth, sixth and seventh centuries has survived, and illustrates the very high quality of artistic achievement that characterized the age. The splendid mosaics of the churches at Ravenna or Rome, the Rossano codex of the gospels, the Syriac gospel book written in 586 by the Mesopotamian monk Rabula (now in Florence), the doors of Santa Sabina in Rome, and many other examples, witness to an artistic renaissance of the first distinction, devoted to the expression of Christian themes and unrestrained by any inhibitions about portraying Christ and the saints. Yet these representations of Christ caused pain to those who remembered an older austerity and reserve. The icons were the object of an undercurrent of mistrust which emerged in the eighth century as the bitter iconoclastic controversy, when the emperor Leo the Isaurian in 726 initiated by edict a full-scale programme of destroying all such pictures. The icons had become an accepted and loved part of church decoration, and were deeply valued by devout souls. The controversy grew into a major conflict between church and State in the Byzantine empire lasting over a century, and (since the emperors were iconoclast and the papacy was not) contributed to a still further widening of the estrangement between Rome and Byzantium.

The strength of the iconoclasts lay less in their theological arguments, which were too technical to be in the long run persuasive,[1] than in their instinct that images were associated with the idolatry Christianity had come to destroy, and that the representations of Christ, the Virgin, and the saints, owed too much to pagan precedents. In this instinct there was a measure of truth. The representation of Christ as the Almighty Lord on his judgement throne owed something to pictures of Zeus. Portraits of the Mother of God were not wholly independent of a pagan past of venerated mother-goddesses. In the popular mind the saints had come to fill a role that had been played by local heroes and deities.

But it was inevitable that iconoclasm should be understood as an attack on aids to devotion which frail mortals needed, and to which they had become accustomed by tolerably long use over more than a century before the outbreak

1. The principal iconoclast arguments were: (*a*) the second commandment; (*b*) man alone is the earthly image of God; (*c*) to portray Christ implies a Nestorian separation of the humanity from the divine nature; or, if not that, it implies a circumscribing and limiting of the divine nature which cannot be so limited.

The iconodules replied: (*a*) we venerate not the icons but those whom they depict; (*b*) honour addressed to Christ's servants the saints is relative, not an absolute worship; (*c*) icons are a necessary consequence of the invocation of saints; (*d*) if value is ascribed to relics, why not also to icons? (*e*) the second commandment was only temporary legislation; (*f*) icons aid devotion and are universally used.

of the controversy. John of Damascus saw iconoclasm as implying a pessimistic, Manichee view of matter. The charge was no doubt very unfair. The exquisite cross in the mosaic of the apse at St Irene in Istanbul, the decoration of which belongs to the iconoclastic period, is in itself sufficient to refute the notion that the eighth-century iconoclasts were utterly indifferent or hostile to aesthetic values. They were not Philistines but conservatives wanting their religion the old way, as it had been in their grandfather's time before the artists had been encouraged to let themselves go. But they were also unconsciously repeating in a new form and a new idiom something of the old attack of the spiritualizing Origenists upon the 'Anthropomorphites' who needed to picture the God to whom they prayed (above, p. 185).

The decision to restore icons was taken by the empress Irene (780-90). In face of strong hostility in both Church and army her firm hand led the second Council of Nicaea (787) formally to condemn the iconoclasts. The failure of Irene and her successors to achieve prosperity for the empire brought a reaction in favour of iconoclasm again from 814 until 843, the iconophile cause being maintained meanwhile by the monks of Studios at Constantinople under their abbot Theodore. But on the first Sunday in Lent 843 the empress Theodora restored the icons for the last time with a procession that in the eyes of posterity marked 'the triumph of Orthodoxy', and made possible the gradual redecoration of the churches under the patriarch Photius from 858 onwards.

Conclusion

THE first historian of the Church, Eusebius of Caesarea early
in the fourth century, saw the story of the emergent Christian
society as one of successive conquests over obstacles and
attacks – over government persecution, over heretical deviation, over paganism. He was tempted to see evidence of the
power of Christianity in its social or worldly triumphs, expressed in the favour of sympathetic emperors, or in the con-
struction of splendid church buildings, or in the adherence of
distinguished intellectuals like Origen. Towards such trium-
phalist assumptions a twentieth-century Christian is likely
to be cool and reserved. But Eusebius was no doubt right in
seeing the successive controversies as making much of the
stuff of church history, and most of the main issues then
faced by the church in its formative period have remained
virtually permanent questions in Christian history – questions which receive an answer but are then reiterated in a
modified shape in each age.

The central questions of the apostolic age turned on the
continuity or discontinuity of the church with Israel. Those
who wanted to assert the continuing validity of the Mosaic
Law, and Gentiles who, at the opposite extreme, urged the
radical abandonment of the Old Testament were alike rejected. The accepted way became St Paul's *via media*. The
Old Testament retained a permanent place in the Christian
Bible as the history of a divine education of the race, a tutor
to bring men to Christ, and a book to be interpreted in the
light of Christ. In consequence the Church may never have
felt completely at home with the Old Testament, but it has
never been able to do without it.

With the sub-apostolic age (roughly 70–140) the Gentile
mission, for whose liberty St Paul had fought successfully
but painfully, passed through a vigorous expansion. The

Roman siege of Jerusalem in A.D. 70 and the final destruction
of the city as a Jewish capital in 135 ended the importance of
the old Jewish Christian congregations, and the centre of
gravity passed to the Gentile churches in the great cities, in
Antioch, in Alexandria, and especially in Rome, where both
St Peter and St Paul had died a martyr's death under Nero.
But the passing of the apostles left huge questions of authority
to be determined: the second century was accordingly the
age when the basic pattern of Christian doctrine began to
be tersely summarized in embryonic creeds, when the ministry achieved its universal threefold shape of bishop, presbyter, and deacon, and when finally the canon of the New
Testament came to be formed. Order and unity were urgently
needed, especially because of the centrifugal tendency of
Gnostic syncretism. The conquest of Gnosticism may be
counted the hardest and most decisive battle in church
history.

The way in which the second-century Church solved the
questions of authority, however, produced its own problems.
Emphasis on the local bishop as the fundamental principle
of unity (Ignatius) and on the sacredness of the 'tradition'
(Irenaeus) was necessary enough for survival, but had its by-
product in a measure of clericalization of the Church. The
part of the people in the sacraments began to become less
important than the acts of the priest in the mystery; and the
priest became rather more remote, especially after the fourth
century, when the Greeks started to veil the altar from the
congregation's view. At least by the eighth century, probably
earlier,[1] the canon of the Latin mass was commonly said in
a low voice not audible to the congregation.

The Gnostic crisis was already beginning to pass its zenith
when the debate with educated pagan critics began to be
taken seriously. Justin Martyr and his successors who wrote
in defence and vindication of the faith marked out the path
for Clement of Alexandria and Origen in making common
cause between Christianity and the highest aspirations of

1. Silent recitation of the great eucharistic prayer is first attested for
fifth-century Syria. It was forbidden by a law of Justinian of 565, but
had become customary at Constantinople by the ninth century.

classical religious and ethical philosophy. To claim Socrates as a 'Christian before Christ', or to speak with Tertullian of man's natural intuition for Christianity, was to see in the gospel a fulfilment of the moral potentiality of man as the creation of God.

In the next generation Irenaeus of Lyons and Tertullian at Carthage began the systematic and coherent statement of Christian doctrine, which they put forward in conscious opposition to heretical deviations. As the first Christian to write his theology in Latin, Tertullian played a part of epoch-making importance in working out a convenient vocabulary for the purpose.

By the middle of the third century (it is presupposed in both Cyprian and Origen) the church was living its life much more in the public eye, and Christianity was making deep penetration among the educated and governing classes. As the old paganism receded, its adherents were thrown on to the defensive and were made conscious of their need to think out a positive alternative in face of the Christian onslaught. The barbarian attacks of the middle years of the third century threatened the survival of the empire for a time, and for a few years persecution fell sharply upon the Christians. But the great persecution under Diocletian was long, unpleasant and much more thorough; it left an unhappy legacy of internal schism, above all in North Africa where the Donatists lived in bitter coexistence with their Catholic brethren until the Islamic invasions of the seventh century.

The conversion of Constantine did not make Christianity the formal religion of the empire. This was first established at the end of the century by Theodosius. The fourth century was the great age of the Greek churches, and later Eastern Christians looked back on Athanasius, Basil, Gregory Nazianzen, and John Chrysostom as teachers possessing a classical status and authority. In a pre-eminent degree these were 'the Fathers' – the acknowledged interpreters of an authoritative tradition. The episode of Julian's pagan revival was too individual and too short to mark a serious recession in progress. The Christians of the age were more disturbed

by the storm of the long Arian controversy. But even the
fourth century was not all tears. That the importance of the
Arian controversy can be exaggerated is evident from
the catechetical lectures of Cyril of Jerusalem (350) whose
pastoral instruction is almost wholly untouched by the fac-
tious slogans of the rival parties of the age. Ordinary church
life went on in tranquillity, largely indifferent to the theologians and the schemes devised by church politicians.

The flood of new adherents to the church during the fourth
century was an element in the withdrawal of the ascetics into
separate communities, the relation of which to the regular
life of the church was a problem not settled in a day. Without
having any such intentions the world-renouncing monks
became, in the West, important transmitters of culture and
education through the chaotic disturbance of the barbarian
invasions. The disintegration of the Western empire into
separate barbarian kingdoms left the church, especially as
represented by the leading Western bishop in Rome, the
only effective instrument of European unity, while in the
writings of Augustine of Hippo the West possessed an intel-
lectually coherent system of thought with intense power.

Once the papacy in the person of Gregory the Great had
recognized that its vocation lay more with the Western barbarians than with the old empire at Constantinople, the
process of widening the gulf between Greek and Latin
churches was accelerated. The sense of tension between
East and West goes back to an early stage in church history,
and understanding was not furthered by the fact that they
spoke different languages and had different social and ecclesiastical customs. But relations were made particularly
difficult by a succession of failures in mutual comprehension,
such as the attitude of the West during the ecumenical
council of Constantinople (381), or Pope Leo's dealings with
the council of Chalcedon (451), or the quiet assumption of
virtually all Greek bishops that the dignity and jurisdiction
of the bishops of Rome were simply analogous to those of an
Eastern patriarch as at Antioch or Constantinople.

The popes turned their gaze westwards at just about the
time when the Greek churches were to face the impact of the

Islamic conquest and to be racked with internal controversy about the legitimate use of icons. The consequences of these events mark an epoch in the history of the church, and there is reason in the convention by which the age of the church fathers is commonly reckoned to conclude with Gregory the Great in the West and with John of Damascus in the East. For thereafter it is much more difficult to write the history of both Eastern and Western Christendom as if it were a single story.

Tension between Latin West and Greek East is pre-Christian. Divergent paths, ranging from the mystery of the Trinity to the date of Easter, took Eastern and Western Christians different ways, and the legacy of that remains. An initially conciliar understanding of synodical authority yielded in the West to a mounting concentration of jurisdiction at Rome in the see of Peter and Paul, especially when there ceased to be a Western Emperor uniting the provinces. Only the papacy represented universality and independence from a secular power. The Greek East continued to think of authority as synodical, under the leadership of the patriarchs, among whom Rome should preside in love. The orthodox emperor acted as a linchpin. The Augustinian *Filioque* (above, p. 236) was and remains in Greek or Russian ears an irreverent addition to the ecumenical faith of the Council of 381, weakening the claim for Rome to be a touchstone of authenticity for the universal Church. At the political level, East–West relations became prickly as Rome and Constantinople competed for possession of the Balkan peninsula. The frontier of jurisdiction shifted in Constantinople's favour, especially with the Slav immigration into Balkan lands. East of the Adriatic, Rome could keep its influence only with the help of medieval Venice, and Slav tribes, Croats and Serbs, were to find themselves on opposite sides of an uneasy ecclesiastical frontier, sharing the same interest only to the degree that both would resent the Islamic Turkish empire. Painful rivalries and unreconciled memories tend to produce exaggerated sensitivity to differences, obscuring the vast area of shared doctrine, institutional structure, and devotional practice common to sister

Churches. Even at moments when relationships were to be most problematic, both East and West knew that, in the phrase of Anselm of Canterbury, despite differences they enjoyed 'substantial agreement'.

Suggestions for Further Reading[1]

GENERAL GUIDES TO EARLY CHRISTIAN LITERATURE

J. Quasten, *Patrology* (1950–86, 4 vols.); B. Altaner, *Patrology* (ET 1960); E. J. Goodspeed and R. M. Grant, *A History of Early Christian literature* (1966); F. L. Cross, *The Early Christian Fathers* (1960); B. Ramsey, *Beginning to Read the Fathers* (1985); A. di Berardino, *Encyclopedia of the Early Church* (1992).

SELECT DOCUMENTS

J. Stevenson (revised by W. H. C. Frend), *A New Eusebius* (1987); *Creeds, Councils, and Controversies* (1989); E. Giles, *Documents illustrating papal authority 96–454 A.D.* (1952); P. R. Coleman-Norton, *Roman State and Christian Church* (3 vols. 1966).

GENERAL SURVEYS

L. Duchesne, *Early History of the Christian Church* (ET 1909–24, 3 vols.); H. Lietzmann, *The Beginnings of the Christian Church*; *The Founding of the Church Universal*; *From Constantine to Julian*; *The Era of the Church Fathers* (ET 1937–51); J. G. Davies, *The Early Church* (1965); W. H. C. Frend, *The Rise of Christianity* (1984); H. von Campenhausen, *The Fathers of the Greek Church* (ET 1963); *The Fathers of the Latin Church* (ET 1964); H. St. L. B. Moss, *The Birth of the Middle Ages 395–814* (1935); J. Daniélou and H. I. Marrou, *The Christian Centuries*, I *The First Six Hundred Years* (ET 1964); A. H. M. Jones, *The Later Roman Empire 284–602* (1964); J. Meyendorff, *Imperial Unity and Christian Divisions* (1989).

On the intellectual and doctrinal history see J. N. D. Kelly, *Early Christian Doctrines* (1958); J. Daniélou, *A History of Early*

---

1. ET = English translation.

Christian doctrine before the Council of Nicaea (ET 1964); A. Grillmeier, *Christ in Christian Tradition* (ET 2nd ed. 1975); D. S. Wallace-Hadrill, *Christian Antioch* (1982); H. Chadwick, *Early Christian Thought and the Classical Tradition* (1966); W. Jaeger, *Early Christianity and Greek Paideia* (1962); R. M. Grant, *The Early Christian Doctrine of God* (1966); H. A. Wolfson, *The Philosophy of the Church Fathers* (1956); M. Wiles, *The Christian Fathers* (1966); R. A. Norris, *God and World in Early Christian Theology* (1965). J. J. Pelikan, *The Christian Tradition* i (1971); Frances Young, *From Nicaea to Chalcedon* (1983); R. A. Greer, *Broken Lights and Mended Lives* (1986); *The Fear of Freedom* (1989).

1: From Jerusalem to Rome

On Judaism in Roman society see E. Schürer, *The History of the Jewish People in the Age of Jesus Christ* I (2nd ed. 1973, by G. Vermes and F. Millar). On the Dead Sea Scrolls and the Early Church see M. Black, *The Scrolls and Christian Origins* (1961); J. Daniélou, *The Dead Sea Scrolls and Primitive Christianity* (ET 1958); F. M. Cross, *The Ancient Library of Qumran* (revised ed. 1961). On the legal and political position of the Church in the Roman empire see W. H. C. Frend, *Martyrdom and Persecution in the Early Church* (1965); A. N. Sherwin-White, *Roman Society and Roman Law in the New Testament* (1963); H. J. Cadbury, *The Book of Acts in History* (1955). On the social and intellectual encounter see A. D. Nock, *Conversion* (1933); *Early Gentile Christianity and its Hellenistic Background* (revised ed. 1964); E. R. Dodds, *Pagan and Christian in an Age of Anxiety* (1965).

2. Faith and order

Gnosticism: see H. Jonas, *The Gnostic Religion* (1958); R. M. Grant, *Gnosticism and early Christianity* (1959); B. Gärtner, *The Theology of the Gospel of Thomas* (1961); W. C. Van Unnik, *Newly discovered Gnostic writings* (1960); A. Harnack, *Marcion* (ET 1989); K. Rudolph, *Gnosis* (ET 1983); J. M. Robinson, *The Nag Hammadi Library* (3rd ed. 1988); B. Layton, *The Gnostic Scriptures* (1987).

The ministry: see H. B. Swete (ed.), *Essays on the Early History of the Church and Ministry* (1918), especially the essay there by C. H. Turner; W. Telfer, *The Office of a Bishop* (1962). The canon: see A. von Harnack, *The Origin of the New Testament* (ET 1926); K. Aland, *The Problem of the New Testament Canon* (1962).

Montanism: G. Salmon's thorough article in the *Dictionary of*

Christian Biography (1882) is superior to anything in English of more recent date. E. Gibson, *The 'Christians for Christians' Inscriptions of Phrygia* (1978).

3: Expansion

K. S. Latourette, *A History of the Expansion of Christianity*, vol. I (1938); A. von Harnack, *The Mission and Expansion of Christianity in the first three centuries* (ET 2nd ed. 1908; the German 4th ed. 1924 is fuller). On Syria see W. Bauer, *Orthodoxy and Heresy in Earliest Christianity* (ET 1971), ch. i; R. Murray, *Symbols of Church and Kingdom* (1975). On Egypt see C. H. Roberts, *Manuscript, Society and Belief in Early Christian Egypt* (1979). On social life and ethics see C. J. Cadoux, *The Early Church and the World* (1925); *The Early Christian Attitude to War* (1919); J. G. Davies, *Daily Life in the Early Church* (1952); A. von Harnack, *Militia Christi* (ET 1981); R. M. Grant, *Early Christianity and Society* (1977).

4: Justin and Irenaeus, 5: Tertullian, 6: Clement and Origen

There are monographs on Justin by E. F. Osborn (1973), on Irenaeus by W. Lawson (1948), on Clement of Alexandria by R. B. Tollinton (1914, 2 vols.), on Origen by H. Crouzel (ET 1989). On Clement and Origen the best single study is C. Bigg, *The Christian Platonists of Alexandria* (2nd ed. 1913). On Origen's Biblical exegesis see R. P. C. Hanson, *Allegory and Event* (1959), and R. M. Grant, *The Letter and the Spirit* (1957). On all these writers the relevant chapters in Harnack's *History of Dogma* remain important. On the synthesis with Greek philosophy in Justin, Clement and Origen, see H. Chadwick, *Early Christian Thought and the Classical Tradition* (1966); *Origen contra Celsum* (1980); B. A. Pearson and J. E. Goehring, *The Roots of Egyptian Christianity* (1986).

7: Church, State and Society

On Cyprian consult M. Bévenot's annotated translation of 'The Unity of the Church' and 'The Lapsed' (*Ancient Christian Writers*, vol. 25, 1957); his *Letters*, ed. G. W. Clarke in this series, vols. 43, 44, 46, 47 (1984–9); G. S. M. Walker, *The Churchmanship of St Cyprian* (1968); M. Sage, *Cyprian* (1975).

8 and 9: Constantine and the Arian Controversy

A. H. M. Jones, *Constantine and the Conversion of Europe* (1948); N. H. Baynes, *Constantine the Great and the Christian Church* (British Academy lecture, 2nd ed. 1973); H. Dörries, *Constantine and Religious Liberty* (1960); S. L. Greenslade, *Church and State from Constantine to Theodosius* (1954); T. D. Barnes, *Constantine and Eusebius* (1981).

On Arianism see A. Robertson, *St Athanasius* (Nicene and Post-Nicene Fathers, 1892), a translation of the principal works preceded by a distinguished introduction; H. M. Gwatkin, *Studies of Arianism* (2nd ed. 1900); N. Q. King, *The Emperor Theodosius and the Establishment of Christianity* (1961); J. N. D. Kelly, *Early Christian Creeds* (1950); E. P. Meijering, *Orthodoxy and Platonism in Athanasius* (2nd ed. 1974); R. P. C. Hanson, *The Search for the Christian Doctrine of God* (1988); R. Williams, *Arius* (1987); T. A. Kopecek, *A History of Neo-Arianism* (1979).

On Donatism see W. H. C. Frend, *The Donatist Church* (1952); S. L. Greenslade, *Schism in the Early Church* (1953).

10: Paganism and Christianity

A. Momigliano (ed.), *The Conflict between Paganism and Christianity in the Fourth Century* (1962), covers most of the field except for Julian. There is a biography of Julian by R. Browning (1975). G. Downey, *Gaza in the Early Sixth Century* (1963); R. L. Wilken, *The Christians as the Romans Saw Them* (1984); J. Geffcken, *The Last Days of Greco-Roman Paganism* (ET 1978). Studies of Julian by R. Browning (1975), G. W. Bowersock (1978), P. Athanassiadi-Fowden (1981). P. Brown, *Power and Persuasion in Late Antiquity* (1992).

On Ambrose see the biography by F. Homes Dudden (2 vols. 1935), and K. M. Setton, *Christian Attitude to the Emperor in the Fourth Century* (1941); J. F. Matthews, *Western Aristocracies and the Imperial Court 364–425* (1975). H. Chadwick, *Priscillian of Avila* (1976). C. Stancliffe, *St Martin and his Hagiographer* (1983).

12: The Ascetic Movement and 13: John Chrysostom

See Owen Chadwick, *John Cassian* (2nd ed. 1968), *Western Asceticism* (1958); Helen Waddell, *The Desert Fathers* (1936); W. K. Lowther Clarke, *St Basil the Great* (1913); K. E. Kirk, *The Vision of God* (1931); D. J. Chitty, *The Desert a City* (1966). P. Rousseau, *Pachomius* (1985); Elizabeth Clark, *Ascetic Piety and Women's Faith* (1986); P. Brown, *The Body and Society* (1988).

On John Chrysostom there is a biography by C. Baur (ET 1959–60, 2 vols.; the translation is at times misleading). The older Life by W. R. W. Stephens (2nd ed. 1880) gives a good introduction. Consult also G. Downey, *A History of Antioch in Syria* (1961); J. H. W. G. Liebeschuetz, *Barbarians and Bishops* (1990).

14: The Christological Controversy

N. H. Baynes, *Byzantine Essays* (1955) ch. VI; C. E. Raven, *Apollinarianism* (1923); J. Meyendorff, *Christ in East Christian Thought* (1985); R. A. Norris, *Manhood and Christ: A Study in the Christology of Theodore of Mopsuestia* (1963); F. Loofs, *Nestorius and his Place in the History of Christian Doctrine* (1913); L. Thunberg, *Microcosm and Mediator* (1965); K. Sarkissian, *The Council of Chalcedon and the Armenian Church* (1965); A. Louth, *Denys the Areopagite* (1989); R. Sorabji, *Philoponus and the rejection of Aristotelian Science* (1987).

15: Latin Christian Thought

There are biographies of Jerome by J. N. D. Kelly (1975), of Rufinus by F. X. Murphy (1945), and of Augustine by J. J. O'Donnell (1985) and P. R. L. Brown (1967). See also F. X. Murphy (ed.), *A Monument to St Jerome* (1952). On the background see S. Dill, *Roman Society in the Last Century of the Western Empire* (2nd ed. 1899). E. Clark, *The Origenist Controversy* (1993).

On particular problems in Augustine see J. J. O'Meara, *The Young Augustine* (1954); F. van der Meer, *Augustine the Bishop* (ET 1962); E. Gilson, *The Christian Philosophy of S. Augustine* (ET 1961); R. Sorabji, *Time, Creation and the Continuum* (1983); G. Bonner, *Augustine, Life and Controversies* (2nd ed. 1986); J. Burnaby, *Amor Dei* (2nd ed. 1991); R. A. Markus, *Saeculum* (1970); H. Chadwick, *Augustine* (1986); *Augustine's Confessions* (1991); G. Corcoran, *Augustine on Slavery* (1985); A. Zumkeller, *Augustine's Ideal of the Religious Life* (ET 1986); R. A. Markus, *The End of Ancient Christianity* (1990). On Apiarius see B. J. Kidd, *A History of the Church to A.D. 461* III (1922), ch. ix. On the Quicunque Vult see J. N. D. Kelly, *The Athanasian Creed* (1964). Pelagius is studied by J. Ferguson (1956), R. F. Evans (1968). On the Western idea of the Church see R. F. Evans, *One and Holy* (1975).

16: The Papacy and 17: The Barbarians

T. G. Jalland, *The Church and the Papacy* (1944); B. J. Kidd, *The*

Roman Primacy to A.D. *461* (1936); J. Chapman, *Studies on the Early Papacy* (1928). Biographies of Leo by T. G. Jalland (1941), and of Gregory the Great by F. Homes Dudden (2 vols. 1905) and C. Straw (1988). Consult also W. Ullmann, *The Growth of Papal Government in the Middle Ages* (1955); J. M. C. Toynbee and J. B. Ward-Perkins, *The Shrine of St Peter and the Vatican Excavations* (1956); R. B. Eno, *The Rise of the Papacy* (1990).

On the barbarians see E. A. Thompson, *The Visigoths in the time of Ulfila* (1966); *Attila and the Huns* (1948); S. Dill, *Roman Society in Gaul in the Merovingian Age* (1926); C. E. Stevens, *Sidonius Apollinaris and his Age* (1933); O. M. Dalton's introductions to his translations of the letters of Sidonius (2 vols. 1915) and of the History of the Franks by Gregory of Tours (2 vols. 1927); M. L. W. Laistner, *Thought and Letters in Western Europe* A.D. *500 to 900* (revised ed. 1957); J. J. O'Donnell, *Cassiodorus* (1979); H. Chadwick, *Boethius* (1981); H. Mayr-Harting, *The Coming of Christianity to Anglo-Saxon England* (2nd ed. 1992).

On Benedict see J. Leclercq, *The Love of Learning and the Desire for God* (ET 1961); Cuthbert Butler, *Benedictine Monachism* (2nd ed. 1924); D. Knowles, *The Monastic Order in England* (1940), ch. 1. There is an annotated translation of the Benedictine Rule by J. McCann (1952).

On Patrick see the biographies by J. B. Bury (1905) and L. Bieler (1949 and 1967), R. P. C. Hanson (1968).

18: Worship and Art

J. H. Srawley, *The Early History of the Liturgy* (2nd ed. 1947); J. A. Jungmann, *The Early Liturgy to the Time of Gregory the Great* (ET 1961), and *The Mass of the Roman Rite* (ET 1959); T. Klauser, *Short History of the Western Liturgy* (ET 1969); A. Baumstark, *Comparative Liturgy* (ET 1958); Gregory Dix, *The Shape of the Liturgy* (1945); V. L. Kennedy, *The Saints of the Canon of the Mass* (2nd ed. 1963); A. A. McArthur, *The Evolution of the Christian Year* (1953); J. D. C. Fisher, *Christian Initiation, Baptism in the Medieval West* (1965); F. L. Cross, *St Cyril of Jerusalem's Lectures on the Christian Sacraments* (1951).

On music consult E. Wellesz, *A History of Byzantine Music and Hymnography* (revised ed. 1961); J. Quasten, *Music and Worship in Pagan and Christian Antiquity* (ET 1983). On Latin hymns, F. J. E. Raby, *Christian Latin Poetry* (2nd ed. 1953).

On art see W. F. Volbach and M. Hirmer, *Early Christian Art* (ET 1961); F. van der Meer and C. Mohrmann, *Atlas of the Early Christian World* (ET 1958); M. Gough, *The Early Christians* (1961); L. Hertling and E. Kirschbaum, *The Roman Catacombs and their Martyrs* (revised ed. ET 1960); D. Talbot Rice, *The Art of Byzantium* (1959); J. G. Davies, *The Origin and Development of Early Christian Architecture* (1952); R. Krautheimer, *Early Christian and Byzantine Architecture* (The Pelican History of Art, 3rd ed. 1979); R. J. Mainstone, *Hagia Sophia* (1988).

On icons see N. H. Baynes, *Byzantine Studies* (1955); E. Bevan, *Holy Images* (1940). P. J. Alexander, *The Patriarch Nicephorus* (1958). C. Mango, *The Art of the Byzantine Empire* (1972), translates selected documents. On the veneration of the saints see H. Delehaye, *The Legends of the Saints* (ET 1962); P. Brown, *The Cult of the Saints* (1981).

Index

READ MORE IN PENGUIN

In every corner of the world, on every subject under the sun, Penguin represents quality and variety – the very best in publishing today.

For complete information about books available from Penguin – including Puffins, Penguin Classics and Arkana – and how to order them, write to us at the appropriate address below. Please note that for copyright reasons the selection of books varies from country to country.

In the United Kingdom: Please write to *Dept. EP, Penguin Books Ltd, Bath Road, Harmondsworth, West Drayton, Middlesex UB7 0DA*

In the United States: Please write to *Consumer Sales, Penguin USA, P.O. Box 999, Dept. 17109, Bergenfield, New Jersey 07621-0120*. VISA and MasterCard holders call 1-800-253-6476 to order Penguin titles

In Canada: Please write to *Penguin Books Canada Ltd, 10 Alcorn Avenue, Suite 300, Toronto, Ontario M4V 3B2*

In Australia: Please write to *Penguin Books Australia Ltd, P.O. Box 257, Ringwood, Victoria 3134*

In New Zealand: Please write to *Penguin Books (NZ) Ltd, Private Bag 102902, North Shore Mail Centre, Auckland 10*

In India: Please write to *Penguin Books India Pvt Ltd, 706 Eros Apartments, 56 Nehru Place, New Delhi 110 019*

In the Netherlands: Please write to *Penguin Books Netherlands bv, Postbus 3507, NL-1001 AH Amsterdam*

In Germany: Please write to *Penguin Books Deutschland GmbH, Metzlerstrasse 26, 60594 Frankfurt am Main*

In Spain: Please write to *Penguin Books S. A., Bravo Murillo 19, 1° B, 28015 Madrid*

In Italy: Please write to *Penguin Italia s.r.l., Via Felice Casati 20, I–20124 Milano*

In France: Please write to *Penguin France S. A., 17 rue Lejeune, F–31000 Toulouse*

In Japan: Please write to *Penguin Books Japan, Ishikiribashi Building, 2–5–4, Suido, Bunkyo-ku, Tokyo 112*

In South Africa: Please write to *Longman Penguin Southern Africa (Pty) Ltd, Private Bag X08, Bertsham 2013*

READ MORE IN PENGUIN

RELIGION

The Gnostic Gospels Elaine Pagels

In a book that is as exciting as it is scholarly, Elaine Pagels examines these ancient texts and the questions they pose and shows why Gnosticism was eventually stamped out by the increasingly organized and institutionalized Orthodox Church. 'Fascinating' – *The Times*

Islam in the World Malise Ruthven

This informed and informative book places the contemporary Islamic revival in context, providing a fascinating introduction – the first of its kind – to Islamic origins, beliefs, history, geography, politics and society.

The Orthodox Church Timothy Ware

In response to increasing interest among western Christians, and believing that a thorough understanding of Orthodoxy is necessary if the Roman Catholic and Protestant Churches are to be reunited, Timothy Ware explains Orthodox views on a vast range of matters from Free Will to the Papacy.

Judaism Isidore Epstein

The comprehensive account of Judaism as a religion and as a distinctive way of life, presented against a background of 4,000 years of Jewish history.

Who's Who of Religions Edited by John R. Hinnells

This detailed and informative dictionary brings together for the first time the biographies of leading men and women of religions both ancient and modern who have had a significant impact on religion.

The Historical Figure of Jesus E. P. Sanders

'This book provides a generally convincing picture of the real Jesus, set within the world of Palestinian Judaism, and a practical demonstration of how to distinguish between historical information and theological elaboration in the Gospels' – *The Times Literary Supplement*

BY THE SAME AUTHOR

THE PENGUIN HISTORY OF THE CHURCH
General Editor: Owen Chadwick

also published:
Western Society and the Church in the Middle Ages   R. W. Southern

In the period between the eighth and the sixteenth centuries the Church and State were more nearly one than ever before or after. Professor Southern discusses how this was achieved and what stresses it caused.

The Reformation   Owen Chadwick

In this volume Professor Owen Chadwick deals with the formative work of Erasmus, Luther, Zwingli, Calvin, with the special circumstances of the English Reformation, and with the Counter-Reformation.

The Church and the Age of Reason, 1648–1789   Gerald R. Cragg

This span in the history of the Church stretches from a time of bitter religious and civil strife before the Peace of Westphalia to the age of industrialism and republicanism which followed the French Revolution.

The Church in an Age of Revolution   Alec R. Vidler

'A most readable and provocative volume and a notable addition to this promising and distinguished series' – *Guardian*

A History of Christian Missions   Stephen Neill
Revised Edition

This volume, the first attempt in English to provide a readable history of the worldwide expansion of all the Christian denominations, has been updated according to the late Professor Neill's intentions by Professor Owen Chadwick.

The Christian Church in the Cold War   Owen Chadwick

In this concluding volume, Professor Owen Chadwick surveys the difficulties encountered by the Eastern and Western Churches from the end of the Second World War and the era of a divided Europe to the fresh global challenges and opportunities facing Christians now.